FITTING SENTENCES: IDENTITY IN NINETEENTH-
AND TWENTIETH-CENTURY PRISON NARRATIVES

JASON HASLAM

Fitting Sentences:
Identity in Nineteenth- and Twentieth-Century Prison Narratives

UNIVERSITY OF TORONTO PRESS
Toronto Buffalo London

ISBN-13: 978-0-8020-3833-3
ISBN-10: 0-8020-3833-6

∞

Printed on acid-free paper

Library and Archives Canada Cataloguing in Publication

Haslam, Jason W. (Jason William), 1971–
   Fitting sentences : identity in nineteenth- and twentieth-century prison
   narratives / Jason Haslam.

   Includes bibliographical references and index.
   ISBN 0-8020-3833-6

   1. Prisoners' writings – History and criticism.   2. Identity
   (Psychology).   3. Imprisonment – History – 19th century – Sources.
   4. Imprisonment – History – 20th century – Sources.   I. Title.

   HV8706.H38 2005   828'.08   C2005-904225-7

University of Toronto Press acknowledges the financial assistance to its
publishing program of the Canada Council for the Arts and the Ontario
Arts Council.

This book has been published with the help of a grant from the Canadian
Federation for the Humanities and Social Sciences, through the Aid to
Scholarly Publications Programme, using funds provided by the Social
Sciences and Humanities Research Council of Canada.

University of Toronto Press acknowledges the financial support for
its publishing activities of the Government of Canada through the
Book Publishing Industry Development Program (BPIDP).

To my mother,
whose laughter, strength, and
gifts of household appliances
have all kept me going

Contents

Closing Statements / Opening Arguments   189

Acknowledgments

The people involved in helping this project through to this point are more numerous than I can possibly list here, but I do want to thank the major players. First, I give my undying gratitude to Dennis Denisoff, who was a supervisor, and is a friend, beyond compare. Without his unflagging support and insight, this project would be a mere shadow of what it is. Any lingering unlit areas are purely mine, and I'm sure he'll loan me a flashlight. Glenn Hendler has also provided me with some excellent comments, questions, discussions, and, just as important as the rest, support. Thanks also to the numerous people who have commented on this work at its various stages: Peter Gibian (who helped from the start), Ioan Davies, Stan Johannesen, Victoria Lamont, A. Lynne Magnusson, Linda Warley, the University of Toronto Press's anonymous readers, and audiences at the various forums at which I have discussed this work have all helped to form this study. Jill McConkey at the University of Toronto Press has been a terrific editor, and the staffs at Dana Porter Library, the other Tri-University group libraries, and the British Library were all extremely helpful.

I would also like to express my gratitude to the organizations that have provided continued financial support for my research: the Social Sciences and Humanities Research Council of Canada, the Aid to Scholarly Publications Programme, and the Northeast Modern Languages Association's Summer Fellowship Program. Thanks, too, to the many gracious readers and letter writers involved in my applications.

An earlier version of chapter 1 appears as '"They locked the door on my meditations": Thoreau and the Prison House of Identity' in *Genre: Forms of Discourse and Culture* 35.3/4 (2002): 449–78; I would like to thank *Genre* and the University of Oklahoma for their permission to print this updated version. An earlier version of chapter 4 appears in *Captivating Subjects: Writing Confinement, Citizenship, and Nationhood in the Nineteenth Century*, edited by Jason Haslam and Julia M. Wright (University of Toronto Press, 2005).

My family deserves the biggest thanks of all. My mother, to whom this study is dedicated, has for her whole life worked harder than most academics can imagine, and she taught me what education is supposed to be. Thanks also to Kim, Chip, Rob, Steph, and Zach for keeping me in books, care packages, and b.b. guns. Friends also kept me sane, and many helped with discussions about and around this work: T'ai W.P. Zimmer, who's been there for me from the beginning and Brian 'Philip' Greenspan; Ian R.S. McKergow, Erika Burger, and the rest of the Montreal gang; and M. Morgan Holmes and Ivan the Terrible, James Allard and Adriana Pagnotta, and all the Ontario folk. There are too many other colleagues and friends to name, but a few stand out for their willingness to discuss these and other matters: Jodey Castricano, Joel Faflak, Michele Kramer, and Jim Weldon. And an honourable mention goes to the folks at Station 24 in the MUC – for the inspiration. And last, but certainly far ahead of least, my endless thanks to Julia M. Wright, who knows that she means more to me than I could fit in here.

FITTING SENTENCES: IDENTITY IN NINETEENTH-
AND TWENTIETH-CENTURY PRISON NARRATIVES

Opening Statements

A history of prisons is a history of prisoners. That may seem like an obvious statement, but, on many levels, a history of prisons is distinctly *not* a history of prisoners. Prisoners have had largely no voice in the formation of prisons, nor have they generally had a role in actively creating policies concerning criminal justice. So, the history of prisons is not a history written by prisoners. It is, however, a history written on and through prisoners. Prisons – and the officials, politicians, and systems supporting them – only gain solidity through the people living in them. Prison policy and practice are engaged in an extensive and constant construction of *the* prisoner, the mythic body and identity of the generic person unfortunate enough to be incarcerated. The general aim of this study is to examine how those constructions are challenged by prisoners themselves. Specifically, I argue that prison writers' refigurings of identity tend to work against notions of the Enlightenment individual, since that construct (so closely linked to the history of autobiography) is intimately related to the structure of prison itself. Nevertheless, this tendency also has drawbacks in connection to the larger social functions of the prison and of civil liberties and Western democracy as a whole (which are of course tied to the notion of the individual), a fact that several of these authors attempt to highlight and problematize, and which I examine most explicitly in the final chapter and closing statements. Overall, my analyses of specific texts are offered to show how their authors textually negotiate the various definitions of identity forced upon them by the dominant society that the prison represents and of which it is a vital component. *Fitting Sentences* demonstrates that these negotiations of identity are, therefore, not simply offered as personal reflections or attempts to gain or create a new sense of self, but are constructed in large part as social critiques.

Before moving on to my readings of the ways in which specific prisoners have dealt with this construction of identity, a brief history of Western penal practices is in order. The prison's history as an institution in the West has been variously defined and problematized not only by historians, but also by philosophers, psychologists, sociologists, reformers, politicians, and others too numerous to list. Their statements take various forms, ranging from those that support incarceration as a proper method of either punishment or reform, to others that combat the efficacy of incarceration in achieving either of those ends. Within the specific limitations of an institutional history, however, some common points arise. First, while the practice in the West of incarceration for criminal activity goes back to the Middle Ages and earlier, it is 'the period at the turn of the nineteenth century when imprisonment first became a general policy,' as David Garland states.[1] Christopher Harding and Richard W. Ireland further write that the difference in the practice of incarceration before and after this period can be seen as a difference between 'method' and 'institution.'[2] The criminal's separation from society and the restriction of that person's movement may have been one form of punishment in the pre- and early modern periods, but it was not yet the socially sanctioned prime method. As John Bender writes in his study of the relations between eighteenth-century fiction and the penitentiary, early prisons 'were temporary lodgings for all but a few,' whereas the justice systems of the late eighteenth and early nineteenth centuries used long-term incarceration as the central punishment.[3] Even after the institutional transformation of incarceration, other methods of punishment were still enforced; today, such punishments as fines and community service are regularly doled out by the courts. As the number of popular television and film crime dramas indicate, though, these rulings are generally seen as alternatives to incarceration, which is perceived as the generally accepted mode of punishment. Thus, studies of prison – and of prison literature – can help further larger projects concerned with the general understanding of modern culture.[4]

Second, within the study of the modern institutionalization of incarceration there are other generally accepted points. The modern prison and its practices are said to arise from a Protestant rhetoric of the individual's ability to reform, a theory seen, as I will discuss in the first two chapters of this study, in the model beginnings of the contemporary prison. These beginnings are usually posited in the American prisons in Auburn, New York, and Philadelphia, Pennsylvania, both constructed in the early nineteenth century (though earlier experiments can be traced back to the late eighteenth century). These institutions were copied and enlarged upon throughout the Western world, a dissemination indicated by, for example, Gustave de Beaumont and Alexis de Tocqueville's study of the American prison system and its potential application to France. Indeed, Frank Lauterbach notes that both the Auburn and Philadelphia prisons

> were visited extensively by foreign penologists in the 1830s (and were written about by many more who had never even visited them at all), an exchange that culminated in the first international prison congress at Frankfurt (Main) in 1846. Among those visitors were Gustave de Beaumont and Alexis de Tocqueville for France in 1831, William Crawford for the United Kingdom from 1832 to 1833, Dominique Mondelet and John Neilson for Canada in 1834, and Nicolaus Heinrich Julius for Prussia in 1835.[5]

While the Auburn and Philadelphia penitentiaries differed from each other in some practices, specifically in their approach to the use of collective or individual labour, both emphasized the necessity of silence as a means of allowing prisoners to reflect on their crimes. As David J. Rothman writes, the 'distinctive feature' of both systems was 'the silence that pervaded the institutions.'[6] According to the humanist philosophy undergirding this practice, as will be explored further in chapter 1, the reflection supposedly inculcated by this silence would then of necessity lead the prisoners to reform their behaviour, to move away from crime and become properly constituted individuals and citizens. The reformatory theories of silence and isolation are further tied, as many prison historians and theorists have shown, to the rise in the West of democracy and the ideas of individual rights.[7] Because each individual has certain 'inalienable rights' within the democratic society, and is capable of understanding and changing her or his actions, incarceration as punishment for crime is normalized and institutionalized as a means of ensuring that those rights not be violated, and of allowing the criminal a chance to change.

While this theory of penitence and reform continued throughout the nineteenth century, and arguably still forms some of the basis for the continuation of imprisoning practices,[8] by the late 1800s theories of the origins of crime and of human behaviour in general began to shift, and the understanding of punitive practices altered with them. In this period, as Martin J. Wiener discusses in his excellent study, the rise of sociological sciences and their concomitant emphasis on the social origins of behaviour – rather than on individual choice or responsibility – radically altered the perception of crime. Instead of choosing to commit a criminal act, and therefore being solely responsible for it, the criminal was seen to be in some ways the product of larger social forces which limited the options available, thus partially sublimating the criminal's personal responsibility. As I discuss in my third chapter, this change was figured in penal policy through a move 'away from deterrence and moralization' towards a more scientific view of criminal activities as generally falling into the categories of statistical, empirical, and medical analyses.[9] Within this scientific understanding, criminals cannot simply alter their behaviour through personal reflection. This change resulted in an intense period of prison and legal reform, in which psychologists, medical doctors, and other 'outside' professionals became more heavily involved in the treatment of prisoners and the organization of prisons.

However, despite the differences in perception and practice that these changes brought about, the general effect of imprisonment, as described by the prisoners themselves, remained fairly constant. Prisoners' own discussions of incarceration, and analyses of those discussions, can help to provide a detailed picture of the split between carceral theory and practice. As I argue in chapter 1, prisons function in large part as alienating and brutalizing institutions which, despite emphases on either reform or scientific cure, use demeaning and often violent forms of punishment to enforce prison codes. Harding and Ireland discuss the treatment of the prisoner as, in one sense, a transhistorical action of transforming the prisoner into a series of objects (largely defined) that can be acted upon. That is, certain possessions – material or otherwise – which relate to the prisoner in some intimate sense are removed, violated, or otherwise negatively acted on in order to punish the prisoner. They detail several important objects in the history of punishment, including the prisoners' bodies, their freedom to move or act, and their ability to engage in social interaction.[10] Such an objectification of people is, in Michel Foucault's words, part of the 'technologies of power,' for which the prison is arguably the major synecdoche. For Foucault, these technologies are figured as attempts to 'determine the conduct of individuals and submit them to certain ends or domination, an objectivizing of the subject.'[11] Within the period covered by my study, roughly the mid-nineteenth century to the present day, and throughout the transatlantic region that I cover, the isolation of the prisoner from society at large and the restriction of that person's movement and ability to act remain generally consistent, and are variously joined with corporal punishment, restrictions on communication, and isolation within the prison itself. As demonstrated in all the chapters, these forms of punishment tend to alienate the prisoner from, among other things, family, friends, and society in general. Further, they serve as attempts to reinforce what the prison officials, and the authorities associated with them, see as the more proper social space for the prisoner to inhabit, thus working towards actively determining the subjectivity of the prisoner.

Related to this discussion of identity reformation, and perhaps arising from prison historians' and theorists' existence within a sociological paradigm, the third general point of agreement among analysts of the prison is that incarceration, and the institutions involved with it, function as part of the larger matrix of society, whether that society is seen as being controlled by the active engagement of a variety of individuals, or as a conglomeration of various institutions which, to a large degree, control the society's members, or as somewhere between these two models. The differences in opinion within this larger understanding account for a significant portion of penological theory.

While there are problems with any attempt to summarize these differences, for the purposes of the present study they can be reduced to two camps. On the one hand, Foucault, in his work *Discipline and Punish*, and those critics who follow from his conclusions, generally argue that prison and incarceration, after the turn of the nineteenth century, form one part of a larger disciplinary system of surveillance, subjugation, and control.[12] As D.A. Miller writes, discipline within such a system was supposedly 'confined to the carceral' only 'in order that it might ultimately be extended ... to the space outside it.'[13] I will briefly recapitulate the salient points of Foucault's well-known text in order to situate both those critics who move away from his reading of the prison as well as my own argument.

Foucault uses Jeremy Bentham's construction of the panopticon as a figure that demonstrates the effectiveness and pervasiveness of the disciplinary mechanisms of society. In general, Bentham's architectural design of this institution allowed for inmates to be constantly watched – or at least feel as if they were – while the inmates themselves could never see the officials in charge of them. This structure, according to Bentham, permits the exercise of complete and total discipline in that it makes those subject to its control feel as if any infraction of the rules will be noticed and the perpetrator punished. Thus, in Bentham's plan, the inmates would be much less likely to commit any misdeeds, and would therefore begin to modify their general behaviour for what he saw as the better. Bentham writes that 'the more constantly the persons to be inspected are under the eyes of those who inspect them, the more perfectly will the purpose of the establishment have been attained.'[14] In his writings on the subject, Bentham argued that the panopticon could be effectively used not only for penitentiaries, but also for *'work-houses, or manufactories, or mad-houses, or hospitals, or schools.'*[15]

Foucault interprets Bentham's plan in terms of its intended effects on the inmates and their relationship to the exercise of social power. He writes that the 'major effect of the Panopticon' was 'to induce in the inmate a state of conscious and permanent visibility that assures the automatic functioning of power.'[16] Foucault details the creation of this automation in a list of the panopticon's organizations and functions, writing that these need to be arranged in such a way that

> the surveillance is permanent in its effects, even if it is discontinuous in its action; that the perfection of power should tend to render its actual exercise unnecessary; that this architectural apparatus should be a machine for creating and sustaining a power relation independent of the person who exercises it; in short, that the inmates should be caught up in a power situation of which they are themselves the bearers.[17]

In other words, Foucault argues that the feeling of being constantly watched leads the inmates of the panopticon to enforce discipline on themselves. Panoptic discipline is, for Foucault, an ideological function that alters the inmates' relation to and understanding of themselves. He writes of the structure that, '[t]hanks to its mechanisms of observation, it gains in efficiency and in the ability to penetrate into men's behaviour.'[18]

That Bentham saw the panopticon as a structure that could be used to modify behaviour in a variety of institutional settings highlights for Foucault that the form of discipline exercised in the modern prison is in fact widely spread throughout society, forming the very heart of the social system of power relations. Foucault refers to this disciplinary system as 'the carceral city,' in which the prison 'is not alone, but linked to a whole series of "carceral" mechanisms which seem distinct enough – since they are intended to alleviate pain, to cure, to comfort – but which all tend, like the prison, to exercise a power of normalization.'[19] Indeed, to take one example, the rise of collateral punishments, in addition to imprisonment, that are handed out by the US justice system to offenders – what Jeremy Travis has called 'invisible punishment' – materializes this carceral city, 'reach[ing] deep into American life.'[20] In Foucault's paradigm, prisons, schools, churches, and other social institutions function to maintain the status quo, to enforce values and codes of behaviour that serve to protect the status of the people who occupy the higher realm of society, be it economic, religious, political, or any of a variety of positions of authority. Activities such as prison reform, which would seem to work against the methods and aims of the carceral matrix, are instead parts of the system itself.

Against this overarching view of social discipline, on the other hand, critics of Foucault's theories argue that his positioning of the prison as part of a larger socio-institutional matrix that serves to reproduce existing power relations (between members of different classes, races, genders, regions, and so forth) is overly deterministic and generalized, and depends on an understanding of social relations that is too reliant on seeing those relations as completely defined by power differentials. John S. Ransom summarizes these arguments, writing that Foucault's critics depict his account of 'Western societies' as 'nothing more than an interlocking system of disciplinary mechanisms.'[21] This critique is occasionally taken even further to suggest that the constant reproduction of hegemonic power structures which Foucault describes is a form of strategic conspiracy that would require far too much organization and intent to remain consistent. David Garland, describing the arguments against Foucault's penological history, writes that, '[i]n the absence of any hard evidence that a strategy with these objectives does really exist, it would appear that Foucault is simply taking the (unintended) consequences of the prison to be its (intended) *raison d'être*.'[22]

Despite the excellence of Garland's body of work on prison history and the social implications of punishment, his summary of the critique against Foucault can be complicated through an analysis of the word 'power.' For Garland, Foucault's assertion that the prison functions within a matrix of power relations which are geared towards maintaining the social status quo necessarily implies that those in 'positions of power' both fully understand and actively deploy strategic uses of institutions in order to maintain their own authority. While Garland makes a passing reference to Foucault's rejection of 'the idea that power is a thing that is "held" by someone,' he insists on treating it as such.[23] But Foucault, as he writes in *The History of Sexuality*, instead uses 'power' to refer to a series of relations among groups, institutions, and people, 'without being exactly localized in them.'[24] Foucault's two texts combined, then, could show this definition of power as the central point that the various functions of the prison highlight. Garland is certainly correct in writing that Foucault's work does not address how those 'people in positions of power' (by which he means positions of authority) 'came to be there,' but his stress on Foucault's lack of emphasis on the intentions of such people can obscure the argument that they, like everyone else, live and act within a matrix of power relations.[25] Thus, Gilles Deleuze can say of Foucault's formulation of power that 'it passes through the hands of the mastered no less than through the hands of the masters' and that 'because it does not itself speak and see, it makes us see and speak ... Seeing and Speaking are always already completely caught up within power relations which they presuppose and actualize.'[26] Those in so-called positions of power do not simply wield force as a means of controlling society, but are part of the larger mechanisms of power that enable both their actions and the actions of those who resist them. The prison officials' intentions, for example, can be seen as less important than the ways in which their decisions and actions, made with whatever motives, carry with them the authority invested in their place in society.

My aim in laying out this debate is not to offer a fully integrated or cohesive theory of punishment and the social functions of the prison, but instead to delimit my theoretical area of concern: the way in which imprisoned authors detail the relationship of the prison to other social institutions, to the members of society, to various forms of the exercise of power, and to the people directly affected by it. I also see Foucault's theoretical construct as problematic, especially in his lack of discussion of the impact of slavery on the formation of the early prison – a connection which I discuss in chapter 2 and which has a significant impact on any understanding of the prison as a modern institution and of its use of both physical and societal violence. Elissa D. Gelfand similarly notes that Foucault's study lacks any discussion of women prisoners.[27] However, I do argue that the basic terms in which Foucault outlines the functions of the prison prove useful, but precisely because they parallel, to varying degrees, the prison authors' depictions of their own incarceration. Beyond this position, though, I would also argue that the figuration of power offered by the 'later Foucault' can be and is used similarly by various prison authors to work against the attempted creation of an overarching penological (and social) discipline. It may be tempting to use this distinction between the 'Foucault of discipline' and the 'Foucault of power' to instigate a discussion of the uses of the author function by recent critics (myself included, perhaps).[28] But, I offer this combination here only to set up my analysis of the multiple and varied ways in which prison writers construct themselves as negotiating the streams of power that pass through their hands – and the hands of those who imprison them – in attempts to analyse and potentially undermine disciplinary technologies and the oppressive power differentials in their societies. While I critiqued my opening sentence by stating that the history of prisons is not written by prisoners, occasionally the history of a prisoner does supersede the history of the prison, making a voice heard through the wilderness of constructions and abuses perpetrated on the person who owns that voice. Henry David Thoreau, Harriet Jacobs, Oscar Wilde, Martin Luther King Jr, Constance Lytton, and Breyten Breytenbach all tend to demonstrate that prisons and related disciplinary institutions work within a larger social, carceral framework, reproducing the oppressive hierarchies and assumptions of their particular societies. While these texts range from the mid-nineteenth to the late twentieth centuries, and were written in American, English, and South African contexts, the general paradigm of institutionalized imprisonment remains largely consistent due to the international dissemination of prison forms throughout the history of the institution, as discussed above.[29]

Therefore, even though H. Bruce Franklin is correct in stating that prison writing 'cannot be lumped in some timeless category ..., as though prisoners of all times and places constituted a society'[30] – an assertion that is supported by the immense range of forms, genres, styles, and other categories of prison writing – the various works written from prison do constitute a different type of unitary group. Rather than being based on formal similarities among texts, the cohesion of this group lies in the situations in and against which the works were composed. In other words, all prison writings comment to one degree or another on the oppressive forces of the prison itself, and of the social structures of which the prison is a part. They complicate the ideological frames that the prison both informs and is informed by. Because of this, prison writings do indeed engage in debates that arise from their own particular settings and origins, but similarities can also be found in the means through which they do so. All of the authors discussed here use the prison both as the ground against which they write and as a metaphor within or synecdoche for larger social discussions – in other words, the authors write against the prison, but their critiques (and my analysis thereof) should not be read as ending at the prison walls: those comments expand to encapsulate – and in some senses are aimed primarily at – the larger societies.

The point of comparison that I will explore, in order to develop a specifically nuanced understanding of the social functions of power, is the manner in which the authors reconfigure notions of identity as a means of combatting the oppressive forces arrayed against them. Before continuing, a brief discussion of my terminology is necessary: Paul Smith's distinction between the terms 'subject' and 'individual' is useful in this context. The term 'individual,' he writes, describes the person as 'undivided and whole,' as the source of 'conscious action'; the subject, however, 'is not self-contained' and is always already in 'conflict with forces that dominate it in some way or another.'[31] For Smith, 'The human *agent*' should be seen as 'the place from which resistance to the ideological is produced or played out, and thus as *not* equivalent to either the "subject" or the "individual."'[32] In this study, 'identity' will be used to demarcate the conceptual space in which the subject, the individual, and the agent are all 'played out.'[33]

All of the texts studied support, in one form or another, the point discussed above, that the prison serves to reconstruct and reconstitute the identities of those under its control. Bender defines this project succinctly, writing that '[t]he penitentiary ... uses the material instruments of architecture and daily regime to *recreate* the convict, who has been sentenced for a crime that signifies failure to extract moral order from experience.'[34] Moving beyond these general schemata, however, each text I examine engages with a different element of this transformative project, demonstrating how the generally uniform carceral practices can be used to attack a number of identifications, be they sexual, racial, economic, or any of a variety of social categories that for disparate reasons fall outside the dominant 'moral order.' The authors' own depictions of identity and the transformations in which their texts engage generally work against the reformative and subjugating premises of carceral discipline.

I have chosen these texts not because they are representative of a larger genre of 'prison literature,' nor because, when studied together, they can tell us *the* overarching meaning of that larger category.

Indeed, given the sheer volume of prison texts and the variety of contexts from which they arise, such a 'representative' choice, as Franklin writes, is both theoretically and practically an impossible project. Instead, each text is presented here because it offers a different entrance point into the larger subject of prison and its relation to identity construction. I do not, therefore, offer a general theory of how prison authors constitute a sense of personal agency through the act of writing: as Wright and I state about a similar move in our volume on narratives of captivity in general, 'such a determination would necessitate a construction of metaphorical boundaries, walls, and constraints, that would work directly against the aims of many of the authors studied here, replicating the discursive and material traditions of captivity.'[35] Instead, I examine here the specifics of each text in order to demonstrate, contextually, how prisoners' texts can try to exploit certain fissures in the imprisoning discourse surrounding them, as well as how these attempts sometimes contain their own difficulties. My study does not posit any utopian notions of the ability to gain agency through writing, nor does it offer its dystopian opposite, a negative formation of the seeming impossibility of escaping the carceral structures of society. Rather, I demonstrate how these specific authors, in responding to similar penal situations (if not societal ones), construct textual negotiations of identity issues in order to critique and problematize the dominant functions of power in their societies.

The texts studied could be divided into those written in the nineteenth century and those composed in the twentieth, where each group deals with the disciplining models of their own time. Such a division could, however, ignore the larger similarity between the prisons of the two periods, possibly creating a space for problematic value judgments about different practices (along the lines of 'prisons now are better than prisons of the past') – practices which, in the end, lead to similar results. An explicitly chronological organization could also result in the silencing of other equally important distinctions, such as those of nationality and gender, and of the differing relations those categories have to the carceral institutions described. Partially in order to avoid these difficulties, while also attempting to structure the larger argument about identity in such a way as to foreground the authors' own comments, I have organized *Fitting Sentences* along more thematic lines, splitting the text into three sections, each of which contains two chapters, each focusing on one author. In this, I am differing from the few major studies of prison writing, including the works of Ioan

Davies, H. Bruce Franklin, and Barbara Harlow: Davies's analysis takes a much broader scope than mine, reading literature that ranges in time from the Middle Ages through to the present day; Franklin's text takes an historical and national perspective, looking at the evolution of American prison writing, widely defined, from slaves' songs through to Herman Melville's maritime work and the contemporary prison narrative; and Harlow's studies look at a wide variety of prison writing within specifically imperial and Third World contexts, as well as in terms of gender. Each of these excellent works analyses vast numbers of texts in an attempt to develop theoretical and socio- and literary-historical approaches to prison writings, providing the groundwork for my more specific analysis of this significant and influential group of works. By more closely examining a smaller number of texts, my analysis may seem necessarily more limited in scope than these others, but it lends further detail to their works. My study therefore deals with the more obscure and intricate ways in which prison authors struggle with their creations and their situations, allowing me to detail their complex analyses of the carceral matrix – analyses which forge critical spaces that can help to alter, or at least point out, the specific oppressive uses of power in their various social surroundings. In addition, my reading of a range of texts from the past two centuries within a transnational Western context helps to retain a more general framework with which to understand the prison and related subjects.

Part 1, 'The Carceral Society,' analyses the ways in which prison writers depict discipline and punishment as informing a variety of institutions and society as a whole. Looking at Henry David Thoreau's 'Civil Disobedience,' the first chapter examines Thoreau's critiques of the market economy, of slavery, and of the American war with Mexico in terms of his reworking of contemporary reformative paradigms of incarceration. Specifically, Thoreau rewrites his arrest and the night he spent in jail as acts that condemn the State that imprisoned him, rather than as acts that reform him into a 'proper' citizen, thus falling into, as Victor Brombert has defined it, the 'happy prison' motif of Romantic writing. My reading of Thoreau's text also demonstrates, however, that his rebellion and use of this motif can, in fact, reproduce some aspects of the carceral matrix itself. His assertion of his identity as an individual who can transcend State oppression runs the risk of reproducing the philosophical and ontological foundations of the modern prison system. Thoreau's text and its wide-ranging influence, conversely, also show the power of such a resistant position. Thoreau's work, therefore, introduces the overall problematic and contradictions of identity that I mentioned in my first paragraph, above, and as discussed in the rest of the book.

The second chapter demonstrates how another social institution that coexisted with, and helped to create, the early prison engages in comparable forms of discipline which serve to reinforce dominant social patterns and hierarchies. Analysing Harriet Jacobs's description in *Incidents in the Life of a Slave Girl* of mid-nineteenth-century American slavery, and her negotiations of the sentimental literary tradition, this chapter further complicates the analysis of the carceral offered by many of the critics mentioned earlier. I demonstrate that practices and assumptions of slavery informed the early prison, as well as the ways in which both engage in comparable forms of discipline that serve to reinforce dominant social patterns and hierarchies. This chapter therefore begins with a discussion of the exact historical connections between slavery and the modern prison, building on the historical and theoretical analyses of H. Bruce Franklin, Angela Y. Davis, and Adam J. Hirsch, among others. My further development of this connection also shows that the theoretical framework used here is not limited to discussions of actual prisons, but can be expanded in order to include a variety of specific issues of social oppression, thus richly widening the scope of the project. My reading of *Incidents* is combined with a critique of contemporary gender biases in relation to disciplinary oppression. The chapter therefore highlights the ways in which different social norms are enacted by varying institutions and ideological frames, and how these frames intermingle to create a complex web of oppression. Beyond this analysis, Jacobs's textual reworking of this web allows her to demonstrate not only its far-reaching implications, but also the ways in which the oppressed author can strategically deploy one set of expectations against another as a means of constructing at least a partial form of freedom within a social critique. The reading of this strategy translates well from Jacobs's slave narrative to the prison texts I examine, and this chapter should be read as the beginning of my analyses of the various means used by the authors subsequently studied to oppose disciplinary practices, while at the same time avoiding the difficulties of a Thoreauvian denial of and supposed transcendence beyond the effectiveness of those practices.

'Writing Wrongs,' the second part of my study, analyses two letters written while their authors were imprisoned. Oscar Wilde's *De Profundis* and Martin Luther King Jr's 'Letter from Birmingham City Jail' were both written ostensibly as means of critiquing the acts of specific individuals, but were also purposively constructed as larger social statements. Both letters, as well, use the portrayal of the authors' imprisonment to critique specific social institutions as figured through previous texts that furthered the prison's disciplinary project. Wilde's letter, addressed to his erstwhile friend, protégé, and lover, Lord Alfred Douglas, combines the fact of Wilde's own imprisonment, as well as more generalized constructions of the prisoner, with a depiction of a conversion in order to oppose and deny the negative valuations of Wilde's sexuality as defined by the courts and the press. In *De Profundis*, Wilde portrays an ideal identity that exists beyond the perception of others, and so beyond the reach of the carceral regime. Unlike Thoreau's transcendent identity, however, Wilde constructs his as being completely private, asocial, and passive, thus avoiding the problems I discuss in Thoreau's text. But, as I show, this construction of identity, like Jacobs's, simultaneously denies Wilde the ability to actively assert himself as an individual, thus also risking a lack of the agential power Thoreau asserts.

In his 'Letter,' King constructs a different notion of self, one that occupies a space of tension between the dominant culture that supports the prison and the oppressed African American populace that King is fighting to empower. Imprisoned because of his demonstrations against the illegal racial segregation in the American South, King wrote his letter as a direct response to another letter by eight clergymen who condemned the demonstrations he was leading. Like Wilde, King uses his letter not only to defend himself, but also to attack another social institution that supports the prison's social project – in this case the white Southern church. By constructing an identity for himself that exists in a space between the dominant and oppressed groups, King attempts to open up the possibility of social, communal action for an ongoing process of social reconstruction.

With the exception of the chapter concerning Thoreau, the first two parts of *Fitting Sentences* examine how authors who are subject to specific dominant forms of institutionalized oppression respond to the prison and the larger carceral society. The two chapters of part 3, 'Privilege, Prison, and Complicity,' deal with texts by authors who are, in different ways, members of the ruling class that governs and controls institutionalized imprisonment. Continuing the critique, in which the other texts participate, of (the biases inherent in) the form of individualism espoused by, for example, Thoreau, both of the authors studied in this final section explore how constructions of a decentred, fragmented identity can help to question and problematize the assumptions of the disciplinary project, assumptions which, the writers contend, are tied to the dominant group's oppression of various 'others.' The fifth chapter reads Lady Constance Lytton's 1914 suffragette prison narrative, *Prisons and Prisoners: Some Personal Experiences*, as an attempt to demonstrate, as Jacobs's text does, the ways in which a person can be conflictingly identified within different but contiguous ideological frameworks. Portraying her upper-class status as being part of the same patriarchal matrix that results in gender oppression, Lytton struggles in her text to remove herself from her class position, while at the same time make her unprivileged position as a woman visible and active in order to make a larger political point about the relations between groups and between the various social classifications of people.

Breyten Breytenbach's *The True Confessions of an Albino Terrorist* explicitly engages in a theoretical renegotiation of identity as a means of undermining the assumptions lying behind the South African apartheid state. Breytenbach was convicted of terrorist activities against the Nationalist government, the racist policies of which he strongly opposed. As an Afrikaner, a member of the dominant racial and linguistic group, Breytenbach's position as a terrorist and a prisoner leads to an even more fragmented portrayal of identity than does Lytton's dual position as an upper-class woman. His consistently self-reflexive comments on this ungrounded and split identity are, in many ways, the inverse of Thoreau's assertion of himself as the transcendent individual. However, Breytenbach's text highlights the dangers of such an identity, which can lead, like Thoreau's rebellion, to a reproduction of the ontological basis of the alienating forces of the prison and the carceral matrix. The final chapter can thus also be read as the first, opening a second reading of the book that cuts across the grain of the larger 'post-humanist' critique.

A series of caveats seems an appropriate intervention here. First, there is a possible concern related to my choice of texts. All of the authors I have chosen to study are well known either for reasons exceeding the specific texts analysed, or because the texts themselves have become canonical, or at least popular, in literary and other academic study. Certainly a question can be raised as to what dynamic such a choice creates within the larger context of the analysis of prison writing. Does my general failure to analyse works written by so-called common prisoners in effect reproduce the silencing effects and policies of the prison? Am I engaging in a process of validation that allows only the voices of those whose position within other social hierarchies already allows them broader access to powerful discursive spaces? Despite my own feelings about such a process, the short answer is 'yes.' Davies presents a defence of his similar choice of such seemingly 'privileged' texts, stating that his study explicitly deals with 'intellectuals whose incarceration came about for political or religious reasons,' since 'the intellectual prisoner of conscience was the only figure who presented a continuous narrative of incarceration.'[36] Such a statement is problematic on two levels. On the one hand, it ignores what is in fact a large body of texts composed by so-called common prisoners. On the other, Davies's definition of the 'prisoner of conscience' problematically equates all such figures. While the second problem is likely a function of the statement's appearance in the introduction of Davies's book, it points to the danger my work courts of reproducing, at least in small part, the homogenizing forces of the prison itself. A study that does carefully analyse the writings of more explicitly non-privileged prisoners would provide an invaluable resource to further our understanding of the social functions of the prison and how to critique them. Indeed, Franklin's study in part answers this need. The writings of prisoners who were 'average citizens' before their arrest, and who were convicted of crimes that were not explicitly related to battles for social justice, also participate in the forms of social analyses that the present study details.

Second, a reading of texts by 'common' prisoners could also engage more explicitly in an analysis of the definition of criminality than I do here. While all the authors I study can be labelled 'criminals' simply because of their status as prisoners, they tend to fall outside of the category of the 'common criminal.' However, this term is not as easily defined as my use of it here may imply. George Jackson, for example, was arrested in California in 1960 for a petty robbery, and was given an indeterminate sentence of one year to life in prison. While incarcerated, Jackson became a political activist whose anti-prison and revolutionary writings inspired countless people. Jackson and two other men were charged for the murder of a guard ten years after his original arrest, and Jackson was himself later murdered by another prison guard. Obviously, Jackson's life story complicates the divisions between the 'common' and the 'political' prisoner. Beyond his case, and moving past the significant period of prison activism in the 1970s, many prison writings by 'common criminals' similarly make explicitly political statements, as I have argued elsewhere.[37]

The importance of a study of writings by problematically termed 'common' criminals does not, however, negate the value of analysing the writings assembled here. All of these works explicitly engage in the relationship between identity construction, the prison, and the larger social frameworks in which those are enmeshed. Moreover, I chose texts that were written by authors whose criminality is more obviously tied to political and social issues in order to demonstrate the centrality and far-ranging influence of the penological system in Western society, even into the ivory tower of canonical literary research. This was especially a consideration for the reader unfamiliar with prison writing as a category. Beyond this, the distinction between 'common' and 'uncommon' prison authors and their relationships to the literary canon is as intensely problematic as the distinction detailed above between 'common' and 'political' prisoners. Harriet Jacobs is a strong case in point: her condition as a slave, and later as an author, was certainly not that of social privilege, and yet her authorship and narrative have, in the past two decades, become intensely studied, written about, and taught at all levels of the academy. Does the burgeoning canonicity of her text work against her historical oppression, or does the privileged space accorded her text within literary institutions threaten to obscure other authors? While a study that can propose answers to these questions is necessary, the choices of texts for the present analysis were made in order to demonstrate more fully some of the ways in which the values of the dominant culture (be it figured through the prison or through the academy) have encoded within them the space for the voice of resistance. This space gives rise to, for example, the newly canonical status (if we can still use that phrase) of Jacobs's text and her use of sentimental discourse, and to Breytenbach's resistance from within his privileged identity.

My section divisions also fall roughly into a generic categorization. This is especially true for the final two parts, which deal with, respectively, letters and somewhat traditional autobiographical memoirs. This leads to my final caveat, with which I will end this introduction and open the main statements of my study. While the authors' negotiations with the genres in question are discussed and figured as part of the larger argument, this study is not intended as a means of exploring the ways in which prison writing can alter our understandings of particular genres. Instead, each text is situated in terms of its specific constructions of the relationships between identity and the social dynamics of incarceration and discipline. This focus is motivated by a desire to avoid positing an overly deterministic structure onto texts that, in large part, attempt to combat such determination. The textual means that prison authors use to critique different forms of oppression in their societies are in fact necessarily myriad, as they are intended to work against the homogenizing, identity-stripping forces of the prison, and as such may actively work against any form of structure used to contain them.[38] Prison texts offer, to appropriate a phrase, 'a plurality of resistances, each of them a special case.'[39] These resistances are analysed here, centrally, in terms of how each author uses definitions of identity as figures through which to critique the dominant and disciplinary society. To reiterate, I do not construct a cohesive, monologic theory of the writing subject, or the way in which prison authors reconstruct their identities. The study as a whole should be looked at as a series of 'opening statements.' I use that legal phrase purposively, for even though in a trial setting a lawyer's opening statements may seem at first to offer the unquestionable 'facts' of a case, in fact they offer only a theory of those 'facts,' a construct that is always under attack by the opposing side. The case, during the trial, is always open-ended and multiple, and this is the way in which *Fitting Sentences* should be read. This is why I set out, above, the two possible readings of this book in the summary of the chapter on Breytenbach. This doubling is certainly not part of a reactionary anti- or a-theoretical stance – anything but. Edward Said, in a recently published book, called for the type of project that I have tried to make *Fitting Sentences*: he argues for a form of analysis that 'is a technique of trouble,' wherein '[t]he task is constitutively an unending one, and it should not aspire to conclusion of the sort that has the corollary and ... deleterious effect of securing one *an* identity.'[40] In this discussion of prisoners' negotiations of identity, I offer arguments and conclusions, certainly, but my point is that I do not offer any *final* conclusions or a set of *deterministic* evaluations of prison writing as a genre, or even of these specific texts, nor do I define a singular form of identity construction in which such writings engage. Instead, I want to engage a dialogue in order to help further understandings of the ways in which the history of prison *is* a history of prisoners, or rather histories, given in their own voices, and which are engaged in meaningful critiques of society to which everyone should listen.

PART ONE

The Carceral Society

CHAPTER ONE

'They locked the door on my meditations': Thoreau, Society, and the Prison House of Identity

Henry David Thoreau's 'Civil Disobedience' is an ideal starting point for my analysis of prison literature, because it offers an explicit interplay between incarceration, politics, and identity. The essay, in which Thoreau explains and justifies his refusal to pay his poll tax – which led to his 1846 arrest – has become one of the most influential political statements of the past one hundred and fifty years. Indeed, it would not be an exaggeration to suggest that Thoreau's discussion of non-violent resistance has helped to shape the current form of American and world politics. Both Martin Luther King Jr and Constance Lytton use Thoreau's ideas and words in their prison texts, and such figures and organizations as Mahatma Gandhi, Leo Tolstoy, and the African National Congress have cited 'Civil Disobedience' as a foundation of their own social philosophies.[1] Despite this range of influences, however, Thoreau's essay and his political thought in general are not without detractors. Discussing the vast amount of critical study on Thoreau's works, Bob Pepperman Taylor bemoans the fact that Thoreau's political ideas have been occasionally figured more as 'a symptom of a problem in the American political tradition – an extreme individualism, say, and moral subjectivism – than as a rich, powerful, and helpful resource to inspire and guide us today.'[2] Taylor's recognition of the split between the critical readings of Thoreau's political works, on the one hand, and their acknowledged influence, on the other, raises the possibility of a problematic contradiction within the texts themselves. If the critical interpretations of Thoreau's work are disjoined from the real-world effects it has had, then it may follow that the writings themselves open up the spectre of opposed interpretations, that they exist as both symptoms of problems and as inspirational resources. If 'Civil Disobedience' is examined not only in terms of Thoreau's other work and its philosophical and literary contexts, but also in the context of nineteenth-century penological and punitive discourses, then the contradiction between Thoreau's transcendental individualism and his more communal political project becomes clear. By tying together his political rebellion and his transcendental subjectivity, Thoreau's essay reproduces the ontological foundations of the carceral matrix (both the actual jail and the society that surrounds it) that he is attempting to critique. Despite this reproduction, though, certain constructions of identity in 'Civil Disobedience' and other texts allow the reader access to a more positive appropriation of Thoreau's rebellious strategies.

1. Prisons, Reform, and Alienation

The overt connection between 'Civil Disobedience' and American punitive practices and penological history has been largely ignored by critics of the essay. Only eleven years prior to Thoreau's one-night confinement in a local jailhouse, de Beaumont and de Tocqueville published, in France and America, *On the Penitentiary System in the United States, and its Application in France*, detailing the methods and practices of the American prison systems, and cementing America's reputation as the world leader in penology. Orlando F. Lewis, in his foundational study of American penal history, notes that 1844 marked the formation of the Prison Association of New York.[3] Moreover, Lewis defines the years between 1844 and 1846, the actual year of Thoreau's arrest, as an especially significant period during 'the formative era of American penology,'[4] a period that included the publication of *Remarks on Prisons and Prison Discipline in the United States* by the highly influential nurse and reformer Dorothea Dix (1845).

As I note in the introduction, prisons had become a centre of both American debate and transnational efforts at a time when American penological practices were defined by the competing, but in many ways similar, Auburn and Philadelphia systems (named after prisons opened in the early nineteenth century at Auburn, New York, and in Philadelphia, Pennsylvania; the latter began at the end of the eighteenth century as a small penitentiary experiment within the Walnut Street jail, and then afterwards expanded into the Eastern State Penitentiary). The practices of and theories behind these systems, as Lewis writes, had become ingrained in American penology: 'principles had become fairly well established; methods were fairly well fixed; traditions had already formed.'[5] While one might expect the jail in the small town of Concord, Massachusetts, not to resemble the larger state institutions much, Thoreau found himself in a fairly large building which served not just Concord, but the surrounding county as well. Thoreau biographer Walter Harding writes that the jail was 'built of granite, three stories high, sixty-five feet long, thirty-two feet wide, and surrounded with a brick wall about ten feet high, mounted with iron pickets. It had eighteen cells, each twenty-six feet long and eight-and-a-half feet high. Each cell had two double-grated windows. A formidable jail indeed.'[6] While even these facts may make the county jail not much more than a rural replica of the institutions at Auburn and Philadelphia, or the notoriously brutal environment of Sing Sing prison, the cultural discourses informing the practice of imprisonment were becoming entrenched in the American imagination. In other words, despite the fact that '[c]ounty and local prisons were almost without exception the centers of callous, unsystematic and ignorant confinement of inmates,'[7] these local jails, like the larger prisons, were seen as sites for the punishment of criminals through confinement. Such punishment, moreover, was understood as a means of deterring further criminal activity (by both the inmate and the general population), and the prisons were, at least theoretically, supposed to be institutions designed to reform the criminal into a civil, socially productive individual.[8]

This construction of reformation and productivity as mutually reinforcing categories was, as Sloop writes, reflected practically in the prison system by the use of 'silence and hard labor: silence in order to allow reflection and redemption, labor in order to make the criminal "productive."' Sloop goes on to note that,

> [i]n early debates about criminal justice, the argument was not over whether prisoners should be silent or work at hard labor but instead, whether their hard labor and silence should be practiced in isolation or in the company of other inmates. Hence, in the Auburn system, the prisoners worked in silent groups, while in the Philadelphia system ..., the prisoners lived and worked in silence and separate from each other.[9]

At the root of the use of silence is the assumption that personal reflection can lead to spiritual redemption, which would bring with it concomitant behavioural changes. De Beaumont and de Tocqueville make this clear when they note that 'communication between' prisoners 'renders their moral reformation impossible,' whereas when a prisoner is '[t]hrown into solitude he reflects. Placed alone, in view of his crime, he learns to hate it.'[10] This emphasis on the individual's innate ability to change is, as mentioned earlier, further discussed by Foucault as a shift in punitive practices which reflects a change in the conception of subjectivity, away from the notion of a thoroughly embodied subject, which reacts mostly to externally enforced punishments, to a subjectivity constituted by an internalized notion of social hierarchies and authorities. Foucault writes of the Philadelphia system that '[i]t is not ... an external respect for the law or fear of punishment alone that will act upon the convict but the workings of the conscience itself.'[11] However, Foucault mistakenly sees a difference between this and the Auburn system which, through the use of 'isolation, assembly without communication and law guaranteed by uninterrupted supervision,' attempted in his view to 'rehabilitate the criminal as a social individual.'[12] Despite the emphasis on working in groups and under supervision, the rule of silence enforced in both systems in fact places the overarching emphasis on the individual prisoner's own abilities to reconstitute the self into a socially acceptable being.

Beyond this theoretical motivation, however, the actual practice of the prisons belies not only the effectiveness of the rule of silence, but also the general notions of human subjectivity that enable it. While the spectacle and practices of corporal punishment do indeed diminish in the nineteenth century, violent physical punishment did not disappear, but was reorganized and shifted in emphasis. Indeed, early in the history of prison reform and speaking in Philadelphia, US founding father Benjamin Rush included both pain and silence as means for reformation: 'The punishments, should consist of bodily pain, labour, watchfulness, solitude and silence.'[13] By Thoreau's time, half a century later, rather than being used primarily as a direct means of punishment or rehabilitation, pain was used in the American prison system in part as a means of enforcing the new prison rules of silence and labour. Lewis describes these problems in both the Auburn and Philadelphia systems:

[T]he unbroken silence in Auburn-type prisons could, in most instances, be maintained only by the inflicting of severe corporal punishments. Floggings became so atrocious in Auburn, and especially in Sing Sing, as to stagger public opinion when finally revealed ... Prisons on the Pennsylvania plan were not without weaknesses ... [T]he Eastern Penitentiary was with increasing frequency charged with a higher rate of deaths, disease and insanity than was alleged to occur in prisons of the Auburn type.[14]

Peter Oliver supports this view, writing that, when officials from Upper Canada were reviewing the Auburn plan with American prison officials before setting up Kingston Penitentiary, 'nothing was said about how men could be forced to work together twelve to fourteen hours a day, month after month, year after year, without ever speaking to each other, or about the punishments that such a system would require.'[15] Georg Rusche and Otto Kirchheimer, writing much earlier, take this conclusion further, bluntly stating that '[p]rison labor became a method of torture.'[16] Rather than following through with the Protestant rhetoric of the possibility of the individual's reformation through meditation and reliance on conscience, these prisons in fact beat, brutalized, and killed more often than they rehabilitated.[17]

The difference between the prisons' theoretical models and their practices raises the question of what the actual relationships were between prison, society, and the inmates whose identities were being actively reformed. Rather than reconfiguring the inmates' identities from deviants and criminals to 'productive citizens' who have authentic relationships with their essential consciences, these prisons consistently brutalized and alienated prisoners, treating them as objects and tools, which points to the American prison's connection to slavery as a model of discipline – a relationship which will be further developed in the next chapter. In the Auburn system, especially, prisoners' welfare and moral reform were only important insofar as they were valuable as marketable products. The Auburn system's primary goal was to be economically self-sufficient through the exploitation of inmate labour. H. Bruce Franklin notes that such prisons 'rapidly shed much of their early pretense of being places of reformation and became frankly acknowledged as places of cheap mass production.'[18] Indeed, the Auburn prisons were so profitable that working groups employed at making the same products as the prisoners held strikes and protests, claiming that the prisons were threatening their livelihoods.[19]

The prisons run on the Philadelphia system were not nearly as profitable as the Auburn prisons, simply because each prisoner was required to remain completely isolated, which rendered factory-like work impossible. Hard labour was, however, still one of the central facets of prison life in the Philadelphia system. Rothman states this explicitly, writing, 'In retrospect, the differences between the two plans do not seem very notable. Both ... emphasized isolation, obedience, and a *steady routine of labor.*'[20] Even though the Auburn system was motivated to a large degree by the desire for profit, hard labour was first and foremost perceived to be a means of rehabilitation. In other words, while modern-day, and even some nineteenth-century, critics easily separated labour as market relation from labour as means for individual salvation, they were not as easily disjoined within the prison context. Auburn proponents could discuss the possibility (and reality) of prisons as profit-making ventures solely because hard labour as a tool of reformation was generally unquestioned, as was silence. In the burgeoning industrial revolution, and in the established republic that was America, both labour and one's innate ability to 'further' oneself went hand in hand.

The result of the emphasis on people's innate reformative ability and the use of labour to aid that ability led to a uniformity of punishment that was embodied in the identical rows upon rows of cells in the panoptic structures of the larger prisons. Prisons became man-factories, churning out supposedly rehabilitated citizens.[21] The stress on the power of the individual effectively removed any notions of individualized punishment. Wiener phrases this contradiction succinctly:

> The advancing individualism of the age had a dark, anarchic side that few failed to sense. Many traditional limitations upon individual freedom of action were being dismantled, while traditional structures of authority were being challenged ... As the brutality of the law was lessened, its reach was extended to cover more persons and more forms of behavior ... In tandem with these changes, punishment was reconstructed so that its discretionary, public, and violent character yielded to forms more calculated to promote the development of inner behavioural controls. In convicted criminals, this reorientation was accomplished through the uniform and impersonal disciplinary regime of the new prisons ... At all levels prosecution was made easier, punishment more certain, and penalties more predictable, impersonal, and uniform. The guiding vision of this reconstructed system of criminal justice was that of the responsible individual.[22]

The power of the single person rapidly degenerates into the uniform treatment of 'the people' as a civic body, each member of which reacts to, and can thus be disciplined by, the universally applicable rulings of the State. Wiener is here discussing Victorian England, but in nineteenth-century America these issues were if anything more pronounced, thanks to the democratization of the country and to the growing popularity of the figure of the rugged individual.[23] Since the individual, and not the State, is endowed with 'certain inalienable rights,' uniform, predictable, and specifically de-individualized forms of punishment are seen as necessary in order to avoid violating those rights.

Prisons and the legal system are thus situated within the socio-political spectrum between the emphasis on the power and rights of each person and the theoretically uniform treatment of the entire populace. The difficulty here is that such uniform treatment, especially when combined with industrial capitalism, leads to the de-individuation of the citizenry. The prisons' treatment of inmates also results in the effective removal of whatever rights those people could claim. In the prison system, as in slavery, oppression is distilled into a brutalizing force that would deny the very humanity of its victims. Sloop argues: 'The prisoner was constituted in some sense as one element of the communal machine, to be taken, repaired, and made to work again, with no question of what the prisoner himself thought was best, with no imagination that a criminal could have rights ... The old penology shaped criminal justice and carried with it the assumption of the prisoner as malleable object.'[24] While Sloop sees this reification of prisoners as a hold-over from earlier forms of punishment, it can also be read as a paradoxical and indirect result of the nineteenth-century emphasis on individual rights and freedoms.[25]

In order to retain personal rights within society, people had to act within (self-)regulated bounds of propriety; if certain individuals did not do so, it became the State's responsibility *to the individual* to readjust him or her. And those bounds of propriety generally fall within the social behaviour of the upper classes who, since they are enfranchised and control economic power, can help form the law.[26] From an emphasis on democracy and people's power to reform their behaviour, then, we come to the position from which that propriety is defined, and through which individual actions and rights are limited. Within this limitation, the most brutal functioning of a hierarchical society is also apparent, where people who act outside 'proper' norms are treated as less than human, and those who are seen as less than human are automatically subject to the prison system.

2. Thoreau and the Disciplining of Society

Given these conclusions, which situate the prison as part and parcel of the alienating forces of nineteenth-century American society, 'Civil Disobedience' and the prison-related context of its writing offer an opening for the voice of the prisoner to be incorporated into the histories of the prison and of the larger social framework. Specifically, what 'Civil Disobedience' does, in conjunction with *Walden* and Thoreau's other writings, is provide us with a connection between the policies of the seminal nineteenth-century prison and the socializing forces of the time.

Thoreau wrote 'Civil Disobedience' as a means of protesting the American war against Mexico, which began on 11 May 1846 as a direct result of Texas's entrance into the Union. The addition of Texas as a slaveholding state was felt to 'increase substantially the influence of the South in national politics.'[27] Because the addition of Texas was seen as an expansion of slavery and because it inevitably resulted in the war with Mexico, many abolitionists and peace advocates opposed it, both before and after Texas achieved statehood in 1845.[28] The year Thoreau's essay was written, 1848, was also an election year, and therefore a pivotal year in the debates that would result in the passing of the Fugitive Slave Law in 1850. This law allowed for the forced return of slaves who had escaped from the South to the supposed 'freedom' of the North. In order to protest the war and the related issue of slavery, Thoreau followed the example of his friend Bronson Alcott, who refused to pay his poll tax and was arrested in 1843. Despite his arrest, Alcott was never jailed, because 'Squire Hoar, [Concord]'s leading citizen, paid Alcott's taxes himself rather than permit such a blot on the town escutcheon'; Hoar paid the same tax for Alcott's friend Charles Lane, who had also refused to pay.[29] Thoreau, though, perhaps due more to the fact that he was arrested at the end of the day than to the seriousness of his crime, did spend the night in jail in late July 1846, and when he was to be released the next day after someone else paid his tax, he tried to refuse to leave.[30]

Thoreau's transformation of his economic protest into a verbal and written form did not occur for a few years. He first delivered an address on the subject at the Concord Lyceum in 1848, and published the essay in Elizabeth Peabody's first and only issue of the journal *Aesthetic Papers* in May 1849.[31] Rather than focus on the explicit issues that resulted in his refusal to pay the poll tax, Thoreau instead offers a complex denunciation of what he perceived to be the alienating effects of the government and the economy of his time. He saw the State and the market-driven economy as mutually reinforcing entities that separated people's actions from their consciences in order to exploit their labour as fully as possible, thus helping the market and the State, as institutions, to reproduce and perpetuate themselves.

The second paragraph of the essay explains this institutional desire for perpetuation explicitly: 'This American government, – what is it but a tradition, though a recent one, endeavoring to transmit itself unimpaired to posterity.'[32] The institution of the State itself, rather than its officers or leaders, is portrayed as an active force that uses people to sustain itself. This is most obvious for Thoreau in the use of soldiers:

> A common and natural result of an undue respect for law is, that you may see a file of soldiers, colonel, captain, corporal, privates, powder-monkeys and all, marching in admirable order over hill and dale to the wars, against their wills, aye, against their common sense and consciences, which makes it very steep marching indeed, and produces a palpitation of the heart. They have no doubt that it is a damnable business in which they are concerned; they are all peaceably inclined. Now, what are they? Men at all? or small moveable forts and magazines, at the service of some unscrupulous man in power? Visit the Navy Yard, and behold a marine, such a man as an American government can make, or such as it can make a man with its black arts, a mere shadow and reminiscence of humanity, a man laid out alive and standing, and already, as one may say, buried under arms with funeral accompaniments. (65–6)

Beginning by tying 'law' and the military together under the single force of 'an American government,' this early passage organizes Thoreau's vision of the relationship between the State and the individual: the State, in effect, erases the existence of individuals, replacing them with a homogeneous assemblage of tools and parts. In the act of homogenizing them, it removes their ability to act on their own, to match properly their movements with their wills, thus transforming them from 'men' to machines that further the State's aim of retaining the slave territories of Texas.

The gothic imagery at the end of the passage, recalling more of *Frankenstein* than of American politics, is the culmination of the description of the alienated, objectified, State-manufactured person, transforming what Thoreau elsewhere calls 'the noblest faculties of the mind'[33] into corpse-like automation. This description of the objectification of people looks forward to Thoreau's description of slavery in 'Slavery in Massachusetts,' his direct response to the passing of the Fugitive Slave Law.[34] Thoreau sees slavery as an issue simply beyond debate; as the legally and socially sanctioned transformation of human beings into objects, it is the ultimate evil. He writes:

> If I were seriously to propose to Congress to make mankind into sausages, I have no doubt that most of the members would smile at my proposition, and if any believed me to be in earnest, they would think that I proposed something much worse than Congress had ever done. But if any of them will tell me that to make a man into a sausage would be much worse, – would be any worse, than to make him into a slave, – than it was to enact the Fugitive Slave Law, I will accuse him of foolishness, of intellectual incapacity, of making a distinction without a difference. The one is just as sensible a proposition as the other.[35]

Exposing not only the evils of slavery, but also what he sees as the foolishness of debating the issue, Thoreau's 'Swiftian modest proposal' (Kritzberg, 545) further emphasizes his vision of State control of the populace as a dehumanizing and even deadly force. Similar arguments allow him to conclude that the citizens of Massachusetts, through passing the Fugitive Slave Law, have turned themselves into slaves of the State: 'There is not one slave in Nebraska; there are perhaps a million slaves in Massachusetts.'[36] Further, if people who recognize these forces still defend them, they are not only serving the State to their own detriment, but also actively splitting their own vision of the world – they make distinctions where no differences exist.

Military activity and slavery are only the most obvious of the State's alienating powers and, as such, Thoreau does not spend much time actively engaging them. Instead, most of the rhetorical energy of 'Civil Disobedience' is devoted to more insidious and pervasive dehumanizing and alienating forces. In keeping with the essay's general theme of explaining the reasons of his arrest, certain taxes are portrayed as State impositions which, when obeyed, result in a splitting of identity, a severance between thought and deed. This is a form of alienation which for Thoreau is the equivalent of a living death. Addressing an audience which he delineates as, in Henry Golemba's words, '"well disposed" to lead a just and moral life,' but 'who comply with the state even though they disapprove' of it,[37] Thoreau reconstitutes the act of paying the poll tax as, instead, an attack on the taxpayer himself:

See what gross inconsistency is tolerated. I have heard some of my townsmen say, 'I should like to have them order me out to help put down an
insurrection of the slaves, or to march to Mexico, – see if I would go'; and
yet these very men have each, directly by their allegiance, and so indirectly, at least, by their money, furnished a substitute ... Thus, under the
name of order and civil government, we are all made at last to pay hom-
age to and support our own meanness. After the first blush of sin, comes
its indifference; and from immoral it becomes, as it were, *un*moral, and
not quite unnecessary to that life which we have made. (71–2)

The exchange of funds between the taxpayer and the State is grounded
on an understanding that those funds will help to perpetuate 'order
and civil government,' but that exchange comes at the expense of the
taxpayer's ability to act in accordance with his own beliefs and values.
Because the equation of the civil government with social order is
unquestioned, acts of immorality are not only tolerated, but seem to
become part of the foundation of civil society. This unquestioning tol-
erance of the State's action results, in Thoreau's logic, in the splitting of
identity of the individual taxpayer into a passive figure who speaks
against the State and the more active subject who supports it by substi-
tuting himself with his tax.

The way in which the State convinces its citizens to alter – or re-form
– their individual consciences points to the direct echoes between Thoreau's vision of society and the nineteenth-century disciplinary, penological model. Thoreau argues that society, like the prison, attempts to
force those under its control to behave in a docile yet productive fashion, removing personal motivations and dulling individual faculties
(be they criminal or 'poetic' as in *Walden*),[38] restructuring those people
as socially acceptable automata. He makes this comparison more
explicit later in the essay, as I discuss below. At this point, however, it is
apparent that Thoreau's portrayal of the State's governing and alienating forces parallels Wiener's summary of recent discussions of criminal
policies, in that both are seen as being 'determined by unacknowledged deep structures of power,' while at the same time their point is
'to reproduce existing social power relations.'[39] Individuals in society
are, for Thoreau, similar to prisoners in that they are constructed or
reduced to a uniform mob, which is then forced to function within dictated bounds of propriety as a means of allowing the institution, or
State, to continue to operate.

Thoreau writes that, given this disciplinary functioning of society, the rule of the majority in a democracy is simply a means of forcing on the minority certain codes of behaviour that, in and of themselves, are not tied to justice or right:

> [T]he people must have some complicated machinery or other, and hear its din, to satisfy that idea of government which they have. Governments show thus how successfully men can be imposed on, even impose on themselves, for their own advantage ... After all, the practical reason why, when the power is once in the hands of the people, a majority are permitted, and for a long period continue, to rule, is not because they are most likely to be in the right, nor because this seems fairest to the minority, but because they are physically the strongest. But a government in which the majority rule in all cases cannot be based on justice, even as far as men understand it. (63–5)

The 'men' referred to in this passage are not individuals of 'integrity,' the unalienated few who are not owned by their possessions. They are 'the mass of men' and so their need to hear the din of government is itself a result of their alienation by the social structures around them. Grammatically, the pronoun in 'their own advantage' refers not to the men who are the objects of the sentence, but to the 'Governments,' which are the agential subjects. Taylor discusses the agency of the State, picking up on a passage in *Walden* which refers obliquely to the construction of the pyramids, noting that 'Thoreau sees our economic life as a new incarnation of an old attempt by nations to assure their place in history by building monuments to themselves.'[40] Or, as Thoreau puts it in 'Civil Disobedience,' governments use complex disciplinary powers in order to force men to impose on themselves, allowing governments to gain even more advantage, thereby helping the State 'to transmit itself unimpaired to posterity' (63).

Because of the hierarchical structure of the disciplinary mechanisms of society, Thoreau's townspeople, like prison inmates, are subject not just to the amorphous structures of power, but to the people who are placed in the upper echelons of the social, or carceral, system. Just as the warden has the ability to decide *exactly* how the discipline of the prison will be enforced, those in positions of power in the government can control the means through which the subjects of the State are controlled. Because the American government 'has not the vitality and force of a single living man ... a single man can bend it to his will' (63). Further, as Donald E. Pease details, such seemingly powerful men were generally idealized in nineteenth-century American popular culture as powerful orators who dictated, rather than listened to, the will of the people: 'The idealization of the characters of the people's representatives ... assumed the early form of a denial of their representative function and in effect reversed the relation between the leaders and the will they were to represent.'[41] These men thus reinforce the separation in the 'mass of men' between thought and deed, or between will and government.

But Thoreau does not allow the leaders of government to become simple scapegoats without whom society would improve. The problem, as he sees it, is with the disciplinary functions of the State itself. Those who are in positions of power, such as 'legislators, politicians, lawyers, ministers, and office-holders' (66), turn their intellect to solving the problems that impede the functioning of the State, thus helping the State to continue, and so, Thoreau writes, 'as they rarely make any moral distinctions, they are as likely to serve the devil, without intending it, as God' (66). Thoreau's use of the word 'intending' (which is italicized in the posthumous version of the essay)[42] reinforces a sense of separation between thought and deed, an alienation which, he implies, affects those at the top of the social hierarchy as much as those on the bottom.

3. Thoreau and the Transcending of Society

The seeming pervasiveness of society's discipline is, however, superficial. For Thoreau, unlike Marx, the means to escape the cycle of discipline, monetary exchange, and alienation are not found in a communal effort, but in a personal rejection of the power of social forces. Relying on the American rhetoric of the power of the individual, and on the philosophical basis provided by his transcendentalist circle, Thoreau constructs a strategic economic and political philosophy that evades the discipline of the State and the alienating forces of the market through a construction of an interior subjectivity which simply denies the State access to the individual. Thoreau details this subjectivity by emphasizing the importance of a simplified mode of living, which is tied to a heavily Romanticized relationship with Nature, which in turn allows for a more direct relationship between thought and deed.

Walden is, of course, the prime example of Thoreau's doctrine of simplification. The infamous passage which contains the command 'Simplify, simplify' continues:

> Instead of three meals a day, if it be necessary eat but one; instead of a
> hundred dishes, five; and reduce other things in proportion ... The nation
> itself, with all its so called internal improvements, which, by the way, are
> all external and superficial, is just such an unwieldy and overgrown
> establishment, cluttered with furniture and tripped up by its own traps,
> ruined by luxury and heedless expense, by want of calculation and a wor-
> thy aim, as the million households in the land; and the only cure for it as
> for them is in a rigid economy, a stern and more than Spartan simplicity of
> life and elevation of purpose.[43]

The entire nation is here depicted as having its integrity destroyed by
the objects of material gain. Beyond this, Thoreau makes the connection between the simplified life in which these objects are stripped
away and an 'elevation of purpose.' This is the common perception of
Thoreau's experiment at Walden Pond; not only by placing himself at a
remove from society, but also by removing the trappings that are valued in that society, Thoreau attempts to construct his life as a Romantic
ideal, where his connection to Nature and its 'Higher Laws' is unim-
peded by the alienation brought about by those objects.

Thoreau explicates the personal nature of his transcendence of the
everyday, and his connection to a more Platonic notion of the universal
right, in a passage in the 'Conclusion' of *Walden*:

> I learned this, at least, by my experiment; that if one advances confidently
> in the direction of his dreams, and endeavors to live the life which he has
> imagined, he will meet with a success unexpected in common hours. He
> will put some things behind, will pass an invisible boundary; new, uni-
> versal, and more liberal laws will begin to establish themselves around
> and within him; or the old laws be expanded, and interpreted in his favor
> in a more liberal sense, and he will live with the license of a higher order
> of beings. In proportion as he simplifies his life, the laws of the universe
> will appear less complex, and solitude will not be solitude, nor poverty
> poverty, nor weakness weakness.[44]

The self-imposition of simplicity is tied to a more complete understanding of 'universal' laws, and both are the direct result of acting
'confidently,' of not allowing anything to come between one's actions
and one's conscience or thought. Economic simplification leads to a
removal of the danger of market- or State-enforced alienation, thus

erasing the personal and ideological boundaries that 'unnaturally,' in Thoreau's view, separate the individual from the 'truly' universal.

The erasure of these enforced boundaries, and the resulting direct relationship between action and conscience, has an immediate and powerful political effect. Shortly following the above passage, Thoreau writes: 'It is a ridiculous demand which England and America make, that you shall speak so that they can understand you ... I desire to speak somewhere *without* bounds; like a man in a waking moment, to men in their waking moments.'[45] The State, for Thoreau, attempts to enforce not only its laws, but also the means and modes of communication. The restrictions placed by the State on people's actions may result in the alienation of those people, but Thoreau argues that each person can learn to speak *'without* bounds'; individuals can remove themselves from the effects of the market through a concerted simplification of their relationships to market and social forces. This, in turn, allows the individual to understand higher and more universal laws than those imposed by the State, and thus allows that person to act, with conscience, against earthly laws.

For this reason, Thoreau writes in 'Civil Disobedience' that '[a]ction from principle, – the perception and performance of right, – changes things and relations; it is essentially revolutionary, and does not consist wholly with any thing which was. It not only divides states and churches, it divides families; aye, it divides the *individual*, separating the diabolical in him from the divine' (72). While Barry Wood notes that '[d]oing *something* means, for Thoreau, resolving the polarities through action which carries dichotomies to a new level where they can be synthesized in a higher unity,'[46] Thoreau's text here functions less in the dialectical form Wood would impose than through a simple binary construction that opposes the degraded society to the principled individual. The step from one to the other may involve a synthesis of action and conscience, but this is perceived as a reinstantiation of a pre-existing natural order, not as a progression to a completely new stage of development. Thus, the person of integrity who has a simplified life and a transcendent connection to the right, cannot simply be a subject of the State, or even an ideal synthesis of the contradictions of society which leads to a new evolution of that society, but is instead a permanent ideal, the Platonic form of the revolutionary figure that is always opposed to the impure social world.

Further describing the transcendental figure, Thoreau writes that, while alienated subjects serve the State with their bodies and others serve with their heads, '[a] very few, as heroes, patriots, martyrs, reformers in the great sense, and *men*, serve the State with their consciences also, and so necessarily resist it for the most part; and they are commonly treated by it as enemies' (66). Only through a denial of alienation and through a transcendent relationship to the higher law can people truly be patriots, and such people are resisted by the government which would impose 'bounds' on the necessarily boundless, universal conscience. James Duban argues a similar point in discussing Thoreau's relationship to Unitarian thought, writing that Thoreau subordinates 'civil authority to the voice of God manifest in private conscience.'[47] This subordination allows Thoreau to write that John Brown, who attempted to steal weapons to arm an antislavery revolt, was 'a transcendentalist above all, a man of ideas and principles' who was not afraid to act on them.[48] Transcendentalism can therefore simultaneously involve the individual's removal from and replacement into the State. The removal from the State 'divides' the person from its alienating effects, and the replacement becomes the necessary rebellion of the transcendentalist against the State. This is true for Thoreau even if that rebellion takes the form of a passive example of living the 'proper' life, because '[i]t is not so important that many should be as good as you, as that there be some absolute goodness somewhere; for that will leaven the whole lump' ('Civil,' 69).

4. 'My Prisons'

'Civil Disobedience' dramatizes the process of the Romantic individual's transcendence beyond the State's disciplinary functions in the section dealing with Thoreau's imprisonment, which he refers to as 'My Prisons.' Offset in a different typeface in most editions, this section explicates Thoreau's disciplinary social model, and the means through which one can escape its imposed alienation, by inverting contemporary penological thought on imprisonment, meditation, and reform.

Thoreau introduces the offset section by describing his arrest, and by creating an explicit synecdochic relationship between the prison and the State as a whole. He writes, 'I have paid no poll-tax for six years. I was put into a jail once on this account,' which leads him to the conclusion that 'the State never intentionally confronts a man's sense, intellectual or moral, but only his body, his senses' (79–80). Thoreau identifies the causal relationship between the tax and the jail, making them both parts of the physical imposition of the State. His continuing references to the State as an alienating force which attempts to deal with people only as physical objects are again stated here, directly reinforcing a previous description of the jail cell: 'as I stood considering the walls of solid stone, two or three feet thick, the door of wood and iron, a foot thick, and the iron grating which strained the light, I could not help being struck with the foolishness of that institution which treated me as if I were mere flesh and blood and bones, to be locked up' (80). Introducing the central prison section, this passage sets up the terms on which Thoreau will critique his night in jail. Specifically, the prison, as a figure of the State, attempts to deal with Thoreau as an alienated, purely embodied tool that is in need of correction. The listing of the physical details of the cell, the close enumeration of its confining space, highlights the ways in which the prison as an institution attempts to affect social reform through isolation. For Thoreau, the 'solid stone' and iron only highlight the State's misapprehension of his identity: as the transcendent individual, he sees himself as being beyond such punishment.

Moving from the State's ineffective attempts to punish him, the central description of Thoreau's night in jail details a specific moment of transcendence which ironically duplicates the reformative rhetoric of the nineteenth-century prison system. This system, especially as perceived in the Philadelphia-style prisons, relied on the assumption that personal reflection could lead to a form of spiritual redemption, which would lead to changes in behaviour that would make the prisoner more amenable to social life. Thoreau plays off of this notion by constructing a moment of personal reflection that *does* lead to a spiritual redemption, but that simultaneously places him at odds with the general social world. He states that, after his cell mate blows out their light, he felt that '[i]t was like travelling into a far country, such as I had never expected to behold, to lie there for one night.' He continues:

It seemed to me that I never had heard the town-clock strike before, nor the evening sounds of the village; for we slept with the windows open, which were inside the grating. It was to see my native village in the light of the middle ages, and our Concord was turned into a Rhine stream, and visions of knights and castles passed before me. They were the voices of old burghers that I heard in the streets. I was an involuntary spectator and auditor of whatever was done and said in the kitchen of the adjacent village-inn, – a wholly new and rare experience to me. It was a closer view of my native town. I was fairly inside of it. I never had seen its institutions before. This is one of its peculiar institutions; for it is a shire town. I began to comprehend what its inhabitants were about. (82)

Rather than being a constricted and confined place, as intended, Thoreau's cell opens up the world to him. The prison cell does indeed become a place of reflection, but instead of receiving a purely internal vision of the impropriety of his past 'criminal' actions, Thoreau's perspective immediately widens, giving him an intimate view of his town and his society. This view is also one in which the society is primitivized, looking backward both temporally and geographically to pre-imperial Europe, a past that America supposedly rebelled against. In other words, while privately reflecting in his prison cell, Thoreau has a condemnatory vision of the degraded character of the outside society.

This vision is a dramatization of Thoreau's transcendentalism, which permits him to condemn the State based on his own Romantic connection to and understanding of higher laws. His censure of society is clarified in the penultimate main paragraph of the prison section:

> When I came out of prison, – for some one interfered, and paid the tax, – I did not perceive that great changes had taken place on the common, such as he observed who went in a youth, and emerged a tottering and gray-headed man; and yet a change had to my eyes come over the scene, – the town, and State, and country, – greater than any that mere time could effect. I saw yet more distinctly the State in which I lived. I saw to what extent the people among whom I lived could be trusted as good neighbors and friends; that their friendship was for summer weather only; that they did not greatly purpose to do right. (83)

Thoreau employs the rhetoric of the reformatory practice of the prison to condemn the brutalizing and alienating effects of the disciplinary institution, which he sees at work in the whole of society. Thus, he uses the institution of the prison itself to reverse the judgmental gaze. His reflective time in prison does change his outlook on his position in society but, rather than reconstruct him as a productive citizen, it highlights for him the hypocrisy and untrustworthiness of his neighbours, and of his country as a whole. A. Robert Caponigri summarizes the philosopher's transcendent, judgmental position, writing that '[t]o the degree to which' a person achieves this position 'he becomes the law-giver to himself, not subservient to any outer law.'[49] Thoreau's prison

vision defines the State and its law-abiding citizens as the true criminals, while Thoreau becomes the transcendental patriot.

This reversal, indicative of Thoreau's writing, is evident in his strategic use of the 'happy prison' motif, wherein the prison cell becomes an
idealized space of freedom. He writes: 'I saw that, if there was a wall of
stone between me and my townsmen, there was a still more difficult
one to climb or break through, before they could get to be as free as I
was' (80). Discussing the late-eighteenth-century prison writing of
British radical John Thelwall, Julia M. Wright notes: 'While [Victor]
Brombert suggests that the "happy prison" in Romantic literature
arises from the identification of solitude with transcendence and cre-
ativity, the prison in Thelwall's writing ... is a "happy" one insofar as it
functions as the site of defiance and reveals the limits of the state's
power.'[50] While Thoreau's essay constructs the prison as 'happy' for
reasons similar to Thelwall's, his reversal of the prison's reformatory
rhetoric implies that the State itself is precisely what enables this rebellion, by 'stripping' the prisoner of all but his necessities. The construction of the second wall between Thoreau and his neighbours –
obviously a moral or transcendental wall – is available to Thoreau precisely because the prison cell offers the preconditions for a transcendental rediscovery of one's own conscience. Like his life at Walden, his
prison life is stripped of all but its essentials, 'Food and Shelter.'[51] And
just as his shack is devoid of an excess of furniture that would 'trap' its
owner,[52] the prison cell is 'the whitest, most simply furnished, and
probably the neatest apartment in the town' (81). The cell offers a life
free of the material objects and market relations, which Thoreau sees as
the precondition for his transcendent moments at Walden Pond.

5. Thoreau as State

Thoreau's history of 'My Prisons' therefore seems to dramatize both
the State's methods of alienation and its impotence in the face of transcendent truths by ironically deploying the rhetoric of reformation that
lies behind the State's prisons. Is his use of this rhetoric actually ironic,
however? The reformative foundations of the original Philadelphia
system and Thoreau's notion of the individual's ability to comprehend
universal truths and act on them are in many ways similar. Both grow
out of a Protestant notion of each person's ability to understand and
receive divine guidance, and both the prisons and his writings are posited as guides toward a better society.[53] Given this, Thoreau's use of the

prison cell as a space of conversion may be ironic in that he uses it to attack the very State that arrests him, but, on a philosophical level, Thoreau's advice to 'simplify, simplify' in order to reach a more authentic relation to the self actually runs parallel to the prison project. The question that needs to be posed, then, is whether Thoreau's philosophical project, like the prison system, results in the alienation and brutalization of its audience instead of their reformation.

Many revisionist readings of Thoreau and of the American Romantics in general support an affirmative answer to this question. Grusin discusses such interpretations of Thoreau's economic critique, noting that they 'have suggested that the economy Thoreau practiced at Walden was not independent of the ideology of American capitalism but made in its image.'[54] Michael T. Gilmore's conclusion about *Walden* provides perhaps the clearest statement on the revisionist position. Gilmore argues that, in Thoreau's critique,

> market society engenders a conflation of history with nature. By presenting its limited, time-bound conventions as eternal, the existing order in effect places itself outside time and beyond the possibility of change. Although Thoreau rigorously condemns his society's 'naturalization' of itself in this fashion, he can be charged with performing a version of the same process on his own life by erasing history from *Walden* and mythologizing his experiment at the pond.[55]

Gilmore argues further that Thoreau's rhetorical and compositional methods in *Walden* duplicate the alienating forces of society from which he is avowing to remove himself. By setting up his experiment as an ideal example, Thoreau's text, Gilmore writes, assumes the ideological functions of the market; 'he is unable,' Taylor writes, 'to escape the type of self-conscious and exploitative manipulation of the world that he criticizes capitalism for'; because of this, 'Thoreau did not solve the problem of how to discipline a free will, how to remain free and yet not fall prey to the vice of pride.'[56] This 'vice of pride,' or individualism, one might say, is closely related to Gilmore's conclusions about Thoreau's naturalization and idealization of his own life.

These conclusions need to be expanded. The problem of the reduplication of the dominant culture in Thoreau's writings, be it in terms of economics or politics, is embedded at the very root of Thoreau's world view, in his construction of his own identity as the basis from which his philosophy evolves. At the beginning of *Walden*, Thoreau defends his use of first-person address, writing, 'In most books, the *I*, or first person, is omitted; in this it will be retained ... We commonly do not remember that it is, after all, always the first person that is speaking.'[57] While the wording of this defence may seem to suggest that Thoreau is setting up a subjective narrative, where the viewpoints expressed are only defensible as one person's opinion, he quickly relates how his viewpoint is a universal one that allows him access to all others. First, he turns his first-person account into one that can speak *for* the reader, offering, 'I would fain say something, not so much concerning the Chinese and Sandwich Islanders as you who read these pages, who are said to live in New England; something about your condition.'[58] Moving from a focus on his own voice, on his own opinion, Thoreau here elaborates that voice to include the specific readers from his region – his 'simple and sincere account'[59] of his life, he implies, will have immediate and important consequences for others.

Thoreau's expanding voice does not stop there. After he enumerates the cost of his shack, he writes, 'If I seem to boast more than is becoming, my excuse is that I brag for humanity rather than for myself; and my shortcomings and inconsistencies do not affect the truth of my statement.'[60] Despite problems with what he writes, his boasting is still universally true. While this is certainly one of the passages that would cause revisionists to cringe, Thoreau's unquestioning assumption of the universal applicability of his particular experiences is not simply the braggadocio of an unabashed egotist. Rather, Thoreau is bringing to the surface the ontological assumptions that are inherent in his transcendentalism. Caponigri details the transcendent moment as one that 'lends to the vision and to the utterance ... of the individual a range and authority far outreaching his personal capacity; indeed it makes these utterances normative for all men.'[61] For Thoreau, everyone has the ability to transcend the particular, to understand the universal laws that are applicable to 'all men.'[62] As Sidonie Smith argues, this neo-Platonic Romantic individual is the foundation of a democratic subject which 'can claim equal access to the universally human.' Smith goes on to detail the central difficulty with this identity:

> Yet within this claim there is implicit a hierarchy wherein what is and is not appropriate, at any given juncture, to the universal subject gets staked out. Founded on exclusionary practices, this democratic self positions on its border ... that which becomes identified culturally as other, exotic, unruly, irrational, uncivilized, regional, or paradoxically unnatural.[63]

What other critics have termed Thoreau's radical individualism, or what George Hochfield calls an 'intense' egotism, the 'maggot in Thoreau's head,'[64] is instead his own take on the naturalization of the liberal, humanist identity. The problem with such a naturalization, as Smith points out, is that it is grounded on an exclusion of the 'other,' which generally denotes, in this context, anyone who is not white, male, and of a certain class.[65] The 'others' left out of such categories are then perceived as being lower on the hierarchical valuation of humanity. Ignatieff places this structuring principle in the prison context, writing that nineteenth-century American penal and criminal policy arises from 'an increasing intolerance towards "deviant" minorities,' an intolerance which was itself characteristic of 'the advent of democracy.'[66] Thus, the supposedly democratic, universally accessible, transcendent subject that Thoreau constructs could be seen as a further privileging of the white, rich, and male subject.

The exclusion of the 'other' is readily apparent in several passages in *Walden*, the most well-known of which is the section describing Irish immigrant John Field. Thoreau describes Field as '[a]n honest, hardworking, but shiftless man' who lived with his family in a shack near Thoreau's.[67] Field becomes, in Thoreau's text, the degraded ground against which Thoreau's own transcendence and idealism is highlighted. This contrast is enabled by Thoreau's bigoted construction of the Irish in general: 'A man will not need to study history to find out what is best for his own culture. But alas! the culture of an Irishman is an enterprise to be undertaken with a sort of moral bog hoe.'[68] Belying his opening statements that his text is to be perceived as an example through which his fellow New Englanders can perhaps improve their lives, Thoreau's depiction of Field is of a permanently alienated figure who is essentially unredeemable due to his nationality (or race):[69] 'With his horizon all his own, yet he a poor man, born to be poor, with his inherited Irish poverty or poor life, his Adam's grandmother and boggy ways, not to rise in this world, he nor his posterity, till their wading webbed bog-trotting feet get *talaria* to their heels.'[70] Field, his entire family, and their future are always already separated from Thoreau's supposedly universally accessible transcendent truth. Thus, while Henry Abelove may be right in concluding that the discourses of the 'white bourgeois family' are left behind 'at least in the aspirations' of *Walden*,[71] in its execution the distinctions inherent in such discourse are all too visible. Field, as a figure of the lower class and of the Irish, is described as nearly subhuman, with physical deformities that match his unending labour, which, notwithstanding Thoreau's critique of the market, is tied not to social forces but to Field's own essential nature.

The grounding of Thoreau's transcendent identity and its relation to a practice of racial othering is also explicit in 'Civil Disobedience.' After he 'came out of prison,' having realized the degradation of his townspeople and that they 'did not greatly purpose to do right,' Thoreau claims 'that they were a distinct race from me by their prejudices and superstitions, as the Chinamen and Malays are' (83). Thoreau can only recognize his new and higher position against the backdrop of an orientalist, racist depiction of the 'mass of men,' who are superstitious rather than transcendent, prejudiced, and therefore limited in their vision rather than having access to the universal; Thoreau is, indeed, made distinct by 'prejudices.'[72]

In addition to the construction of an 'other' against whom he contrasts his own idealized identity, Thoreau also occasionally describes the transcendental itself in hierarchical terms. In the chapter of *Walden* called 'Reading,' he describes the authors of 'the oldest and the best' books (which he, of course, reads in the original languages) as 'a natural and irresistible aristocracy in every society,' who 'more than kings or emperors, exert an influence on mankind.'[73] Classical texts and the truths they exhort are part of a natural hierarchical power structure to which Thoreau, and similarly educated men of his class, have special access: 'Those who have not learned to read the ancient classics in the language in which they were written must have a very imperfect knowledge of the history of the human race.'[74] The 'natural and irresistible aristocracy' is thus transmitted to the actual and problematic 'aristocracy' of the privileged classes of nineteenth-century America. Given Thoreau's conclusions here and his debasement of John Field, it should come as no surprise when he writes a passage that states: 'Sometimes, when I compare myself with other men, it seems as if I were more favored by the gods than they ... I do not flatter myself, but if it be possible they flatter me.'[75] Thoreau's transcendentalism is itself based on these comparisons, which exclude and vilify while simultaneously claiming universality.

In 'Civil Disobedience,' the hierarchical implications of Thoreau's transcendentalism are figured in the heavily symbolic ending of the dramatized prison section:

I was put into jail as I was going to the shoemaker's to get a shoe which was mended. When I was let out the next morning, I proceeded to finish my errand, and, having put on my mended shoe, joined a huckleberry party, who were impatient to put themselves under my conduct; and in half an hour, – for the horse was soon tackled, – was in the midst of a huckleberry field, on one of our highest hills, two miles off; and then the State was nowhere to be seen. (83–4)

This passage, I argue, must be read as being symbolically paired with the transcendent moment in the jail cell when Thoreau sees his town with a 'closer view' than ever before, thus gaining a new insight into its functioning and its institutions. That insight immediately places him in a position from which to judge and condemn the State, and therefore remove himself from its power. The same movement is figured spatially in this passage, with Thoreau climbing 'one of our highest hills,' a vantage point from which he escapes the panoptic gaze of the prison and the State. Such an allegory would certainly be in keeping with Thoreau's transcendental politics as a critique of State power. This removal, however, is decidedly not constructed in purely individual terms. Thoreau's exit from prison, his escape from the alienating forces of society, is directly paired to his control over others. This is not the 'point of vantage' that lies 'at the redemptive margin,' the liminal space between society and the wilderness which John Hildebidle argues that *Walden* lauds,[76] but is instead a removal from the State's power and from the town's institutions, and a replication of that power in the figure of Thoreau. People wait for him, 'impatient to put themselves under my conduct.' Given the energy Thoreau devotes to constructing his audience at the beginning of the essay (as Golemba details), I would argue that this image of people listening to and following Thoreau's lead should be read allegorically, as an intradiegetic representation of the 'proper' behaviour of the audience. Like the townspeople, the audience should be impatient to "put themselves under [his] conduct," that is, "follow" Thoreau, reject the State, and gain a more authentic connection to themselves through Nature (symbolized, in this allegorical reading, by the huckleberries which, as Thoreau notes in *Walden*, lose their 'ambrosial and essential part' when taken to town [173]).[77]

The difficulty with this representation crystallizes the problems with the exclusionary nature of Thoreau's 'universal' transcendentalism. Moving from the town to the hill, Thoreau's huckleberry party, and any converts in his audience, could be read as merely exchanging one dominating power for another. And, since Thoreau's transcendentalist rhetoric mirrors the prison's alienating, reformatory rhetoric of 'universal' codes of propriety, which in turn support the reproduction of the means of production for the dominant culture, Thoreau's political statement may replicate more than it rebels. D.A. Miller points towards this problem when he writes that 'the difference between liberal and carceral camps is not substantive.'[78] Thoreau's inability to see the State from the hill is, in this reading, a duplication of his critique of 'Statesmen and legislators, standing so completely within the institution' that they 'never distinctly and nakedly behold it' (86). Reading the text in this way (against the grain, so to speak) rings especially sound since the essay ends with Thoreau asserting that there is 'a still more perfect and glorious State, which also I have imagined, but not yet anywhere seen' (90). Thoreau cannot see the extant State, because he is capable of – and wrapped up in – the creation of a State of his own, which his transcendent nature allows him to encapsulate in his imagination, in a sense ruling over the people in his party and his audience.

I began this chapter, however, with a brief enumeration of the positive political influence that Thoreau's essay has had. To conclude with the assertion that Thoreau's rebellion is a stand-in for State power would seem to ignore not only his own critique of such power but his text's actual historical impact, including its undeniably positive impact on the authors I discuss in the rest of this work and on the different civil rights and social struggles in which they took part. The disparity here arises from the two distinct ways in which 'Civil Disobedience' and Thoreau's opus can be read – both of which are enabled by Thoreau's textual construction of his identity. On the one hand, he becomes the ideal that dictates to people what they 'should be,' thus reinforcing the dominant values and forces of the State.[79] On the other hand, Thoreau can be seen as constructing a fictional persona toward which people can aspire, and which can be used strategically as a means of instigating political action. This form of reading allows Hildebidle, in *Thoreau: A Naturalist's Liberty*, to transmute *Walden*'s contradictions into a self-reflexive criticism, and Thoreau's 'Transcendental egotism' into a form of 'inspiration and reassurance' that Thoreau's audience 'may draw from being shown that the goal is attainable.'[80] What the goal is, exactly, is left up to those who are 'inspired.' As a strategic textual example, 'Thoreau' is not only separated from the rhetorically persuasive, domineering, and socio-economically specific position of the historical Thoreau, but also from the historically oppressive ontological ramifications of the transcendent identity. Using 'Thoreau' as an example, other authors can replace his 'universal' laws with different ones, and the danger of replicating the oppressive hierarchies implied thereby is emptied out.

Those activists and authors who engage in strategic uses of Thoreau's essay need to remain aware of the possibility that the ideals or laws they espouse may engage in the same problematic motion of reproduction as Thoreau's essay. While Hildebidle is right in noting that Thoreau does use some contradictory statements intentionally as a means of critique (such as the reversal of criminals and law-abiding citizens), less easy to solve is the overarching contradiction between Thoreau's exclusionary and hierarchical transcendentalism and his political critique of the exclusionary and hierarchical disciplinary functions of the State. Both readings of 'Thoreau,' one in which he is figured as the domineering, State-like figure, and the other that uses 'Thoreau' strategically as idealized textual example, are viable and do not necessarily easily meld together.[81] The contradictory axes of interpretation arising from these paths are what allow both the revisionist and non-revisionist camps of opinion in Thoreau criticism to continue. Thus, Thoreau's great American political descendant, Martin Luther King Jr, as we will see in chapter 4, can use Thoreau as a political example and strategist, while ignoring the emphasis on individual power, constructing instead a shifting notion of subjectivity which he hopes can settle into a more communal identity. Indeed, all of the other prison authors examined in the present study deal with the difficulty of constructing an account of a rebellion from within prison which functions as an example, but which also seeks not to reproduce the rhetoric, hierarchical ontology, and alienating power of prison. Because this difficulty is such a central one for these authors, recognizing the problem in 'Civil Disobedience' should not cause us to cast the essay aside; nor should we ignore the problem altogether. Rather, recognizing this problem allows readers to appreciate the political and theoretical centrality of Thoreau's attempt, while also highlighting the difficulty – for other prison writers and for people at large – of escaping the carceral matrix.

CHAPTER TWO

'Cast of Characters': Problems of Identity and *Incidents in the Life of a Slave Girl*

While not a prison text per se, Harriet Jacobs's slave narrative, *Incidents in the Life of a Slave Girl*, contains several elements that are consistent with prison texts as they are traditionally conceived. Like Thoreau, Jacobs deals with the subjugation of a significant portion of the nineteenth-century American populace by the dominant culture. More explicitly than Thoreau, however, Jacobs, as a fugitive slave author, deals with this subjugation as it is epitomized within the chattel slavery system of antebellum America. Born a slave in 1813 in North Carolina, Jacobs was later sexually abused by her owner, a practice that, as Jacobs and other women slave narrators and abolitionists have detailed, was rampant in antebellum America and other slaveholding nations in the West.[1] Unable to find a means of escaping, she hid in a constrictive garret in the eaves of her grandmother's house for approximately seven years, until a way was found for her to escape to Philadelphia, and later to Boston and New York.

Jacobs's depiction of slavery in *Incidents* demonstrates how it functioned along a track of surveillance, isolation, and punishment that ran parallel to the practices of the panoptic penitentiary, which had already arisen in the United States by the time of publication of *Incidents*. In addition to this historical convergence of practice, a reading of Jacobs's narrative also reveals the ideological similarities of identity construction and subjugation in both slavery and imprisonment. Indeed, Douglas Taylor (in an article published as this book goes to press) argues that 'Jacobs ultimately ends up producing one of the few slave narratives that might also be read as a kind of proto-prison narrative, which anticipates the themes and concerns of twentieth and twenty-first century African American prison narratives.'[2]

Taylor goes on to detail the relationship with Jacobs's master and early, influential American penologist and signer of the Declaration of Independence, Benjamin Rush, discussing the ways in which Jacobs's narrative revises and critiques Rush's theories of punishment. Beyond Taylor's excellent reading, and building on the relationship discussed in my previous chapter between the supposedly humanist intentions of the prison project and its actual brutalizing effects, this chapter demonstrates how such a relationship is visible within the larger society, and how the supposedly democratic social processes of the West in fact produce a variety of oppressive hierarchies and power differentials. Specifically, Jacobs's narrative not only exposes the obvious oppressions of slavery, but also provides the reader with a depiction of how racial and gender biases meet within the 'enlightened' practices of the antebellum Northern states. Like slavery and the prison, the larger social structure posits a series of identifications upon its subjects through an oppressive gaze that serves to isolate and discipline certain members of the populace.

By constructing a sense of community and enacting an ironic mimicry of slavery designed to expose the system's internal contradictions, however, Jacobs's text fights the discursive forces that would define African Americans and women as non-human. Because such forces are so powerfully embedded in the social framework, Jacobs must also deal with the ways in which they are both reproduced in her very acts of resistance and reflected in the so-called freedom of the North and in the textual practices of such abolitionists as her editor, Lydia Maria Child. In the end, Jacobs's negotiations of the sexist and racist identificatory regimes of slavery and of 'freedom' show the impossibility of reaching a Thoreauvian transcendence beyond the enforced oppression of the disciplining discourse. As Carolyn Sorisio argues, Jacobs's life 'as a slave woman taught her to question Emerson's and Thoreau's transcendental individualism.'[3] My reading of *Incidents* in the context of the panoptic discipline that slavery and the larger society perpetuate enables me to show how Jacobs opts for an in-depth social critique articulated through her own complex negotiation of subjectivity. Jacobs's repositioning of her identity within the determinative discourses of race and gender – as opposed to Thoreau's transcendental removal from other such discourses – provides an excellent framework for perceiving similar movements within the diverse range of repositionings offered by the prison texts examined later in this study.

1. Slavery and Prison

The history of the abolition of slavery and the simultaneous rise of the prison as an institution allow us to see that Jacobs's text, as Taylor states, but also the slave narrative taken generally, is a precedent for contemporary prison writings. While the relationship between slavery and prison is a directly historical one in America – and internationally as well, due to the dissemination of American penal practices – there is also a more general correspondence between the two, especially in terms of how they each conceive of subjectivity. Both systems function in part through physically and mentally oppressing their victims in attempts to create servile subjects. To a large degree, both also serve to create a captive source of labour. Finally, apologists for each system frame their arguments within a paternalistic discourse of moral education and social harmony, even while denying the possibility of a future where criminals/slaves can be educated or 'reformed' so as to disallow the necessity of the paternalistic institution.[4]

The relationship between slavery and imprisonment is also a more detailed and specifically historical one. H. Bruce Franklin draws the connection between the enslavement of African Americans and their imprisonment, writing that '[t]he most intense collective experience in Afro-American history was that of slavery. This experience did not stop with Emancipation, however ... Certainly the prisoners throughout the South who were literally chained together while they worked and while they ate and while they slept had an experience no less oppressive and no less collective than their ancestors in chattel slavery.'[5] The relation between enslavement and imprisonment is also, as Franklin and others point out, explicitly made in the 13th Amendment to the US Constitution, which abolishes slavery while simultaneously reinstantiating it within the purview of the penal system: 'Neither slavery nor involuntary servitude, except as a punishment for crime whereof the party shall have been duly convicted, shall exist within the United States.' Commenting on this rejustification of slavery even at the moment of its banishment, Angela Y. Davis argues:

> The abolition of slavery thus corresponded to the authorization of slavery as punishment. In actual practice, both Emancipation and the authorization of penal servitude combined to create an immense black presence within southern prisons and to transform the character of punishment

into a means of managing former slaves as opposed to addressing problems of serious crime.[6]

Prison becomes a centralized locus to which the heretofore 'naturally savage and unpredictable' black populace can be banished.[7] In addition, the convict lease system began to be used systematically, meaning that prisoners could be leased out or used by the incarcerating institution for the purpose of 'forced labour.' The coding of a range of 'black crime,' and the subsequent ideological criminalization of blackness, especially in the South, when combined with the convict lease system, thus recreates slavery within the auspices of the American penal system.[8] The modern prison's appropriation of slavery's methods is enabled by the fact that both arose in the same paternalistic paradigm of punishment and labour, which were used in order to cultivate and maintain the 'proper' social order, while in the process brutalizing and alienating those who fell on the wrong end of the social hierarchies. When one institution passes away, then, its functions and place in society can be replaced by the other.[9]

An understanding of the racialized practices of the American justice system can also lead to the conclusion that African American prison narratives are renegotiations of the genre of the slave narrative.[10] The connection between slavery, prison, and the narratives arising from both is in fact noted by several African American prison authors, especially those tied to the political and civil rights movements of the 1960s. As these authors point out, prison continues the system of subjugation and oppression originating in slavery. In writing about their imprisonment, these authors and others continue the resistance to the dominant culture that was formed through slave narratives.[11]

This resistance takes many forms, and one cannot homogenize through generic or other generalizations the several acts of resistance represented and embodied in slave and prison narratives – such a project would be, as I wrote in my 'opening statements,' both theoretically and practically impossible. In her text, Jacobs specifically argues against such homogenization which, even at the time of her writing, threatened to silence black voices, and black women's voices in particular, through the enforced repetition of certain generic and 'white' forms such as the sentimental novel. Similarly, the slave narrative genre was generally connected to the male voice, which further marginalized the stories of slave women.[12] Jacobs's text, therefore, permits us to see how the rebellions and social critiques of slave narratives can be joined with and problematized by those of women's narratives, and vice versa. In the process, her text does not become representative of a specific genre or a specific group, but instead demonstrates how sustained critiques of the carceral matrix are entered into from a variety of particular points. And yet, this particularity – incarnated in *Incidents*'s generic variances from the slave narrative and from the sentimental novel – does not negate a reading of the text that demonstrates the general connections between prison, slavery, and gender oppression.

Published in 1861, the year the Civil War began, Jacobs's text takes the form of a sentimental slave narrative, told through the perspective of the pseudonymous narrator, Linda Brent. *Incidents* is, therefore, one of the last antebellum slave narratives. Like the prison texts which they give rise to, these slave narratives were engaged in a battle against not only the brutalizations of slavery, but also the expectations of (white) audiences, both apologist and abolitionist. Interesting to note in this context is the fact that, as Hirsch writes, 'many of the same persons who lobbied for the construction of penitentiaries ... also stood at the forefront of the antislavery movement. The impulse to break down plantations, it seems, was often accompanied by a longing to build up prison walls.'[13] Women's slave narratives, moreover, tend to explicitly demonstrate the further relationships between slavery, gender oppression, and 'freedom.' By negotiating her way through these various interpellating discourses, Jacobs offers a thoroughgoing critique of various forms of racial and gender bigotry in America immediately before the Civil War. This critique, like Thoreau's, highlights the disciplinary function of social institutions and mechanisms, including generic, familial, and gendered structures, demonstrating that a disciplinary model of identity formation is socially ubiquitous.[14] An exploration of Jacobs's negotiation provides further means through which to understand the techniques used and represented by prison authors in their texts to critique a range of disciplinary identifications. In what follows, I will detail the connection between prison and slavery, and then add to the discussion by examining their relationship to gender.

2. Defining Slavery

In addition to the historical connections between slavery and institutionalized imprisonment, there is also a significant similarity in the ways in which the two systems construct the subjectivities of their victims. Both slaves and prisoners are treated as silent objects, devoid of individuality and agency, existing solely for the perpetuation of the systems themselves and the power of the controlling authorities. 'Although it is true that prison punishes delinquency,' writes Foucault, 'delinquency is for the most part produced in and by an incarceration which, ultimately, prison perpetuates in its turn.'[15] Paul Gilroy similarly argues that 'slavery depends' for its existence on the slave's 'continuing condition of inhumanity,' a condition which slavery itself creates.[16] Prison and the Atlantic slave trade as institutions both exist within the Enlightenment ontology which, as shown in the previous chapter, claims a universal human nature while denying that nature to certain groups, including slaves and prisoners. In order to engage in this cycle of self-reproductive oppression, both prison and slavery see their victims as 'mere flesh and blood and bones,' to use Thoreau's words ('Civil,' 80). The laws and practices of slavery, as Martha J. Cutter argues, 'deny slaves' humanity.'[17] Once ideologically dispersed, this relegation of slaves to the status of mere bodies becomes its own justification; in such a formulation, blacks are not legally human as are white people, and are therefore slaves, but because blacks are enslaved, they cannot be treated as legally human. The end result of this tautology is the denial of the humanity of slaves, and the justification of a system of abuse designed to brutalize and oppress them.

This brutalization could lead to the slaves' unwilling internalization of the ideology of slavery because it functions, like the contemporary penitentiary, as a panoptic and therefore programmatically internalizing force of constant surveillance. In his original writings on the panopticon, Jeremy Bentham argues that, whatever the purpose behind the prison (be it education, punishment, simple confinement, etc.), 'the more constantly the persons to be inspected are under the eyes of the persons who should inspect them, the more perfectly will the purpose of the establishment be attained.' In order to achieve this constant surveillance, it is only necessary that the observed person 'should *conceive* himself to be' perpetually watched.[18] Describing in his slave narrative the process of being 'broken' by Edward Covey, Frederick Douglass notes that Covey created this feeling of constant surveillance, resulting in the slaves' conclusion that 'it was never safe to stop a single minute.'[19] Covey's panoptic power leads to Douglass's internalization of slavery's oppressive definitions of him: 'My natural elasticity was crushed, my intellect languished, the disposition to read departed, the cheerful spark that lingered about my eye died; the dark night of slavery closed in upon me; and behold a man transformed into a brute!'[20]

In Douglass's case this internalization is temporary, and it is of course not a universal transformation on behalf of all slaves, but it does signal the oppressive physical and ideological power of the panoptic gaze of the slaveholders.[21] Hirsch points out a startling similarity between Bentham's justification of the penitentiary and apologist justifications of slavery:

> Though he opposed coercive labour, Bentham recommended a prison sys-
> tem that was coercive in other respects. His simple solution was to link
> such coercion with other forms of punishment: 'All punishment is an
> infringement on liberty: no one submits to it but from compulsion.'
> Whether knowingly or not, Bentham's line of reasoning ran parallel to
> one used by slaveholders to justify slave dependancy: 'All government is
> restraint; and this is but one form of restraint.'[22]

Slave authors such as Jacobs fight against this brutalization of their identities, while at the same time combatting the 'universal' codes imposed on them by the white dominant culture, attempting instead to reconstruct identities that are personally and culturally their own.

Like Douglass, Jacobs's narrator, Linda Brent, describes both the system and the constructions of identity against which she writes. At the end of the first chapter of the text, Brent depicts the sale of many members of her family, an event that took place when she was quite young: 'Notwithstanding my grandmother's long and faithful service to her owners, not one of her children escaped the auction block. These God-breathing machines are no more, in the sight of their masters, than the cotton they plant, or the horses they tend.'[23] Brent uses the economic and resource-oriented language of the southern plantation to show how slaves are treated not only as property, but as machines which function to tend other property. The juxtaposition of the legal equation of 'slave' and 'animal' with the assertion of the slave's actual inherent humanity is commonly used in slave narratives. Franklin traces its use in Douglass's narrative as not only a means of asserting Douglass's own humanity, but also as an attempt to reverse the roles of slave and master, by depicting the slaveowner as the animal.[24] Jacobs also uses this technique, with Brent referring throughout the text to the slave-holding and slavecatching 'bloodhounds,' both North and South.

At this early point, however, Brent only describes the systemic equation of slave and inhumanity – even the 'God-breathing' is done by machines. Despite the implied textual recognition of her own humanity, Brent does not represent herself here as asserting this sense of self within the larger structure of slavery. Thus, even though the well-liked and avowedly 'kind' (7) mistress of Brent's childhood had promised to set her slaves free in her will, when the will is read the slaves are bequeathed with the other property. Brent describes how the slaves' hopes 'vanished,' and notes that her 'mistress had taught me the precepts of God's Word: "Thou shalt love thy neighbor as thyself." "Whatsoever ye would that men should do unto you, do ye even so unto them." But I was her slave, and I suppose she did not recognize me as her neighbor' (8). Deborah M. Garfield writes that this passage 'frustrates the affinity between slave and "neighbor,"' while Karen Sánchez-Eppler argues that '[t]he asymmetry of social place that allows the mistress to appear almost as a mother while the slave is not recognizable as a neighbor instantly disentangles familial and plantation relations.'[25] Indeed, this passage points to the impossibility of a position that is at once 'slave' and 'neighbour.' The inability of the mistress to view her slaves as human beings, not property, her inevitable misrecognition of slaves as non-neighbours, is not only a result of the ideological system of slavery, but is also the means through which that system is reproduced and disseminated: after her death, her slaves 'were all distributed among her relatives' (8).

Brent describes the violence that can result from such definitions. If the label 'slave' can only and always signify a piece of property, just as 'prisoner' is equated to a lack of citizenship and rights, then nothing can shield the slave from whatever form of abuse in which the master decides to engage. The most violent of these resultant actions are collected into the chapter 'Sketches of Neighboring Slaveholders.' After detailing the torture and murder of one man, who was 'placed between the screws of the cotton gin' (48) – in an hyperbolic mimicry of the relation between slavery, abuse, and the cotton trade – Brent describes him as exhibiting a certain 'manliness and intelligence' which were what 'made it so hard for him to be a plantation slave' (49). Such qualities work against the proprietorial nature of the slave as defined by the slaveholding society. To such an 'object,' masters could have 'less feeling than would have been manifested for an old house dog' (49). Because the man placed in the cotton gin was a slave, 'the feeling was that the master had a right to do what he pleased' (49). Beyond the violent subjugation of the slaves, Brent argues that slavery also redefines those who are in control of it: 'slavery is a curse to the whites as well as to the blacks. It makes white fathers cruel and sensual; the sons violent and licentious; it contaminates the daughters, and makes the wives wretched' (52).[26] Slavery is thus constructed as an oppressive matrix in which the humanity of the slave is brutally erased, while at the same time the slaveholders are corrupted and denied the status of 'human beings with immortal souls' (52). But because of the slaveholders' position in the power structure, their corruption can remain largely invisible and unspoken; hence they can still be described as neighbours in the chapter's title, while slaves are, in turn, denied that status.

Brent's main focus in the early part of her narrative is the disciplinary subjugation of the slave population. The opening chapter enforces the understanding that slaves were legally, socially, and individually denied the status of being human, and were relegated to an existence as mere property. Brent also demonstrates how this understanding was forced onto the slaves themselves through a form of panoptic gaze. Later in the text, Brent compares her owner's gaze to that of a 'jealous lover,' one who never 'watched a rival more closely than he watched me' (81). For her mistress, the slaves 'were the objects of her constant suspicion and malevolence' (31). This perpetual gaze of ownership can result in an internalization of the label 'slave.' Garfield summarizes this process as it occurs in the early sections of *Incidents*, writing that, 'though the slave child naively imagined the "name" of slave and one's essential "nature" as mutually exclusive, the experienced narrative voice recognizes that the white world forces the slave *name* to imply slave *nature*.'[27] This implication is explicitly discussed in 'The Slave Who Dared to Feel Like a Man.' In this chapter, Brent's brother, Benjamin, escapes to the North and away from a brutal master, after an earlier, unsuccessful attempt. Both of the escape attempts and the desire for freedom lying behind them are placed in opposition to Brent's master's view of slavery. This master, Dr Flint, who rapidly becomes the central villain of the narrative and a synecdoche for slaveholders in general, tells Brent that she 'was made for his use, made to obey his command in *every* thing; that I was nothing but a slave, whose will must and should surrender to his' (18). According to Flint, Brent's being, the 'purpose' for which she was made, is to be his tool, an extension of his desires and nothing else.

This singular and all-encompassing equation of slave and object has further implications in terms of gender, of course. The main facet of Brent's life in slavery, as she describes it, is her sexual abuse by Flint. Because the two oppressed categories of 'slave' and 'woman' meet in the patriarchal matrix of slavery, Flint's sexual abuse also falls into the slaveholder's justification of violence, that 'the master had a right to do what he pleased' (49). Christina Accomando cites antebellum case law to describe the general understanding of the position of the female slave in terms of sexual abuse. She notes that, in the 1859 *George v. State* case in Mississippi (which dealt with the rape of a girl under ten), a lawyer 'argued, successfully, that the rape of a slave was essentially not rape.'[28] Accomando writes, moreover, that 'the law failed to protect slave women from forced sex committed by white men' and 'also generally failed to protect slave women from rape committed by other slaves.'[29] Slave women, because they 'had no subjectivity to speak of,'[30] are constructed as mere bodies that can be acted on in any way without fear of official reprisal.

3. Disruptions of Community

The denial of agency and the brutalization through which it was enacted were not completely unassailable. As Accomando deftly demonstrates, slaveholding discourse is full of contradictions that are exploited by slave authors and abolitionists alike: 'The official line on slavery declared that slaves had no subjectivity to speak of, yet there is tremendous anxiety that there be no public arena where such a subjectivity might somehow speak.'[31] Indeed, Flint's very abuse of Brent is what spurs her to act against him. The passage cited from the chapter 'The Slave Who Dared to Feel like a Man,' when quoted in its entirety, demonstrates this relationship: 'When he told me that I was made for his use, made to obey his command in *every* thing; that I was nothing but a slave, whose will must and should surrender to his, never before had my puny arm felt half so strong' (18). Because Brent rebels against Flint's sexual overtures, he is forced to voice the generally unspoken proprietorial relationship between himself and his female slave, thereby allowing Brent a possible space for a feeling of rebellion, for a rebuttal of his statements.[32]

This liberating potentiality within slavery is exploited by Brent and others through their attempts to build a community that functions both within and against the dominant slaveholding culture. Opposed to Thoreau's individualist rebellion, community and relationships in *Incidents* can, in Winifred Morgan's words, 'support and nourish the individual and contrast with the contrived and unreasonable bonds of slavery.'[33] As we will see in later prison texts, especially in King's and

Lytton's works, community can serve a similar function for prison authors, working against the isolation forced on them by penal structures and policies. Indeed, in Jacobs's work, the contrast between the isolating effects of slavery and those of community often binds the black community more strongly together, just as Flint's verbal definition of Brent as his property allows her to feel a modicum of strength. Discussing her grandmother, a freed black woman who is known in the town as Aunt Marthy, Brent writes:

> My grandmother had, as much as possible, been a mother to her orphan grandchildren. By perseverance and unwearied industry, she was now mistress of a snug little home, surrounded with the necessaries of life. She would have been happy could her children have shared them with her. There remained but three children and two grandchildren. Most earnestly did she strive to make us feel that it was the will of God: that He had seen fit to place us under such circumstances; and though it seemed hard, we ought to pray for contentment ... She always met us with a smile, and listened with patience to all our sorrows. She spoke so hopefully, that unconsciously the clouds gave place to sunshine. There was a grand big oven there, too, that baked bread and nice things for the town, and we knew there was always a choice bit in store for us. (17)

Brent's grandmother's faith in God's plan, as well as her love for her grandchildren, allows her to construct a seemingly ideal domestic space in which the clouds of slavery can be transformed into the sunshine of community. In addition, the seemingly ideal familial community pictured in the grandmother's house is placed at the heart of the larger community, as the 'grand big oven' sends its domestic product throughout the town, while also nurturing the slave children. '[D]espite their legal erasure,' Accomando writes, 'slave families survived, though often in altered forms.'[34] The altered space of black community in Jacobs's text, then, not only supports Brent's family against the oppressive force of slavery, but also creates a sense of civic community that functions as an alternate space of black–white relations.[35]

Brent does not, though, posit the redefinition of black–white interaction within the grandmother's house as an image of a universalizing and harmonizing force of community. Rather than bring about a harmony between slaveowner and slave, such depictions are generally placed in opposition to the white power structure, echoing Thoreau's use of the 'happy prison' motif. During her first escape attempt, Brent gains strength through a symbolic construction of a black community of resistance:

> The graveyard was in the woods, and twilight was coming on. Nothing broke the death-like stillness except the occasional twitter of a bird ... A black stump, at the head of my mother's grave, was all that remained of a tree my father had planted. His grave was marked by a small wooden board, bearing his name, the letters of which were nearly obliterated. I knelt down and kissed them, and poured forth a prayer to God for guidance and support in the perilous step I was about to take. As I passed the wreck of the old meeting house, where, before Nat Turner's time, the slaves had been allowed to meet for worship, I seemed to hear my father's voice come from it, bidding me not to tarry till I reached freedom or the grave. I rushed on with renovated hopes. My trust in God had been strengthened by that prayer among the graves. (90–1)

Brent here combines memories of her parents, of Nat Turner's 1831 rebellion, and of the black community in general (through the meeting house) in order to support her own decision to rebel and escape.[36] Brent's voice is added, writes Hazel V. Carby, 'to a history of slave rebels,' and thus, Sidonie Smith states, Brent 'places herself in a noble family lineage ... characterized by spiritual, moral, and social heroism despite the degrading circumstances of slavery.'[37] In spite of the deaths of her parents and of Nat Turner, and the destruction of the meeting hall by whites (described earlier in her text), the community they signify continues in Brent and her living family, and still voices a desire for freedom and rebellion. As Beth Maclay Doriani writes, freedom for Brent 'involves a relationship to others, interdependence.'[38] By situating her own identity within the continuing community of her black ancestors and their acts of resistance, Brent is strengthened against the destructive force of slavery that results in a 'death-like' state.

Aunt Marthy's house, another image of black community, is more often a temporary refuge from and space of rebellion against Flint's violence than it is a space of ideal domestic and racial peace. While staying with her grandmother after the birth of her second child, Brent describes a meeting between Flint and Rose, an ex-slave who had been purchased and given her freedom by friends after '[s]he had been torn from all her family':

Dr. Flint always had an aversion to meeting slaves after he had sold them. He ordered Rose out of the house; but he was no longer her master, and she took no notice of him. For once the crushed Rose was the conqueror. His gray eyes flashed angrily upon her; but that was the extent of his power. 'How came this girl here?' he exclaimed. 'What right had you to allow it, when you knew I had sold her?' I answered 'This is my grandmother's house, and Rose came to see her. I have no right to turn any body out of doors, that comes here for honest purposes.' (82)

Not only does an act of community legally gain Rose's freedom from slavery, but similar acts allow her to assert that freedom against Flint's attempt to reinforce his authority. Brent asserts that the space of Aunt Marthy's house and Rose's act of visiting are not just beyond Flint's power, but actually remove that power. His panoptic, oppressive gaze is reduced to an impotent flash of anger, while Rose rises to the status of 'conqueror.' This potential for a reversal of power is duplicated by Brent's use of dialogue itself, a linguistic and literary form which, as Andrews argues, 'often became a liminal phase in the master-slave relationship, when neither master nor slave was in full control of the situation, when they implicitly agreed to an "indeterminacy" of outcome to their verbal combat.' 'Within such indeterminacy,' he writes, 'lies a margin of freedom, even for slaves that would seem to be the most powerless.'[39] Brent's use of the pseudo-legal language of rights and purposes also serves to divest Flint of the authority of the slave system. Beyond Flint's inability to remove Rose, she has the legal right to be there; Aunt Marthy's domestic space performs the function of a sanctuary from slavery.

Like the ways in which the redemptive rhetoric of the modern penitentiary is undermined by the violence used to enforce prison regulations, the power of community and of dialogue is mitigated by the fact that slavery as a system functions in part through the disruption and denial of black community, often through violent practices. Flint's and Brent's conversation about Rose, for example, ends with Flint hitting Brent. Although Aunt Marthy arrives and forces Flint to leave, his violence and his references to Brent's illegitimate children work against the 'peace and contentment in that humble home' – peace and contentment which are denied by 'the demon Slavery' (83). The possibility of a self-empowering and perpetuating black community itself enrages Flint. When Brent's romantic relationship with a free black man is discovered and ended by Flint, she takes comfort in her filial relationship with her brother, but even this relationship is subject to Flint's will: 'If he had known how we love each other, I think he would have exulted in separating us' (42). Just as community inside the prison is viewed as a disruptive and corruptive force, as leading prisoners even more deeply into their criminal identities, all black community in the slave-holding society is potentially dangerous to the white power structure, and the disruption of any form of that community is therefore pleasurable to Flint.

Empowering Flint's individual violence towards the black community, the slave system as a whole denies slaves their families and community, thus creating a form of isolation. Brent explicates the systematic separation of parents and children, and the breaking of the slaves' spirits as a result, in a description of the slave auctions held each New Year's Day. One slave woman has seven children sold and taken away from her. Brent describes talking with her afterwards, stating that the woman 'wrung her hands in anguish, and exclaimed, "Gone! All gone! Why *don't* God kill me?" I had no words wherewith to comfort her. Instances of this kind are of daily, yea, of hourly occurrence' (16). The sale of children, and the destruction of family it brings, results in anguish for that family and leads to a further disruption of the entire community. Brent recognizes this disruption when she cannot find any words with which to reassure the woman. The denial of communication duplicates the near erasure of the words on Brent's father's headstone; here, however, there is no communal voice to be heard over the destruction. Stating that this type of occurrence happens hourly reinforces the sense of despair and the difficulty involved in overcoming the oppressive forces of slavery.[40]

There is a more direct way in which disruptions of slave communities and the resulting isolation serve to reinforce the structures of slavery. Since children of slave mothers were by law property of the woman's owner, the widespread rape of slave women led to many slaveowners being the legal owners of slaves who were their own children. Caroline Levander writes that slave mothers in Jacobs's text 'attempt to counteract this dehumanizing maternity in order to nurture their children, but ... are constantly frustrated by owners who demand that slave women produce "stock."'[41] As Jacobs describes it, this situation leads to a simultaneous denial and affirmation of the familial relationship between master and slave, resulting in a violently enforced silence. When a slave mother is overheard arguing with her husband about the paternity of one of her children, Flint savagely whips the man and then sells both of them: 'When the mother was delivered into the trader's hands, she said, "You *promised* to treat me well." To which he [Flint] replied, 'You have let your tongue run too far; damn you!' She had forgotten that it was a crime for a slave to tell who was the father of her child' (13). The existence of a familial relationship between slave and master is dangerous to the latter because it brings with it the possibility of a familial *bond*, signified by the reference to Flint's 'promise' to the slave woman. In order for the master to retain power, such a promise must be violently and immediately denied.

The constant negotiations and fluctuations of community between blacks, whites, and each other, and the concurrent disruptions of these groupings, are detailed through the depiction of Brent's grandmother. Aunt Marthy and her family come to represent, in part, not only the difficulties of forming a black fellowship that resists the oppression of the slaveholders, but also the strains placed on both white and black communities by slavery. Brent describes the 'tangled skeins [of] the genealogies of slavery' (78), informing the reader that '[m]y mother's mistress was the daughter of my grandmother's mistress. She was the foster sister of my mother; they were both nourished at my grandmother's breast. In fact, my mother had been weaned at three months old, that the babe of the mistress might obtain sufficient food' (6–7). Just as Aunt Marthy's house provides sustenance for the whole town, white and black, free and enslaved, her genealogical history acts as a nexus for familial connections that cross racial lines. But, as Harryette Mullen writes, the 'reciprocal relationship' figured through the feeding of the children 'is betrayed by the white child's entry into the patriarchal symbolic of law, property, and inheritance.'[42] The familial connections, like the space of the house, are not completely free from the oppression of slavery, because Aunt Marthy must wean her own child in order to provide for the master's daughter.

Aunt Marthy's position in society does, however, allow her occasionally to disrupt the forces that would confine her and her family. While she was a slave, she was allowed to sell some of her baking, the money from which 'was saved for a fund to purchase her children' (6). This money was 'borrowed' by her mistress and never repaid. Despite this betrayal, Aunt Marthy believes her mistress's promise to set Aunt Marthy free in her will – a promise that is not fulfilled, and Aunt Marthy is put up for sale:

> Dr. Flint called to tell my grandmother that he was unwilling to wound her feelings by putting her up at auction, and that he would prefer to dispose of her at private sale. My grandmother saw through his hypocrisy; she understood very well that he was ashamed of the job. She was a very spirited woman, and if he was base enough to sell her, when her mistress intended she should be free, she was determined the public should know it. She had for a long time supplied many families with crackers and preserves; consequently, 'Aunt Marthy,' as she was called, was generally known, and every body who knew her respected her intelligence and good character. (11)

The position of respect in the town which Aunt Marthy creates for herself ultimately leads to her freedom. When she defies Flint and mounts the auction steps, the crowd shouts 'Shame!' and allows only one bid to be made: 'It came from a maiden lady, seventy years old, the sister of my grandmother's deceased mistress' (11–12). The woman then sets Brent's grandmother free. Aunt Marthy's connection to the larger community of the town, as well as her pseudo-matrilineal and familial connections to her owner, allow her to assume her definition as property in order to escape the actual reinstantiation of that definition.

Aunt Marthy's powerful place within the community thus serves occasionally to frustrate the supposedly socially sanctioned power of the slaveholder. Andrews describes her position as one that 'lay on the margins of the power wielded by the white patriarchy of the South.'[43] Because of the respect that Aunt Marthy gains through her creation of a domestic and economic space connected to both white and black communities, she develops a position for social interaction that is somewhat separate from the types of interaction dictated by slavery. This separation allows her to inhabit a discursive space that helps construct an identity that is not delimited by the practices of slavery, thereby giving her the power to act directly against Flint's slaveholding authority. Brent tells the reader of Aunt Marthy that, '[t]hough she had been a slave, Dr. Flint was afraid of her. He dreaded her scorching rebukes. Moreover, she was known and patronized by many people; and he did not wish to have his villainy made public' (29). The grandmother's discursive access to the white community allows her to reverse Flint's verbal power. The fact that she can make his villainy public allows her to deliver scorching rebukes.

Aunt Marthy's agency, however, is limited to its specific position within domestic spaces and relationships. As Krista Walter notes, this position is also directly associated with Aunt Marthy's replication of the 'values of true womanhood and its rigid morality.'[44] Aunt Marthy's power is based to a degree on the emphasis she places on family and on 'proper' domesticity, as that was defined by the strict moral code of the cult of true womanhood.[45] According to Walter, Aunt Marthy's power to combat Flint derives 'solely from the status she has achieved among the whites in the community as "good" slave as well as surrogate mother, caretaker, and baker. To retain this power, she clings to the ideals associated with respectable Christian womanhood.'[46] Aunt Marthy can gain her freedom because of her 'long and faithful service in the family' of her owner (11), and she retains Brent's respect in part because she was 'very strict' on sexual and other domestic and familial issues (29).

This emphasis on family and domestic propriety can also inadvertently reproduce the conditions of slavery. When Brent first decides to escape, her grandmother convinces her instead to remain a slave:

'Nobody respects a mother who forsakes her children; and if you leave them, you will never have a happy moment. If you go, you will make me miserable the short time I have to live. You would be taken and brought back, and your sufferings would be dreadful. Remember poor Benjamin. Do give it up, Linda. Try to bear a little longer. Things may turn out better than we expect.' My courage failed me, in view of the sorrow I should bring on that faithful, loving old heart. I promised that I would try longer, and that I would take nothing out of her house without her knowledge. (91)

The grandmother's domestic power allows her to convince Brent not to escape and gain her freedom. Brent's connection to family, emphasized by Aunt Marthy, may be 'a source of strength,' writes Sorisio, but 'it also stands as a substantial roadblock on her journey to freedom.'[47] Relying on discourse that arises 'straight out of the sentimental tradition,'[48] Aunt Marthy uses Brent's position as a mother, as well as the social responsibilities attached to that position, in such a way as to inadvertently reinforce Brent's status as a slave.

Rather than Aunt Marthy's reliance on domestic culture and social positions, however, it is Flint's awareness of these traditions that allows him to attempt to cement fully Brent's existence as a slave. After Brent's 'escape' into the hiding place in her grandmother's house, Flint preys on Aunt Marthy's belief in the values of domesticity and the family. When Brent writes a letter to Flint, falsely addressed in order to confuse him as to her whereabouts, Flint replaces it with a letter of his own. Using this false letter from 'Linda,' Flint tries to convince Aunt Marthy that Brent has 'repented of her rashness' and that if she came back from the North, he would allow her to be 'sold to her friends,' so Aunt Marthy could have 'a happy family' (129–30). Flint attempts to regain control of Brent by mimicking Aunt Marthy's wish for family, just as Aunt Marthy gains control of him earlier by strategically mimicking her own status as slave.

In addition, earlier in the text Flint and his son attempt to make Brent fully submit to her status of slave by moving her children to the plantation on which she was working. Imitating Aunt Marthy's emphasis on the importance of remaining with one's children, the Flints try, in Brent's words, 'to fetter me to the spot' by bringing her children to her (93). In another section of the work, Flint attempts to use his knowledge of the importance that Aunt Marthy and her relatives place on family bonds by, significantly, placing Brent's brother, aunt, and two children in jail in order to force Brent's 'relatives to give some information about' her (101). While this is just a small-town jailhouse, the fact that Flint is able to use it to exploit feelings of community, in order to bolster his own power, reinforces not only the historical connection between slavery and prison, but also the ideological connections between the two institutions. This scene also demonstrates how both institutions can use other ideological social structures, such as domesticity and the family, to further their disciplinary ends. Therefore, while community and domesticity can function as means of resistance against the slaveholding hegemony, they can also be used *by* the slaveholders as further means of subjugating the black population within a disciplinary social matrix that continues through the convict lease system and the modern prison.

Brent's questions concerning the oppressive and disciplinary functions of the social institutions of family, domesticity, and slavery, and of the person's place within them, closely duplicate the concerns raised by prison authors, including Thoreau. On the one hand, like Thoreau's conclusions about the relationship between slavery, capitalism, and the prison in terms of the similarities of their alienating effects, Jacobs's text demonstrates how the ideological apparatus of the family can work to alienate people and frustrate their desires for freedom. Unlike Thoreau, on the other hand, but looking forward to later prison writers, Brent denies both the paternalistic and oppressive discourse of slavery and the Romantic notion of an ideal, uncomplicated resistance which always functions in opposition to the oppressive hegemony.

4. Disruptions of Concealment

Because she is hiding in her grandmother's house, Brent is aware of Flint's falsification of her letter. She is also aware of his perverse use of the construction of a black community to further disempower that very group. In order to evade this use of her family and friends, Brent must ironically duplicate the isolating forces of slavery in order to provide a space for her final escape. As Douglas Taylor argues in general, 'Jacobs blurs the boundaries between imprisonment and slavery in order to demonstrate the ways that these concepts' (and I would add the institutions themselves) 'functioned within the slaveholding south to legitimate and subvert the status quo.'[49] Just as community can function as both an empowering and a disempowering force, isolation and concealment can perform a similar dual function.

Brent's use of isolation is most obvious in her seven-year concealment in a crawl space in the eaves of her grandmother's house. She describes the garret as 'only nine feet long and seven wide. The highest part was three feet high, and sloped down abruptly to the loose board floor. There was no admission for either light or air' (114). While the garret was intended as a temporary refuge from Flint while Brent's friends searched for a means for her escape, it became in itself a source of freedom. Even though, as Walter suggests, the depiction of this garret 'more closely resembles a description of the middle passage'[50] than it does a space of freedom, Brent notes that, no matter how horrible her hiding space is, it is still better than her 'lot as a slave' (114). While it replicates the worst and most brutalizing aspects of cellular confinement, the garret provides her a means of avoiding Flint's verbal and sexual abuse by removing her from his gaze. The way in which she is removed from the slaveowner's sight is by hiding within his supposed domain:

> The opinion was often expressed that I was in the Free States. Very rarely did any one suggest that I might be in the vicinity. Had the least suspicion rested on my grandmother's house, it would have been burned to the ground. But it was the last place they thought of. Yet there was no place, where slavery existed, that could have afforded me so good a place of concealment. (117)

While it is tempting to see here a further empowerment of the black community, as figured through the grandmother's house, Brent's assurances that it would be 'burned to the ground' if her presence was even suspected belies this. The garret protects her not because of its proximity to her grandmother or to the larger black community, but because of its connection to the system of slavery. Since Flint assumes that the grandmother's house is within his complete panoptic power due to its placement in an area 'where slavery existed,' he and others cannot conceive of it as a tenable hiding place.[51]

Brent's ability to hide in plain sight is made more explicit when she describes her first Christmas spent in the garret:

> On this occasion, I was warned to keep extremely quiet, because two guests had been invited. One was the town constable, and the other was a free colored man, who tried to pass himself off for white, and who was always ready to do any mean work for the sake of currying favor with white people. My grandmother had a motive for inviting them. She managed to take them all over the house. All the rooms on the lower floor were thrown open for them to pass in and out; and after dinner, they were invited up stairs to look at a fine mocking bird my uncle had just brought home. There, too, the rooms were all thrown open, that they might look in. (119)

Both the white carceral and punishment system, as seen in the constable, and the internalizing effects of this system's panoptic force, figured through the black man trying to pass as white, are represented as being literally unable to see the possibility that Brent is hiding within their range of vision. Slavery's system of supposedly constant surveillance and the brutalization it effects are mocked by Brent's 'loophole of retreat' just as assuredly as these two individuals are mocked by Brent's uncle's pet bird.

The effectiveness of Brent's garret arises not only from its denial of the strength of slavery's surveillance, but also from Brent's reversal of that surveillance. As Thoreau transforms his cell from a site of isolation to a means of seeing his town anew and of reversing judgment, Brent uses her isolating garret to allow her to become the gazing subject, rather than the object controlled by the gaze; both spaces offer, as Walter points out, a 'special vantage' on their communities.[52] After a short time in what she sometimes calls her den, Brent carves a small hole into the wall through which she can see the street. This view, combined with the fact that she can hear people's conversations, allows her to survey the town in a way somewhat similar to that whereby the slaves' actions are surveyed by their owners, giving her a form – albeit very limited – of panoptic vision. She states that 'Southerners have the habit of stopping and talking in the streets, and I heard many conversations not intended to meet my ears. I heard slave-hunters planning how to catch some poor fugitive' (117).

Her constricted existence in the garret, an extension of the physical, mental, and social constrictions placed on her as a slave, gives her less restricted access to the functionings of the power structures of slavery. The potential power of Brent's use of this panoramic sight exists in conjunction with a similar use of linguistic tools.[53] Flint and Brent engage in a letter-writing duel in which Brent has the upper hand because she can observe his various actions while also controlling all of the information he receives. She knows, therefore, when he attempts to take advantage of her grandmother's belief in family by replacing one of her letters with his own fabrication. Writing a letter to him which was addressed from New York but states that she lives in Boston, she not only further convinces Flint that she is in the Free States, but also manipulates him into stating his convictions, as well as proving that he 'had not given me up' (128). Knowing Flint's mind in this way, Brent concludes, heightens the possibility of her physical escape from slavery, so she resolves 'to continue to write letters from the north from time to time' (132).

The garret is obviously not a space from which Brent can gain absolute freedom from slavery. Just as faith in the strength of the black community can function to support its destruction by the slaveholders, and just as Aunt Marthy's domestic space can help to replicate the unequal relations of slavery, so too can the garret replicate the isolating and physically abusive problems to which slaves were subject. Michelle Burnham argues that Jacobs escapes Flint's surveillance 'only by going into a captivity that in many ways enacts the condition of slavery on a hyperbolic scale.'[54] Beyond its obvious echoes within my project to the violence and brutalization associated with imprisonment, Brent's hiding space can also be seen as a replica of the space in the cotton gin used to punish and ultimately kill the slave as described in the chapter 'Sketches of Neighboring Slaveholders' (48–9). At one point, Brent does come near death, and as a result her 'tongue stiffened, and I lost the power of speech' (122), an echo of Flint's enforced silencing of the slave whose tongue had 'run to far' (13).

The hiding space – and cell – also forces an isolation onto Brent that closely resembles the separation of family members by slavery. When she becomes ill because of her living conditions, her grandmother also falls ill 'under the weight of anxiety and toil' (123). Brent tells the reader that the 'idea of losing her, who had always been my best friend and a mother to my children, was the sorest trial I had yet had' (123). Immediately following this passage, she describes seeing her son through her peephole after he was attacked by a dog, a situation that causes her to respond, 'O, what torture to a mother's heart, to listen to this and be unable to go to him' (123). The juxtaposition of her grandmother's illness, caused by Brent's isolation, and Brent's inability to help her children for the same reason, recalls earlier descriptions of the ways in which slaveholders violently separate children from parents and abandon elderly slaves (16). Brent of course understands the failings of her garret and recognizes that it is not a space to be lauded for the potential resistance it allows. Such readings, writes Carla Kaplan, miss the fact of 'Brent's *inability* ... to "reverse" the power structures which bind her,' an inability which 'is the lived meaning of slavery for Linda Brent.'[55] As Brent notes, the seven years that she spent in such a cramped space 'is a fact; and to me a sad one, even now' (148). Despite the fact that her seven-year retreat does eventually lead to her freedom, she does not see it as a freeing experience in itself, 'for my body still suffers from the effects of that long imprisonment, to say nothing of my soul' (148). Refusing to set up a transcendent, Thoreauvian imprisonment, where her body's constraint is figured as unimportant, Brent ties her physical suffering to a more profound spiritual one, thus highlighting the connection between the social oppression visited upon her and her ontological status as an embodied black and female subject. Here, the constraint of the cell and of the body leads to its replication in a constraint of subjectivity, rather than to a freeing reformation.

5. The Slave Mother

To see Brent's time in the garret as overarchingly negative, however, is to ignore the safety and escape it provides, just as to emphasize only this safety is to ignore the damage it perpetrates on her. Brent's life in the garret and her descriptions of the power of community must be recognized as negotiations between the gaining of agency and its removal by surrounding subjugating forces. Samira Kawash states that Brent's 'condition of ... security is simultaneously the absolute deprivation of freedom.'[56] The assertion of a self-determining identity can, at the same time, be a denial of that identity. These negotiations are further entrenched into her narrative through her textual construction of her identity as a 'slave mother.' If community both empowers slaves and replicates slavery, and if isolation both replicates slavery and provides a refuge and means of escape, then Brent's sentimental construction of herself as a 'slave mother' both gives her an identity and erases it. Brent's negotiations of 'isolation' and 'community,' and of 'slavery' and 'freedom,' take place through her construction of 'slave woman' or 'slave mother' as an ineffable identity that allows her to complicate the expectations of her readership.

As several critics have noted, Jacobs's text generally follows the generic conventions of sentimental fiction.[57] In *The Theory of Moral Sentiments* (1759), Adam Smith concludes that sympathy is a universal human response through which all individuals are to a degree interested 'in the fortune of others.'[58] Smith looks forward to Bentham's models of the penitentiary, in that both base their thoughts on ideas of the universal nature of human conscience, and on people's ability to reform themselves through reflection.[59] Smith argues that, when viewing another person's suffering, especially if it is caused by actions resulting from 'improper' motives, 'we then heartily and entirely sympathize with the resentment of the sufferer,' which seems to call for 'a proportional punishment' to the person who caused the suffering.[60] Relying on this relationship between sympathy and action, sentimental fiction can be read as an attempt to spur action against certain injustices including, for example, slavery and the oppression of women.[61]

The relation between sentimental fiction and slavery is formed at the nexus of sympathy and action. The form of the sentimental novel, already common to such abolitionist authors as Harriet Beecher Stowe and Jacobs's editor, Lydia Maria Child, allows Jacobs to spur her readership to engage directly in anti-slavery action. Depicting her own suffering at the hands of Flint and in her garret, Jacobs engages a response designed not only to connect her to her readership – a community of free women – but also to involve that community in her own political enterprise.

Sentimental fiction was closely related to the expectations of the cult of true womanhood and to the constructs of domesticity.[62] Doriani writes: 'As *Godey's Lady's Book* and other women's magazines described her, the "true" American woman was pious, pure, submissive, and domestic. These were standards by which white women apparently judged themselves, and were judged by, forming the core of womanhood valued by the prosperous and growing middle class.'[63] As Doriani goes on to note, and as *Incidents* makes clear, these standards, with the notable exception of submissiveness, are precisely what are denied to slave women. Slaves are not allowed families, and their domestic spaces are subject to abuse; slave piety, figured through their relations with the Church, is to be used solely as a means of furthering their subjection to slavery, or else it is destroyed (as the black meeting hall is in Brent's town); and purity, expressly constructed as sexual purity, is violated by sexually abusive slave-owners like Flint, who rape slave women with legal impunity in order to increase their slave holdings. As the relation that Bender draws between prison and theory of sensibility details, both prison and the sentimental novel function as disciplinary institutions. But, just as the isolation and labour used by the nineteenth-century penitentiary alienates and brutalizes prisoners rather than reforming them, sentimental fiction, because it is based on similar ontological hierarchies, can replicate the sexist and racist discourse it attempts to undo.

The sentimental novel's emphasis on purity in particular creates a tension in Jacobs's narrative. She uses sentimental discourse in order to bind her white, middle-class readership to her and to spur them to political action, but if she is to adhere to her promise to make her narrative 'strictly true' (1), she must confess her consensual sexual relationship with a white man, Mr Sands, the father of her children. This confession risks alienating her readership – the self-confessed 'true women' of the North whose sexual purity, if not an actuality in the particular, was at least an unquestioned assertion in the general. Jacobs's editor, Lydia Maria Child, voices the recognition of this danger in her introduction to the text, writing that 'the experiences of this intelligent and much-injured woman belong to a class which some call delicate subjects, and others call indelicate' (3–4). Child's statement belies the uneasy marriage of the slave narrative's generic emphasis on suffering and domestic fiction's 'true woman.' While Brent is a 'much-injured woman,' a description which should elicit her audience's sympathy, such sympathy may be curtailed by the (in)delicacy of those injuries. In other words, the sexual abuse of Brent, when reconfigured as her sexual identity, negates the sympathy it elicits, which results in a silence surrounding that abuse – in Child's introduction, the 'delicate subject' is never named. This delicacy to a degree also silences discussion of non-sexual abuse. In her introduction to the text, Yellin quotes

Child's discussion of one of her few major editorial changes to *Incidents*, which was, in Child's words, to 'put the savage cruelties into one chapter ... in order that those who shrink from "supping on horrors" might omit them' (xxv). Such silences duplicate the enforced silence surrounding abuse, and specifically sexual abuse, that slavery itself perpetuates. Garfield writes: 'The cautious reader finds a shocking alter-ego in Flint. She would tie Jacobs's tongue as surely as he bullies his slaves into muteness.'[64] Like the slave woman Flint sells, Garfield is arguing, Brent is again in danger of letting her tongue 'run too far.'

Recognizing this problem, Brent exploits the silence surrounding the sexual abuse of slave women created by the combination of the discourses of true womanhood and sentimental politics in order to create an inviolable space for herself. She navigates, in Carby's words, 'the tension between satisfying moral expectations and challenging an ideology that would condemn her as immoral.'[65] Brent's construction of the subject positions of 'slave woman' and 'slave mother' simultaneously elicits sympathy and evades the moral judgments of her readers. Describing the aftermath of the birth of her second child, she states that Flint made her stand and listen to him heap 'upon me and my little one every vile epithet he could think of' (77); this diatribe goes on for so long that Brent faints. She then states:

> I suffered in consequence of this treatment; but I begged my friends to let me die, rather than send for the doctor. There was nothing I dreaded so much as his presence. My life was spared; and I was glad for the sake of my little ones. Had it not been for these ties to life, I should have been glad to be released by death, though I had lived only nineteen years. (78)

The abuse that Flint hurls at her is, according to him, the direct result of her sexual 'impropriety,' an action which, according to the values of true womanhood, would also be disdained by her reader. Brent thus makes Flint's abuse the moral equivalent of the readers' potential disdain. However, she leaves open another possible response for her readers through the figures of her friends, who are forced to watch her suffering and do nothing. Rather than dismiss the text due to its author's sexual history, readers are invited to recognize the suffering forced on her because of her condition as a slave mother. Further, they are asked not to engage in a duplication of Flint's violence by metaphorically reproducing the act of sending for the doctor. Instead, the reader is told to focus on the suffering while Brent heals on her own terms.

To ask the readers merely to recognize Brent's suffering is not enough to remove her from their judgmental gaze, since this audience was inundated with images of suffering which coexisted with images of purity; as others have argued, these two images coalesced for black women as the figure of the 'tragic mulatta' – a figure which found its demonic equivalent in the equally racist construct of the 'black woman as an innately sexual Jezebel.'[66] In order to escape the image of the 'tragic mulatta,' Brent refuses her audience a full grasp of her suffering. At points throughout the text, she refers to the impossibility of readers reaching a full understanding of her sufferings. When Brent's daughter leaves to be a servant to her own father's family, Brent writes, 'I heard the gate close after her, with such feelings as only a slave mother can experience' (141). When discussing Flint's verbal abuse of her, she informs the reader, 'I would not describe them *if I could*' (77; my emphasis). These ineffable sufferings even result in her audience's inability to participate in her happy moments. When her son meets her in New York after her escape, she asks, 'O reader, can you imagine my joy? No, you cannot, unless you have been a slave mother' (173). The most extended of her deliberations on the impossibility of fully communicating her suffering occurs immediately after she informs the reader of her affair with Sands:

> Pity me, and pardon me, O virtuous reader! You never knew what it is to be a slave; to be entirely unprotected by law or custom; to have the laws reduce you to the condition of a chattel, entirely subject to the will of another. You never exhausted your ingenuity in avoiding the snares, and eluding the power of a hated tyrant; you never shuddered at the sound of his footsteps, and trembled within hearing of his voice. I know I did wrong. No one can feel it more sensibly than I do. The painful and humiliating memory will haunt me to my dying day. Still, in looking back, calmly, on the events of my life, I feel that the slave woman ought not to be judged by the same standard as others. (55–6)

Rather than use sentimentality to 'figure the possibility [of] social unity' through 'the perfect communicability of intense feeling,' as Nudelman describes abolitionist textual practice,[67] Brent highlights the permanent and unnavigable gap between herself and her readers, emphasizing, in Robyn R. Warhol's words, that which the reader 'has not experienced.'[68] Nudelman argues that Brent 'places a barrier between her experience and the reader's own,' one which 'den[ies] the possibility of any empathic response from her readers.'[69] I would argue, however, that Brent constructs her suffering as being of an unimaginable magnitude, thus opening up a space of ultimate sympathy that can never be fully expended. The use of second-person address in this passage highlights this dual action: Brent places the reader in the narrator's place with the use of 'you,' thus encouraging a sympathetic bond between narrator and reader, but she also denies the experience to this person with the use of the negative, 'You have never ...' The reader is forced to sympathize as per the generic conventions of sentimental novels, but is told that such sympathy is inexhaustible. The ineffability of Brent's suffering disallows her readers' judgments of her actions, permitting Brent herself to occupy the only authoritative space from which to critique her actions. This leads to her creation of a system of sympathetic ethics beyond those tied to 'true womanhood,' which permits slave women to be judged on their own terms.

Brent's construction of her own system of sympathy allows her to speak about her sexual history. Directly addressing her reader, Brent states that she entered into the sexual relationship with Sands 'with deliberate calculation,' desiring to 'enrage Dr. Flint' (54, 55). Beyond this form of revenge, however, Brent also tells the reader, 'It seems less degrading to give one's self, than to submit to compulsion. There is something akin to freedom in having a lover who has no control over you, except that which he gains by kindness and attachment' (55). Brent rejects portraying herself as a merely passive victim, refusing, in Walter's words, the 'stereotypically feminine position with regard to her own fate.'[70] She may not be able to claim the social power associated with chastity, but she does claim 'something akin to freedom' through her action.

Her ability to lay hold of this qualified freedom and her position beyond the judgment of white women also reverse her relationship with her readers, allowing her to judge their failings. Because she describes her abuse as being far beyond their knowledge and experience, Brent not only becomes an authority on the suffering of slave women and slaves in general, but also creates a powerful space of continuous suffering, and therefore of permanent sympathy, which gives her a potentially unending hold on her audience. She translates her authority and her control of the audience's sympathies into a judgment of the suffering visited on blacks in the so-called freedom of the North. Brent notes the racism of the North when condemning the Jim Crow laws and segregation on the railways, in hotels, and at her son's workplace (162–3, 175–7, 186). Her most vehement remarks are reserved for the Fugitive Slave Law, passed in 1850, which permitted slave-owners to remove their runaway slaves from the Free States. In the penultimate chapter of the narrative, entitled 'The Fugitive Slave Law,' Brent notes how the passing of the law not only changes her legal status back into one of being a slave, but also alters the character of the Northern states. She describes meeting a slave she had known in the South: 'I was peculiarly glad to see him on Northern soil, though I no longer called it *free* soil' (193). Brent also describes, as does Thoreau in 'Slavery in Massachusetts,' the Northern states as being 'owned' by the South:

> But even in that dark region, where knowledge is so carefully excluded from the slave, I had heard enough about Massachusetts to come to the conclusion that slaveholders did not consider it a comfortable place to go to in search of a runaway. That was before the Fugitive Slave Law was passed; before Massachusetts had consented to become a 'nigger hunter' for the south. (131)

Noting that this relationship was formed by 'consent,' Jacobs echoes Thoreau's distaste both for such a support of slavery and for the individuals of the populace who do not actively remove such consent.

Brent discusses how the African American community in the North reacted against the Fugitive Slave Law in terms strongly reminiscent of her escape to the garret. Just as Brent's peephole allows her to evade and gain some control over the panoptic gaze of slavery, so too does the black community use their collective gaze to fight the slave-catchers who are empowered by the new law. After discussing how the law affected the black people in New York, forcing them to live in 'incessant fear,' Brent informs the reader:

> This state of things, of course, gave rise to many impromptu vigilance committees. Every colored person, and every friend of their persecuted race, kept their eyes wide open. Every evening I examined the newspapers carefully, to see what Southerners had put up at the hotels. I did this for my own sake, thinking my young mistress and her husband might be among the list; I wished also to give information to others, if necessary; for if many were 'running to and fro,' I resolved that 'knowledge should be increased.' (191–2)

While the North is no longer a space free from slavery, the black community, recreated in the North despite slavery's attempt to decimate it in the South, uses its own form of policing to frustrate the execution of the Fugitive Slave Law. Brent's quotation from the biblical book of Daniel enforces this use of the power of knowledge against the behaviour of the slave-owners. The biblical source refers to the Christian end times, when the 'wise shall shine as the brightness of the firmament' while the wicked will receive 'shame and everlasting contempt.' Further, in the section from which Brent's quotation is taken, Daniel is told that the names of the wicked and the wise can all 'be found written in the book.'[71] As the biblical book of judgment simultaneously condemns some and saves others, the newspaper allows Brent to both recognize slave-owners and help ex-slaves to continue to evade their grasp.[72]

Outrage over the passing of the Fugitive Slave Law was common in abolitionist and other reactionary discourse, of which Thoreau's 'Slavery in Massachusetts' is one example. What makes Brent's critique stand out is not her attack on the law and the North, but her parallel attack on her readership – people who would supposedly agree with her arguments – as a group whose sexual politics duplicate the ostracism and duplicity of the Fugitive Slave Law. 'To be bound to the conventions of true womanhood,' writes Carby, 'was to be bound to a racist, ideological system.'[73] Brent makes this connection explicit in a conversation she has with a black minister upon arriving in the North. After explaining her past to him, including telling him 'frankly ... some of the most important events of my life,' specifically concerning her children and their father, the minister replies, 'I did not question you from idle curiosity. I wanted to understand your situation, in order to know whether I could be of any service to you, or your little girl. Your straight-forward answers do you credit; but don't answer every body so openly. It might give some heartless people a pretext for treating you with contempt' (160). Just as the Fugitive Slave Law provides the basis for black people's re-subjection to the panoptic power of slavery (as enacted by slave-catchers), so can the discourse of sexual purity allow for the condemnation and rejection of Brent's life and narrative. Walter describes the seemingly inescapable trap this creates, writing that 'whether she shields herself in the dominant values of white womanhood, or openly exposes her predicament as a female slave, as the author-figure of the narrative, Brent knows she is subject to contempt or dismissal from all sides.'[74] While Brent's quotation from Daniel allows her to imply that slave-owners and their lackeys in the post-1850 North are wicked people who will receive 'everlasting contempt,' the minister tells her that her honesty about her sexual history could result in the same treatment for her.

Brent responds to the minister's statement, and therefore indirectly replies to those who would treat her with contempt, by again describing an identity of ineffable suffering, a space which should, according to her own construction of sentimental politics, create a feeling of sympathy that transcends such judgment:

> That word *contempt* burned me like coals of fire. I replied, 'God alone knows how I have suffered; and He, I trust, will forgive me. If I am permitted to have my children, I intend to be a good mother, and to live in such a manner that people cannot treat me with contempt.'
>
> 'I respect your sentiments,' said he. 'Place trust in God, and be governed by good principles, and you will not fail to find friends.' (161)

The scene from which this passage is taken, in which Brent details the events of her life, can be read as a depiction of the act of reading the *Incidents* of her life. When Brent refuses to be the object of judgment for those who exclude her from their construct of womanhood, she is denying her readers the right to judge her on terms to which she does not consent. Rather than ask for forgiveness or accept the role of the 'tragic mulatta,' Brent removes her identity from the matrix of subjugating and judgmental definitions. Walter describes a similar dynamic, specifically in the context of Brent's refigurations of domestic constructs, writing that 'Brent's use of womanhood and motherhood is not so much a strategy of locating herself within the existing discourses of selfhood as it is a strategy of dislocation.'[75] By relying on the politics of sympathy which undergird the sentimental tradition she is exploiting, Brent constructs an identity for herself that at once depicts the suffering necessary to gain sympathy and removes her identity from the gaze of others. 'God alone' is permitted a vision of her and his view is seen as forgiving. Brent attempts to construct a relationship based on respect, where she is in control of the moment of judgment, through denying the reader a depiction of her suffering, as it is indescribable, thus bringing the sentimental reader into a continual bond of sympathy.

While Douglas Taylor does not examine Jacobs's use of sentimentality in this particular way, my reading could be paired with his analysis of Benjamin Rush's theories of punishment. Taylor argues that Rush advocated the removal of the punishment of criminals from the public gaze in order to make such punishment *more* frightening to the populace:

> Secrecy surrounding the site of the prison, Rush argued, would generate speculation in the form of rumor, superstition, and popular fiction. Such speculation, Rush believed, would be worse than the actual realities of punishment, and would continue the work previously done by the spectacle of public punishment in spreading a crime-inhibiting terror among the multitude.[76]

Taylor does see Jacobs's use of sympathy (and her own isolation) as a redeployment of Rush's theories, in an attempt to create a 'counter-terrorist narrative,' but he also reads her 'silence surrounding sexual abuse' as a 'concession' to the mores of her readership, in an attempt to secure 'a forum' to show the evils of slavery.[77] In addition to this creation of a public forum, I would argue that Jacobs's creation of an ineffable, unending sympathy could be read as the mirror image of Rush's unending terror. *Incidents* could thus be read as inverting the disciplinary, discursive power represented by the prison, collapsing it in on itself.

This textual space of ethical control does not, however, allow Brent to escape completely the unequal power relations that exist between her and the white women of the North. While she creates a nearly transcendent sympathy for herself on behalf of the reader, such a sympathy does not remove the economic, social, and physical obstacles that are placed in front of her because of her race and gender – she cannot transform her garret into Thoreau's Walden Pond shack. Like the garret, Brent's construction of a sympathetic identity may allow her respite from judgment and the ability to visit judgment on others, but it does not allow her to escape her subjugation. This lack of complete freedom is signalled by the means through which she gains her legal freedom from slavery. The final chapter, 'Free at Last,' is not, as one might expect, a reversal of the power relationships Brent describes in the previous chapter, 'The Fugitive Slave Law.' Rather than fully celebrating her final escape from the clutches of slavery and the fugitive law, Brent instead shows how even her legal freedom is tainted by unequal social distinctions. In order to save Brent from her owners and to remove her from the legal purview of the 1850 law, her employer, Mrs Bruce, buys the slave and then frees her. Brent details her reactions upon hearing of this transaction in the following oft-cited passage:

> So I was *sold* at last! A human being *sold* in the free city of New York! The bill of sale is on record, and future generations will learn from it that women were articles of traffic in New York, late in the nineteenth century of the Christian religion ... I well know the value of that bit of paper; but as much as I love freedom, I do not like to look upon it. (200)

Despite Brent's attempts to remove herself from the panoptic surveillance of slavery, and despite her similar attempts to escape the judgmental gaze of the North, her freedom ultimately reinscribes the unequal power relations that result from and support both systems. In her discussion of Thoreau's and Jacobs's uses of the language of liberalism, Anita Goldman writes: 'Whereas Thoreau finds freedom in jail, arguing that the Massachusetts prison is "the only house in a slave-state in which a free man can abide with honor," Jacobs finally insists upon the limits of freedom afforded her by existing social conditions.'[78] Indeed, Brent's freedom only comes when money is used to replace her as a slave, and Mrs Bruce, while fully sympathetic, is constructed as falling outside of the respect which Brent earlier hopes to gain from people. Rather than mutual friendship and respect, Brent is bound to Mrs Bruce by 'Love, duty, and gratitude' (201), and Brent's employment, looking after the Bruce children, closely mimics her duties while a slave.[79] In addition, Brent does not have her own home, a symbol of the motherhood she says she desires when talking to the minister.

While Brent does point to these problems, she still recognizes the benefits of her position, but these benefits can only be acknowledged when paired to a critique: 'I and my children are now free! We are as free from the power of slaveholders as are the white people of the north; and though that, according to my ideas, is not saying a great deal, it is a vast improvement in *my* condition' (201). Just as her life in the garret, while not ideal, is better than her life as a slave, Brent's legal freedom, while still subject to class and racial divisions, can be used as a means of critiquing the northern society in which she is still a member of an 'oppressed people' (201). Hirsch points out another way in which Northern freedom was not ideal, writing that nineteenth-century 'northern penitentiaries contained a disproportionate number of blacks, many of them manumitted slaves. These persons must have found northern freedom, at best, a mixed blessing.'[80] Brent's ultimately indescribable suffering and the sympathy she generates through it invests her with an authority which allows her to critique the Northern white populace, but, though this power to critique may be 'akin to freedom,' it is not equal to it.

6. The Writing of Linda Brent

There is one final means through which 'Linda Brent' attempts to gain a freedom from the constraining discourses and situations around her, be they those of slavery or of the cult of true womanhood. She does this by denying access to the historical identity of the 'slave girl' of the narrative's title. By being Linda Brent, Harriet Jacobs attempts to remove her life's story from the gaze of others. Like Douglass's refusal in his *Narrative* to give details of his escape from slavery, Jacobs's fictionalization of herself and the other figures in her life protects those who helped her who still live in the slave territories: 'I have concealed the names of places, and given persons fictitious names. I had no motive for secrecy on my own account, but I deemed it kind and considerate towards others to pursue this course' (1). Belying her denial of personal motives for this secrecy, though, is her statement at the close of the text that, while the memories of her grandmother give her solace, in general it is 'painful ... to recall the dreary years I passed in bondage. I would gladly forget them if I could' (201). While she is not able to forget, Jacobs's creation of Linda Brent can be seen as a means of creating a form of separation between Jacobs and her narrator, much like the 'dislocation' of identity that Walter discusses. The fictionalized identity of 'Linda Brent' provides her readers with the sentimental abolitionist narrative that attempts to spur them to action, while at the same time it allows Jacobs to retain a form of privacy from her 'true-women' readers of the North by protecting her 'real' identity. Jacobs's narrative negotiations of author, narrator, and sentimental figure re-enact her escape from slavery. While that escape is in part brought about through her mimicry of slavery's isolation in her garret, her escape from the potentially hostile gaze of her audience is enacted through her self-concealment, in Linda Brent, as a slave narrator and sentimental figure.[81]

However, just as her years in the garret are not an unproblematic removal of herself from the abuses of slavery, Jacobs's textual identity as 'Linda Brent' does not provide her with an unproblematic identity that is at once fully public and fully private. At the time of the publication of *Incidents*, Jacobs was often referred to by abolitionists 'as Linda Brent, or, at best, Linda Jacobs,' and the 'fictionalizing' of names and places in *Incidents* becomes 'as significant in Jacobs's life as it is in her text.'[82] Jacobs's renaming moves from an attempt to gain privacy and secrecy to being another indicator of her problematic position within the generic, legal, and other identificatory practices of her time, a position which at once allows her a form of social power and removes that power.

Even contemporary critical studies of Jacobs's text fall into the problem of identification. Jean Fagan Yellin's extensive research into the publication history of *Incidents* and Jacobs's letters proved that *Incidents* was not the fictional piece some had assumed it to be, an assumption stated in John W. Blassingame's well-known critique of the text.[83] Before Yellin's studies, Jacobs's authorship and text were often dismissed and ignored in an unwitting echo of the ways in which slaves were forcibly silenced. Yellin identified the historical figures behind Jacobs's fictional constructs, and thus both inaugurated and enabled contemporary studies of Jacobs and her work. Despite the value of these studies, however, the 'Cast of Characters' which Yellin provides at the beginning of her edition has been used in problematic ways. While some critics refer to the protagonist of the text as 'Linda Brent,' and separate this figure from the author, many simply identify the two figures, referring to Jacobs as both author and protagonist. Although, as Foreman notes, Jacobs herself perpetuated this slippage, many critics combine this identification of Jacobs and Brent with a silence surrounding the other historical figures fictionalized in the text. People write about Jacobs's battles with 'Dr Flint,' for example, rather than her battles with 'Dr Norcom,' the historical figure on whom Flint is based. Studies that engage her text on these terms provide the slave-owner with anonymity and the security it provides, while subjecting Jacobs to the full, scrutinizing gaze of historical criticism. Carla Kaplan discusses this problem:

> The shift ... from Brent's narrated acts to Jacobs's act of narration, may be a troubling one. Not only because it seems to require us to talk about the author as well as her narrator, but because it reminds us that we, as readers, are implicated in the problem we are analyzing ... This raises an important methodological question for recuperative work: what will it

mean for us to recover or recuperate Jacobs's agency when we, as readers, are problematically and unavoidably implicated in the process of its construction?[84]

Kaplan goes on to note that this issue becomes 'particularly troubling' since the place of Jacobs's reader runs 'parallel' to that of Dr Flint in many of the scenes of Brent's narrative.[85]

Beyond this textual parallel, referring to Brent as Jacobs, combined with the silence surrounding 'Flint's' or other characters' historical bases, results in a duplication of a panoptic gaze which renders Jacobs visible while leaving her oppressors and readers hidden. This is the precise form of gaze that Brent/Jacobs was attempting to escape through her existence in the garret and flight to the North. Just as those actions are shown to be inadequate, *Incidents* – with the troubles of fiction and fact, silence and speech – raises the fact that analysing slave (and prison) texts is equally problematic. *Incidents* thus critiques the panoptic gaze that exists in several forms within the carceral society, be it in terms of gender or racial oppression, or in terms of the positioning of texts within the academy. What Jacobs *and* Brent offer us is the understanding that, while a complete Thoreauvian individual transcendence above the oppressive identificatory practices of society is impossible for everyone, no matter what social space they occupy, people can still engage in critiques of those practices. Sorisio notes that Jacobs's narrative may extend 'the privilege of a Romantic self to African American women,' but it also 'checks its optimistic transcendence through embodied experience.'[86] Taking care to analyse the transformations of identity in which Jacobs engages on her own terms, while noting that there can never be a full vision of her negotiations of identity, allows us to recognize that, while it may be impossible to achieve complete freedom, we can create 'a vast improvement' (201) in specific conditions.

While Jacobs's narrative deals with some issues that do not specifically apply to prison texts, her overall project resonates with them. Prison authors also struggle with walking the line between freedom and oppression, between resisting the carceral society and furthering its aims. The resulting constructions of identity take many different forms, though, so while my reading of Jacobs's project is intended to offer an introductory example of the rewriting of identity from within a disciplinary and carceral environment, it cannot be seen as wholly representative of all such rewritings, be they slave narratives or prison texts – and, as I have argued, no prison text should be seen as serving such a fully representative function. As the next chapter demonstrates, prison authors' methods of writing their freedom can also take the form of, among other possibilities, a partial negation or erasure of identity. Whereas the texts examined in this section of the study were written in order to offer somewhat general critiques of the disciplinary institutional functions of society, Oscar Wilde's and Martin Luther King Jr's prison letters, to be studied in the next section, were composed in direct response to specific occurrences and pre-existing texts, in attempts to right the wrongs that the authors saw within the larger social world. However, both letters respond to the ways in which these situations or other documents help to reproduce the disciplinary functions of the prison, and to the fact that this reproduction is also evident on the 'outside,' thus continuing Thoreau's and Jacobs's definitions and critiques of the carceral society. Furthering my analysis of the particularities of this complex process as part of a larger attempt to understand the necessary multiplicity of possible responses, I examine the letters alongside the occurrences and materials against which they were written.

PART TWO

Writing Wrongs

CHAPTER THREE

'To be entirely free, and at the same time entirely dominated by law': The Paradox of the Individual in *De Profundis*

Ah! Happy they whose hearts can break
   And peace of pardon win!
How else may man make straight his plan
   And cleanse his soul from Sin?
How else but through a broken heart
   May Lord Christ enter in?

The Ballad of Reading Gaol, 5.79–84

In a letter to Robert Ross, Oscar Wilde writes that *The Ballad of Reading Gaol* 'suffers under the difficulty of a divided aim in style. Some is realistic, some is romantic: some poetry, some propaganda.'[1] Upon reading the above stanza, one could transform Wilde's description by saying that the poem is also divided by the difficulty felt under suffering – a difficulty that is summed up by the statement that a broken heart leads to happiness. While this phrase may at first seem melodramatic, if not clichéd, it takes on a much larger and more complex meaning in the letter to Lord Alfred Douglas commonly known as *De Profundis*. Written while Wilde was in prison, this long letter complicates notions of suffering and happiness, of sin and redemption, and of a person's place within each of these dichotomies. *De Profundis* is, as Jay Losey writes, an account 'of an artist's struggle to preserve his identity' presented 'in terms of a conversion.'[2] This preservation, like Jacobs's, takes the form of a complex negotiation between concepts of identity as individuality and concepts of identity as entirely subjugated to external social forces. Wilde's problematization of identity does not end there; *De Profundis* makes the seemingly impossible argument that only through a complete loss or rejection of both agency *and* of the constructions placed on one by others can one reach a truly personal perspective.[3] Unlike the universal access to transcendence which Thoreau describes, Wilde depicts an identity in *De Profundis* that only he can interpret, and this interpretation may not be apprehended by others. In a manner resembling Jacobs's use of an ineffable position of suffering, Wilde attempts to create an identity that is wholly separate from the determining forces around him. Within my larger project of analysing how each text of a range of prison writings engages in a unique critique of the identificatory practices within the generally uniform carceral system, this chapter demonstrates how Wilde reworks the disciplinary, identificatory practices of the legal system and the related ideological institution of the press. Wilde also rewrites the Protestant conversion rhetoric that accompanied the construction of the modern prison – detailed in the first chapter of my study – as it was transmitted throughout the West with the proliferation of prison theory in the nineteenth century. Enhancing our understanding of how these general negotiations of identity in which prison authors engage can be used as social critiques, Wilde specifically uses his prison text to reassert or defend the sexual identity for which the carceral society punished him, just as Jacobs critiques racial and gender oppression in her narrative. In order to explicate Wilde's definition of self, this chapter will first discuss the context of his imprisonment and trials as they were depicted through newspaper reports, which therefore, in and of themselves, form part of the disciplinary mechanisms of the carceral matrix. Second, I will examine the way in which Wilde constructs his identity in *De Profundis* against its portrayal in the media. Lastly, Wilde's construction of the ideal individual will be explicated through the letter's discussions of Christ.

1. Prison, the Press, and the Pose

As Regenia Gagnier argues in *Idylls of the Marketplace, De Profundis* must be contextualized in terms of Wilde's imprisonment – and the Victorian prison system in general – before it can be interpreted. Gagnier writes:

> [I]n prison Wilde lived under the contemporary regulations of solitary cellular confinement for two years; his daily routine was determined by a rigorously enforced timetable, and he was not permitted to talk. The self

in his letter is a self constructed in a particular imaginative act of resistance against insanity and against the material matrix of prison space and time – that is, confined, segmented space and timelessness.[4]

Defining the 'material matrix' and philosophical underpinnings of the Victorian prison, Wiener argues that the penal system in England, as in America, underwent a transformation that was conjoined with a new emphasis on the power of the individual. He writes that the 'reformed criminal policy' that began in the early Victorian period

> was to be carried out by overhauling the institutions of police, trial, and punishment, creating a visible force for social surveillance, a more predictable and systematic hearing process, and a prison system subjecting its inmates to a discipline that would without violence both deter and build character. It was to serve not only the immediate practical aim of crime control, but even more importantly the ultimate goal of public character development by reinforcing a new structure of values. Given prevailing views of human nature and of the role of law, the aims of deterrence and moralization seemed by no means incompatible.[5]

These 'prevailing views of human nature' in the early nineteenth-century prison were, in both America and Europe, concerned in large part with the ability of each person to recognize and act according to certain 'natural' behavioural codes. Relying on Bentham's model of the panopticon and its partial enactment in the American penal system as seen in Philadelphia, early Victorian prisons began to rely increasingly on a silent and isolating system of confinement as a means of awakening people to these 'inherent' codes.[6]

Moving into the late nineteenth century, when Wilde's imprisonment occurred, Wiener sees a further transformation in penological methods, in this instance reflecting a move away from the emphasis on the individual that we see in the early Victorian and early nineteenth-century American systems. This shift occurs due more to the temporal difference than to the national one, since, as noted in the first chapter of this study, the institutionalization of the prison was an international phenomenon. Arising from new scientific and philosophical theories, such as Marxism, psychology, and Darwinism and its sociological descendants, the new methods reflected a growing scepticism about personal integrity and agency. As Wiener writes, 'The sea change in constructions of human nature and social agency encouraged both a relaxation of moralizing pressures on the individual and a new anxiety about individual ineffectuality.'[7] Within criminal and social policies, this change was figured through a move 'away from deterrence and moralization' towards a medicalization of criminal behaviour[8] – a view of criminal activities as a sign of an illness (be it biological or social) that the criminal cannot simply alter through force of will. Wilde himself engages in this reformulation of crime, writing in 'The Soul of Man Under Socialism': 'When there is no punishment at all, crime will either cease to exist, or, if it occurs, will be treated by physicians as a very distressing form of dementia, to be cured by care and kindness.'[9] Moving away from early nineteenth-century depictions of individual responsibility, Wilde sees all crimes as effects of 'the misery and rage and depression produced by our wrong system of property-holding,' rather than as direct and conscious acts of individuals.[10] This change in the notion of the origin of criminal behaviour, however, does not alter the prison's role as a disciplinary mechanism. No matter the cause of criminals' behaviour, the prison is seen as the solution, as a means of altering people's identity in order to 'normalize' their behaviour.

This conceptual 'sea change,' like all those before and after it, did not happen overnight and was not all-encompassing. Despite their occurrence near the end of Victoria's reign, Wilde's trials and conviction have much more to do with the moralizing, surveilling, and disciplining apparatuses of earlier penal forms than they do with analyses of social, medical, or otherwise impersonal forces. Wilde's homosexuality and his relationships with Alfred Douglas and other younger men, which form the legal justification of his imprisonment, were treated in explicitly moral terms even while his own writings exist within the new paradigm.[11] Wilde addresses the events surrounding his trials and arrest in the second paragraph of De Profundis, stating to Douglas, 'Our ill-fated and most lamentable friendship has ended in ruin and public infamy for me.'[12] Wilde not only uses the letter as 'an act of resistance against ... prison space and time,' as Gagnier argues,[13] but also as a defence against the 'public infamy' instigated by the moralizing discourse surrounding his sexual identity.

As elucidated in Ed Cohen's studies of Wilde, this infamy was promulgated mostly through the newspaper reports of Wilde's three trials. I would expand this conclusion to argue that the newspapers in fact functioned as part of the surveillance of the carceral system, providing the public, and possibly the jury itself, with partisan reports on the trials. Wilde earlier notes this disciplinary aspect of the press in

'The Soul of Man,' writing that '[i]n the old days men had the rack. Now they have the Press. That is an improvement certainly. But still it is very bad, and wrong, and demoralising ... The tyranny that it proposes to exercise over people's private lives seems to me to be quite extraordinary.'[14] Part of what Wilde is writing against is the public image that was created around him, in part by this tyrannical power.

Cohen argues that the constructions of Wilde's character in the newspaper reports of the trials help, as Foucault writes, to allow for 'an *incorporation of perversions* and a new *specification of individuals.*'[15] Cohen demonstrates that 'in the course of representing the libel proceedings in *Wilde v. Queensberry*, the newspapers effectively (re)produced the possibility for designating Wilde as a kind of sexual actor without explicitly referring to the specificity of his sexual acts, and thereby crystallized a new constellation of sexual meanings predicated upon "personality" and not practices.'[16] Tying this project to the legal system, Jane Wood states that the newspaper reports of the Wilde trials helped to create 'a sophistical leap which permitted a Victorian middle-class judiciary to formulate a category of deviance.'[17] Cohen argues specifically that, because the newspapers do not name the act of sodomy in their reports on the trial (in order to avoid offending public mores), Wilde's transgression of normative sexual codes gets transferred from the acts he allegedly commits to his 'pose' or identity. In the first trial, in which Wilde charged the Marquess of Queensberry with libel, what had to be proven against Wilde was not that he committed acts of sodomy, but that he 'posed' as someone who would commit those acts. Cohen writes: 'By mediating between the defense [i.e., Queensberry's] interpretation and the popular limits for (sexual) representation, the newspapers reiterated the defense's attempts to construct a new category of sexual transgression that could be signified not by reference to specific 'unnameable' sexual acts but by the depiction of a certain type of sexual actor.'[18] The newspapers, and the anti-Wilde side in all of the trials, take the proof of aberrant acts out of the act itself, and place it on a 'type' of person, thus furthering the normalizing, disciplinary project of the courts themselves. This typing, however, inadvertently helps to construct an identity (which then becomes a stereotype) for people engaging in specific, but unnamed, sexual acts.

Cohen goes to great length to show how Wilde is constructed through various newspaper reports as 'extra-ordinary,' 'extravagant,' 'indecent,' 'immoral,' and various other counter-normative terms. To elaborate on this argument, in order to connect these statements to my project, a few examples here will show how Wilde's character was constructed by the press as part of the disciplinary social processes, and why, at the beginning of *De Profundis*, he makes a point of positioning the letter as a defence against his 'public infamy.' These examples will also help to show why Wilde would be adamant about not wanting to see his identity as something that is socially overdetermined and subjugated; while the newspaper reports may be the beginning of a new discourse of sexuality, they are anything but positive about the identity they construct for Wilde. Regressing to an early Victorian moralizing discourse, the newspapers attempt to portray Wilde as an active and wilful deviant who must be disciplined. While Cohen discusses an identity that arises unintentionally from the newspapers, I will argue that Wilde responds to the intentions behind the articles.

Defending the witnesses who were accused of being involved with Wilde, the *Times* states, 'But let those who were inclined to condemn these men for allowing themselves to be dominated, misled, and corrupted by Mr. Oscar Wilde remember the relative position of the parties, and remember that they were men who had been more sinned against than sinning.' Later in the same column, the witnesses were further described:

> There were general observations applicable to all the cases; there was, in point of fact, a startling similarity between each of them on his own admission which must lead the jury to draw most painful conclusions. There was the fact that in no one of these cases were the parties on an equality in any way with Mr. Wilde; they were none of them educated parties with whom he would naturally associate, and they were not his equal in years. The jury would have observed a curious similarity in the ages of each of them. Mr. Wilde had said that there was something beautiful, something charming about youth which led him to adopt the course he did. It was absurd; his excuse in the witness box was only a travesty of the facts.[19]

These descriptions indicate that Wilde is domineering and active in his approach to 'sin' (which is used possibly to rejoin notions of 'gross indecency' with the religious injunction against sodomy, as discussed by Cohen), that his reasons for associating with young men cannot be defended by his 'excuses,' and that the 'unnatural' 'course' he 'adopted' was one which would be 'painful' to the moral sense of the jury which, like both the *Times* and its readers, is capable of discerning the 'facts' behind Wilde's defence. Thus, as Cohen discusses, Wilde is constructed as the antithesis to the sexual identity of the so-called normal male – a construction portrayed in explicitly moral terms. This counter-normative construction of Wilde is made even more explicit in a later *Times* article, in which the reader is told that 'the jury must deal with the evidence on the one hand and their duty to the public on the other,' placing Wilde in opposition to the public at large – the site of the normative value system.[20]

This opposition is one of the immediate contexts of *De Profundis*. Obviously, Wilde saw the negative manner in which his identity was constructed by the media. He writes that he gave his name 'to brutes that they might make it brutal' (458). His name, when placed into a public forum, takes on what he sees as the negative connotations of the public itself. This is accentuated by the use in the public court of his private letters to Douglas, which were portrayed as proof of their 'improper' relationship. Oliver S. Buckton, quoting Jonathan Dollimore, delineates Wilde's recognition of the effects of public attention, writing that 'Wilde was able to perceive the ideological effects and limits of his society, and ... his work as a whole "recognizes the priority of the social and the cultural in determining not only public meaning but 'private' or subjective desire."'[21] Because of this recognition, Wilde realizes that he must somehow construct an identity for himself in opposition to the negative one that has been defined for him by the ideological functioning of the press and the penological system. Indeed, Julia Prewitt Brown goes so far as to write that 'Wilde's abhorrence at being labeled, at having the wealth of his language and his temperament reduced to such paltry material, is no doubt one reason he became involved in the libel suit in the first place.'[22]

This 'abhorrence at being labeled' is not, however, a denial of his sexual identity. As Wilde writes in *De Profundis*:

A great friend of mine – a friend of ten years' standing – came to see me some time ago and told me that he did not believe a single word of what was said against me, and wished me to know that he considered me quite innocent, and the victim of a hideous plot concocted by your father. I burst into tears at what he said, and told him that while there was much amongst your father's definite charges that was quite untrue and transferred to me by revolting malice, still that my life had been full of perverse pleasures and strange passions, and that unless he accepted that

fact as a fact about me and realised it to the full, I could not possibly be
friends with him any more, or ever be in his company. (502)

Working against what David Foster sees as Wilde's attempt in *De
Profundis* to 'disguise the erotic implications of his relationship with
Douglas,'[23] Wilde here does not deny his sexual identity: his 'strange
passions' constitute a 'fact about' his self-conception. Rather, he denies
the negative constructions that Queensberry, the newspapers, and the
trials associate with him. Describing what he refers to as Wilde's 'fatal
effeminacy,' Joseph Bristow situates Wilde's response against such
determinizing in terms of the larger normative discourses of the time,
of which prison was a part, writing that '[t]o fix, to name, and to classify "homosexuality," as the sexologists were attempting to do in the
1890s, was for Wilde to sign its death warrant.'[24] As Wilde says near
the end of the letter: 'What lies before me is my past. I have got to make
myself look on that with different eyes, to make the world look on it
with different eyes, to make God look on it with different eyes' (511).
Wilde transforms the type of strategic identity construction Jacobs creates – an identity defined by the ineffability of suffering experienced
under oppressive determination – into a definition of identity that
attempts to avoid external determination altogether. He wants to
change actively the definition and perception of the past, and therefore
of himself.

2. Puppets with Passions, or, The Paradox of Identity

Wilde starts to create the 'different eyes' by reversing the roles of
definer and defined, and of corruptor and corrupted, as the newspapers, the Marquess of Queensberry, and the trials and prison constructed them. He does this specifically through the construction of his
relationship to Alfred Douglas. Reversing the use of his letters at trial,
Wilde writes *De Profundis* as a means of potentially reclaiming his
name, or at least of denying others' use of it.

  Discussing the mediational aspect of epistolary discourse, Janet Gurkin Altman writes: 'As an instrument of communication between
sender and receiver, the letter straddles the gulf between presence and
absence ... The letter lies halfway between the possibility of total communication and the risk of no communication at all.'[25] In *De Profundis*,
Wilde plays with the ways in which this aspect of the letter can alter
notions not only of presence and absence, but also of the very different

notions of authority and agency. It could be argued, in fact, that Wilde's epistle functions as an anti–love letter. If, as Linda S. Kauffman defines them, love letters 'have been instrumental in disguising relationships of power,'[26] Wilde's text makes those relations its primary topic. One of the recurring ways in which Wilde does this is to construct his relationship with Douglas as one in which Wilde had no effective agency. Indeed, he begins the letter by excusing the fact that he has taken on the action of writing: 'Dear Bosie, After long and fruitless waiting I have determined to write to you myself, as much for your sake as for mine, as I would not like to think that I had passed through two long years of imprisonment without ever having received a single line from you, or any news or message even, except such as give me pain' (423–4). Wilde has taken an active role in his relationship with Douglas in writing *De Profundis*, but only because Douglas's treatment of Wilde during his imprisonment has had negative effects on both of them. Buckton stresses this, writing that 'Wilde invokes the conventional "mea culpa" of confessional remorse, only immediately to displace the cause of his "ethical degradation" on to Bosie himself.'[27] According to Wilde, if he had not written this letter, his relationship with Douglas would have continued with the younger man actively defining a passive Wilde: 'and you yourself will, I think, feel in your heart that to write to me as I lie in the loneliness of prison-life is better than to publish my letters without my permission or to dedicate poems to me unasked, though the world will know nothing of whatever words of grief or passion, of remorse or indifference you may choose to send as your answer or your appeal' (424). From the beginning, the writing of *De Profundis* is an act of regaining a sense of agency from what Wilde depicts as a passive relationship on his part.

Wilde goes on to describe this relationship as one in which he was forced to act against his will. This description, however, takes the paradoxical form of Wilde's statement that all of the blame rests squarely on himself:

> I will begin by telling you that I blame myself terribly. As I sit here in this dark cell in convict clothes, a disgraced and ruined man, I blame myself. In the perturbed and fitful nights of anguish, in the long monotonous days of pain, it is myself I blame. I blame myself for allowing an unintellectual friendship, a friendship whose primary aim was not the creation and contemplation of beautiful things, to entirely dominate my life. From the very first there was too wide a gap between us. (425)

At this early point in the letter, Wilde blames himself for not acting against the friendship, and instead passively allowing an unproductive relationship to dominate him. Wilde adds that this power dynamic lying behind the relationship no longer exists. He does this by blaming himself for the abuse of power: while Wilde describes Douglas as having the semblance of control in their earlier lives, in the letter Douglas is not even allowed the action of taking the blame. This reversal of the nature of the relationship becomes more obvious when Wilde writes, 'I blame myself without reserve for my weakness' (427). The act of writing the letter is such an effective tool of gaining a sense of agency that Wilde even asserts that he was never really powerless to begin with – all of the blame must lie with him. David Foster similarly notes that even Wilde's 'most abject yieldings are represented as acts of commission.'[28] Wilde seems to accept the 'blame' which the newspapers lay on him, including the statements about the gaps between Wilde and the witnesses used against him, who were not 'on an equality in any way with Mr. Wilde.'[29] By situating this blame within a passive nature, however, Wilde gains a level of agency denied to him by Douglas and by the legal and penological systems. This use of passivity is mirrored in the second half of the letter, where Wilde asserts that the only way to gain a sense of self-identity is through complete humility.

Despite this paradox, his construction of his relationship with Douglas is effective in placing Wilde in the role of the passive victim of an 'ethical degradation' that Douglas visits on him (429). The young lord is depicted in *De Profundis* as having controlled and altered Wilde's personality. 'The basis of character,' Wilde writes, 'is will-power, and my will-power became absolutely subject to yours' (429). Wilde expands on this statement, stating:

> I had always thought that my giving up to you in small things meant nothing: that when a great moment arrived I could reassert my will-power in its natural superiority. It was not so. At the great moment my will-power completely failed me. In life there is really no small or great thing. All things are of equal value and of equal size. My habit – due to indifference chiefly at first – of giving up to you in everything had become insensibly a real part of my nature. Without my knowing it, it had stereotyped my temperament to one permanent and fatal mood. That is why, in the subtle epilogue to the first edition of his essays, Pater says that 'Failure is to form habits' ... I had allowed you to sap my strength of char-

acter, and to me the formation of a habit had proved to be not Failure merely but Ruin. (430)

Wilde's failure to assert his will is the ruin of his character, leading him to conclude that his character can be formed by all of the 'small' things in his life. Like Thoreau's damning of the desperate lives of the mass of men, Wilde states that all objects or events of a person's surroundings and life have equal effects on forming that person's character or 'mood.' Unlike Thoreau's statements about identity in his essay, however, Wilde's assertion of his individual will power is not enough to overcome the determination of character forced on him. Wilde's will becomes, he says here, merely an imitation of Douglas's 'supreme vice' of 'shallowness' (425).

If Wilde's pre-prison, but post-Douglas character is only an imitation of the younger man's own personality, then Wilde's portrayal of his lover takes on major importance. Beyond the overt accusations and subtle implications that Douglas was simply presumptuous in his association with Wilde, being 'by [Wilde's] side always' (426), the young lord is portrayed as being profoundly shallow, where shallowness is defined as a lack of self-reflectiveness and, interestingly, a lack of personal strength and will. Wilde reminds his addressee of where the letter is written from:

> Even the spectacle of me behind the bars of a wooden cage could not quicken that dead unimaginative nature. You had the sympathy and the sentimentality of the spectator of a rather pathetic play. That you were the true author of the hideous tragedy did not occur to you. I saw that you realised nothing of what you had done. I did not desire to be the one to tell you what your own heart should have told you, what it indeed would have told you if you had not let Hate harden it and make it insensate. Everything must come to one out of one's own nature. (448)

Douglas is here described as a spectator; he is placed in the passive role that Wilde assumes throughout most of the narrative. Even though Douglas is 'the true author,' he still 'realised nothing.' Wilde reiterates the message that a person's will power or, as described here, 'heart' or 'nature' should be the defining principle of that person's character, but, for both Douglas and Wilde, it never seems to be. Douglas does not recognize even the ideality of the control of 'heart' or 'nature,' and instead blindly watches life through an 'insensate' and 'dead' nature.

Wilde is again playing with an apparent contradiction surrounding agency. Douglas may have completely usurped Wilde's own identity, but Douglas never had an individual position from which to act in the first place. Not only is the younger man's personality insensate and dead but, because of this, his identity, like Wilde's, is constantly being subjugated by others, especially his father. Wilde quotes Douglas's mother as saying that Lord Alfred was 'the one of my children who has inherited the fatal Douglas temperament,' and Wilde adds to this by writing to Lord Alfred that the Marquess's 'hatred of you was just as persistent as your hatred of him, and I was the stalking-horse for both of you, and a mode of attack as well as a mode of shelter. His very passion for notoriety was not merely individual but racial' (433, 446–7). Wilde also describes Douglas's specific traits as being mere copies of his father's, when he mentions 'that dreadful mania you inherit from your father, the mania for writing revolting and loathsome letters' (429). Picking up on the deterministic sciences of the late nineteenth century, Wilde removes Douglas's agency. Just as the criminal justice system was beginning to see criminal acts as determined by social or biological realities, Wilde portrays Douglas's actions as not originating with himself. Lord Alfred becomes in *De Profundis* a non-individual; he is simply a vessel that gets filled with his 'racial' heredity.

Wilde recognizes and explains the difficulty of having his will subsumed by Douglas's non-will, thereby complicating notions of subjectivity that would posit an easy determining/determined dichotomy. First, he writes about various of Douglas's 'incessant scenes,' which 'were the origin and causes of my fatal yielding to you in your daily increasing demands. You wore one out. It was the triumph of the smaller over the bigger nature. It was the case of that tyranny of the weak over the strong which somewhere in one of my plays I describe as "the only tyranny that lasts"' (429). Here Wilde is again reasserting, through *De Profundis*, his own strength of will and personality over Douglas, while still maintaining that Douglas's weaker nature overpowered his own. Wilde defines this problematic relationship of wills as a 'mystery':

> It makes me feel sometimes as if you yourself had been merely a puppet worked by some secret and unseen hand to bring terrible events to a terrible issue. But puppets themselves have passions. They will bring a new

plot into what they are presenting, and twist the ordered issue of vicissitude to suit some whim or appetite of their own. To be entirely free, and at the same time entirely dominated by law, is the eternal paradox of human life that we realise at every moment; and this, I often think, is the only explanation possible of your nature, if indeed for the profound and terrible mysteries of a human soul there is any explanation at all, except one that makes the mystery more marvellous still. (443)

Wilde's dual construction of identity as both entirely free and entirely subjugated can be read as an indication of the transformation from early Victorian to late Victorian notions of identity, which are also played out in criminal policies. Wiener writes that '[a]s the effective reach and force of the individual's actions grew, so too did the reach and force of others' actions grow to impinge upon the individual.'[30] For Wilde, this dual motion means that identity can both be constructed from the outside and arise from inside the self. Unlike Thoreau's assertion that the individual can transcend what Wilde calls being 'dominated by law,' Wilde argues that this type of transcendent freedom does not negate, but instead coexists with subjugation. Jane Wood writes that Wilde 'develops, extends, explores, and manipulates' this and other paradoxes 'in an attempt to defer the moment of realization' which characterizes the classic tragedy, a generic classification of his life that Wilde is attempting to avoid, despite its applicability.[31] Wilde goes beyond 'deferral,' however, showing that 'the paradox of human life' is eternal – it is 'profound and terrible' since it has no possible resolution. Like Jacobs, who critiques Northern society at the end of her narrative by asserting that there is an improvement in her specific conditions even though she does not feel a complete freedom, Wilde sets up the unattainable 'entirely free' existence as a positive force, whereas the 'entirely dominated' personality is cast negatively. Wilde's character was, with respect to Douglas, to the public, and to the criminal justice system, of the latter kind.

This dual theory of identity formation is parallelled in a statement by Lord Henry in *The Picture of Dorian Gray*:

[T]o influence a person is to give him one's own soul. He does not think his natural thoughts, or burn with his natural passions. His virtues are not real to him. His sins, if there are such things as sins, are borrowed. He becomes an echo of someone else's music, an actor of a part that has not been written for him. The aim of life is self-development. To realize one's nature per-

fectly – that is what each of us is here for ... I believe that if one man were
to live out his life fully and completely, were to give form to every feeling,
expression to every thought, reality to every dream – I believe that the
world would gain such a fresh impulse of joy that we would forget all the
maladies of mediaevalism, and would return to the Hellenic ideal – to
something finer, richer, than the Hellenic ideal, it may be.[32]

This passage illuminates the natural/constructed dichotomy of identity that Wilde raises again in *De Profundis*. The influenced person,
according to Lord Henry, is someone whose identity is forced upon
him by outside sources, and thereby any semblance of agency that that
person may have had is removed. Indeed, the notion of self is all but
removed. A person under the influence of another does not even have
a soul. This is the tyranny of the press that Wilde describes in 'The
Soul of Man Under Socialism': the newspapers, as part of the surveilling carceral matrix which also includes trials and the prison, take
over 'people's private lives' in an endless reproduction of 'insatiable
curiosity.'[33] The influencing agent (be it a person or an institution)
becomes the original, which is then copied by those it influences.
Moreover, people so influenced cannot realize their 'own' natures;
they do not even have natures, and so cannot fulfil the aim of life –
self-development.

What is important about this passage for a reading of *De Profundis* is
Lord Henry's belief that if only 'one man' lived as an individual
beyond influence, then the world would be transformed into an ideal:
this is an echo of Thoreau's desire for 'some absolute goodness somewhere; for that will leaven the whole lump' ('Civil,' 69). For Lord
Henry, however, no one, at least since Hellenic times, has achieved this
ideal.[34] Everyone is constructed, according to Lord Henry, in the manner he describes, and no one has yet lived only for and by 'himself.' No
one has a fully realized personality, one that has not been formed or
influenced by outside forces. Therefore, no one even has a nature to
assert.

3. And the Oscar goes to Jesus

Wilde attempts to construct the fully realized identity as an ideal goal
for himself during his incarceration, a goal which he wishes to take
with him into the world outside of prison once he is released. In order
to do so, he tries in *De Profundis* to construct an identity that can exist

completely without society while still living in it. In discussing Wilde's definition of just such an identity for the critic in 'The Critic as Artist,' Lawrence Danson writes that

> Wilde draws on (and acknowledges) a recently published translation of the ancient Chinese philosopher Chuang-tzu, who preached 'the great creed of Inaction, and ... the uselessness of all useful things.' With the help of this otherwise-improbable source, Wilde transforms the dandy's insolent languor ... into a sublime detachment ... [T]he non-productive dandy becomes the critic who is dedicated to self-culture and loves truth for its own sake. The transformation helps the dandy – that is, Wilde himself – move from the raffish edge of society towards a new centre which Wilde's criticism is in the process of defining.[35]

For Danson, this new identity is completely passive. A distinction must be drawn, however, between the passivity that Wilde berates himself for having shown to Douglas and the passivity that leads to the creation of the self-realized identity. The passivity that Wilde allowed himself in front of Douglas was a social passivity; that is, it was a passivity that Wilde enacted in a social, power-structured setting. The passivity to which Danson refers and, I argue, that Wilde defines in *De Profundis*, is an asocial passivity that exists outside of the possibilities of being subjugated to another's will (as Wilde says was the case with his relationship to Douglas) or of having oneself defined against one's own objections (as with Wilde's portrayal in the newspapers and as demonstrated in his imprisonment). It is the state of being passive and inactive which leads to the individual's removal from the power structures of society as a whole.

The example Wilde uses to construct this passive identity is that of Christ:

> And, above all, Christ is the most supreme of Individualists. Humility, like the artistic acceptance of all experiences, is merely a mode of manifestation. It is man's soul that Christ is always looking for. He calls it 'God's Kingdom' ... and finds it in everyone. He compares it to little things, to a tiny seed, to a handful of leaven, to a pearl. That is because one only realises one's soul by getting rid of all alien passions, all acquired culture, and all external possessions be they good or evil. (479)

Wilde's choice of the traditional and socio-politically acceptable image of Christ as his model can be read as an attempt to regain some of the cultural capital that was taken from him during the trials, during which, as Dennis Denisoff writes, Wilde's use of aesthetic discourse 'as the source of his identity lacked the frame of any conventional depth model.'[36] Dollimore sees Wilde's use of Christ as precisely such a depth model, but I would disagree with his assertion that this use necessarily 'involves a conscious renunciation of his transgressive aesthetic,' since Wilde interprets the image of Christ not to remove himself from, but rather to explicate, his artistic and sexual identity.[37] In contrast to his passive non-resistance to Douglas's attacks, Wilde depicts Christ as an individual who rejects all outside influences ('possessions' in this passage referring to both property and spiritual domination by an outside source). Wilde's Christ, unlike Thoreau's construction of the undominated person who necessarily influences others, exists outside of all power structures, be they economic, social, or personal. Christ's passivity, understood through this isolation, is rather a non-activity – Christ does not act in the world because he exists completely outside of it. Thus, Buckton's assertion that Wilde 'can only recognize "himself" ... in the mirror "image" Bosie' is complicated by what he recognizes as Wilde's 'self-dissolution,'[38] what I am calling his construction of an asocial passivity. The dichotomous relationship of 'interdependence' that Buckton sees in the depiction of Douglas and Wilde is exploded by the non-social being of Wilde's construction of himself through the ideal passivity of Christ. Interdependence cannot exist in the isolated and non-discursive space Wilde attempts to create. For Wilde, because Christ managed to exorcise his various possessions, he also managed to escape what we would today call the discourses surrounding him – Christ stepped outside his episteme.

To posit as an ideal an existence in which one can leave one's episteme is obviously problematic. Such an existence would involve rising out of all of the discourses surrounding one, thus rendering oneself incapable of communicating in any language, be it scientific, legal, bodily, or any of a variety of institutional or social forms. Wilde realizes the difficulty of this movement, but it does not deter him from setting up Christ as the ideal or, to use his own word, a 'type' (481):

To the artist, expression is the only mode under which he can conceive life at all. To him what is dumb is dead. But to Christ it was not so. With a width and wonder of imagination, that fills one almost with awe, he took the entire world of the inarticulate, the voiceless world of pain, as his kingdom, and made of himself its eternal mouthpiece. Those of whom I have spoken, who are dumb under oppression and 'whose silence is heard only of God,' he chose as his brothers ... And feeling, with the artistic nature of one to whom Sorrow and Suffering were modes through which he could realise his conception of the Beautiful, that an idea is of no value till it becomes incarnate and is made an image, he makes of himself the image of the Man of Sorrows, and as such has fascinated and dominated Art as no Greek god ever succeeded in doing. (481)

Wilde does construct Christ as voiceless, but with a difference. For Christ, to be silent, or not understood, is not to be without meaning, and is not quite an indication of what Jane Wood sees as 'an almost masochistic desire for self-destruction and for the epic finality which that would accord.'[39] Rather, to fully realize himself – that is, to exist outside of the social system of influence and possession – Christ had to turn voicelessness and suffering into art. Leon Chai sees this dynamic at play in *De Profundis*, writing that 'within it, all past moments are finally collected and shaped into an artistic composition.'[40] Art, for the Wilde of *De Profundis*, is that which is completely useless. In the letter, however, the aesthetic concept of 'art for art's sake' takes on a political edge. As Brown writes, 'Art is "useless" because, in a pervasively utilitarian society, it *must* be so in order to endure ... If it is to do its work, it must be in some measure out of reach.'[41] Conceptualizing art as existing only for its own sake does not simply create a privatized discourse for knowledgeable artists and critics. Rather it removes art from the possibility of completely existing in or for *any* discourse of its time, unlike Thoreau's presently alienated but always universally accessible transcendent individual. For Wilde, art is the non-possessed, non-possessing ideal entity. This definition is explicated elsewhere in his corpus. In 'The Decay of Lying,' Vivian states that '[a]rt finds her own perfection within, and not outside of, herself. She is not to be judged by any external standard of resemblance.'[42] Wilde expands this definition of artistic isolation in 'The Critic as Artist,' in which Gilbert argues about the aesthetic critic, the ultimate artist: 'From the high tower of Thought we can look out at the world. Calm, and self-centered, and complete, the aesthetic critic contemplates life, and no arrow drawn at a venture can pierce between the joints of his harness ... Thought is degraded by its constant association with practice.'[43] The relationship that is implied in these two passages between art and social isolation as a means of escaping determinism is made explicit at the beginning of 'The Soul of Man Under Socialism,' where Wilde writes that '[n]ow and then' a great artist is 'able to isolate himself, to keep himself out of reach of the clamorous claims of others, ... and so to realize the perfection of what was in him.'[44] In *De Profundis*, Christ, as an incarnated image of the voiceless and completely asocial, becomes the perfect image for Wilde's ideal individualist. Citing Norbert Kohl, Jane Wood argues that, in his '"aestheticising of Christ," Wilde envisages the supreme individualist, the anti-traditionalist, who reached out beyond the rule of law (of secular law at least).'[45] Wilde's Christ may exist outside of discourse, but that does not mean he exists outside of meaning, for meaning can be constructed in terms of the 'conception of the Beautiful,' a finally ineffable, yet always extant, concept.

Wilde also makes his point about needing to reach a state of absolute individuation by constructing an image that lies in contrast to that of Christ. This image is the prisoner, or rather, those who are imprisoned, for the prisoners of the various institutions in which he has been incarcerated are never individualized or singular. Prisoners, unlike Christ, can never escape time, just as Wilde cannot escape Douglas, nor the definitions imposed on him by the newspapers and the courts. Directly opposing Gagnier's assertion of the 'timelessness' of prisoners' existence, Wilde writes:

> Three years ago is a long time for you to go back. But we who live in prison, and in whose lives there is no event but sorrow, have to measure time by throbs of pain, and the record of bitter moments. We have nothing else to think of. Suffering – curious as it may sound to you – is the means by which we exist, because it is the only means by which we become conscious of existing; and the remembrance of suffering in the past is necessary to us as the warrant, the evidence, of our continued identity. (435)

Prisoners exist not outside of time, nor outside of the episteme, as Christ does; instead they embody the passage of time due to what Gagnier describes as prison's 'rigorously enforced timetable.'[46] Wilde's use of legal and courtroom metaphors – 'evidence' and 'warrant' – serves to show how prisoners are only identified by that which defines them from the outside, caged and determined by the legal and cultural framework surrounding them. Later he makes this clear, stating that he 'had no name at all. In the great prison where I was then incarcerated I was merely the figure and letter of a little cell in a long gallery, one of a thousand lifeless numbers, as of a thousand lifeless lives' (454).[47]

Christ is the supreme individual; the prisoner is the repeated number and, for Wilde, 'all repetition is anti-spiritual' (483). Against those definitions forced on him by Douglas, Queensberry, the courts, and the press – all functioning within and as the carceral city – Wilde uses the type that he discovers in Christ as the supreme individual and applies it to himself.

For Wilde to reach this ideal, however, he must make a Dantean journey through the non-individualized prisoner. Beyond his direct allusions to Dante's work, Wilde imitates the overall structure of the *Divine Comedy* to show how the supreme individual always has the possibility of rising, even out of the depths of subjugation.[48] This becomes most obvious when he writes about the legal loss of his son:

> I bore up against everything with some stubbornness of will and much rebellion of nature till I had absolutely nothing left in the world but Cyril. I had lost my name, my position, my happiness, my freedom, my wealth. I was a prisoner and a pauper. But I still had one beautiful thing left, my own eldest son. Suddenly he was taken away from me by the law. It was a blow so appalling that I did not know what to do, so I flung myself on my knees, and bowed my head, and wept and said 'The body of a child is as the body of the Lord: I am not worthy of either.' That moment seemed to save me. I saw then that the only thing for me was to accept everything. Since then – curious as it will no doubt sound to you – I have been happier. It was of course my soul in its ultimate essence that I had reached ... It is tragic how few people ever 'possess their souls' before they die. 'Nothing is more rare in any man,' says Emerson, 'than an act of his own.' It is quite true. Most people are other people. Their thoughts are someone else's opinions, their life a mimicry, their passions a quotation. (479)

Becoming a prisoner, becoming a non-self, is for Wilde both a general condition of members of the larger society, and a step in a journey that leads to the possibility of becoming a complete individual. The isolation and silence that the prison forces on him may be an attempt to transform his identity according to social and prison codes, but this is also the necessary step towards Wilde's means of escaping external determination and domination. Further, this escape is an attempt to avoid the dangers of exercising and reproducing authoritative structures – as Thoreau's essay occasionally does – since it also comes at a moment when he completely rejects action and agency – he falls down, vulnerable before the Lord, so to speak. Like the prisoners in *The Ballad of Reading Gaol*, through Wilde's 'broken heart / May Lord Christ enter in.' Wilde reproduces the discourse of prison reform, but, as Brown writes, he does so in order to show that '*Re*formations that are based on obedience to some external precept [as, for example, prison codes or court sentences] are meaningless because the *trans*formation must come from within.'[49] And this transformation must take place not within traditional institutional frames of discourse (such as the Church, the prison, or even the press), but through Wilde's 'isolationist' interpretation of Christ.

Wilde therefore reproduces the moral discourse of early Victorian prison reformation in order to avoid the definitions imposed on him by the carceral society. Like Thoreau, and relying on their common Emersonian sources,[50] Wilde depicts his imprisonment as leading to his escape (if only momentary) from the definitions placed on him by Douglas, the courts, the newspapers, and society as a whole, allowing him to 'possess [his] soul.' While this statement may also seem to fall into the same trap as Thoreau's essay does of replicating the problems of the transcendent identity and of prison rhetoric, there is a subtle difference. Wilde's individual, his Christ, is not universally accessible, and does not attempt to enforce specific codes of conduct. This is not the self-regulation envisioned by early Victorian prison reformers, nor the deterministic 'fixing' of the social subject of later Victorian science and penology. Neither is it the 'affirmation of nonexistence' that Foucault sees as a function of Victorian repression.[51] An identity that always and only exists in relation to itself cannot therefore be defined in the ultimate or finalizing matter to which prison discourse usually regresses; for Christ, 'there were no laws: there were exceptions merely' (485). Wilde's statements about his soul and individuality, as Jane Wood writes, are not 'so much soundings of the depths of subjectivity as the voiding of remnants of the material realities which shackle him to the particular and the predictable.'[52] Wilde's individual cannot be defined by anyone or in any words, for it becomes art.

Despite Wilde's assertions of his own perceptions of his 'soul in its ultimate essence,' we do not see, therefore, Wilde's essential nature in his 'confessions'; such a nature cannot be communicated, as all discourse leads to the imposition of determination. Miss Prism, in *The Importance of Being Earnest*, notes the ease with which such essentialist confessions can be labelled, defined, and dismissed, saying, 'These sudden conversions do not please me. They belong to Dissent. They savour of the laxity of the Nonconformist.'[53] *De Profundis*, then, is not 'a celebration of the protagonist's spiritual salvation,' as William E. Buckler writes,[54] as much as it is a critique of externally imposed definitions of one's identity. 'Far from reflecting or prescribing for the true nature or essence of man,' Dollimore argues, individualism for Wilde 'will generate the cultural difference and diversity which conventional morality, orthodox opinion and essentialist ideology disavow'; it is therefore 'the public voice ... which seeks to police culture' that Wilde writes against.[55] Wilde's individualism *constructs* a space beyond discourse that is rooted in the traditional figure of Christ in order, in part, to ground both his refusal to deny his sexuality and his denial of the imposed and bigoted definitions of that sexuality. I generally agree with Buckton's conclusion that 'far from being a work in which Wilde repents of his crimes and confesses his guilty secret, the letter is a celebration of the power of secrecy to free desire from the banal or violent invasions of public scrutiny';[56] however, I would argue that what Buckton sees as secrecy's freedom from scrutiny is instead a denial of the very ability to scrutinize, as all such perceptions exist in the realm of public discourse and are therefore at a remove from Wilde's individual. The narrator of *Dorian Gray* makes a point that is easily applied to Wilde's self-construction in *De Profundis*, noting, 'There is a luxury in self-reproach. When we blame ourselves we feel that no one else has a right to blame us.'[57] While confidential letters were used in the trial to publicly humiliate Wilde, he now uses a letter with a potentially public audience (as he did plan to publish it) in order to assert an inviolable privacy.

Nevertheless, the fact that Wilde did write about this non-discursive subject, and did plan to have the letter read by others, points to a slippage that echoes Thoreau's reproduction of the prison's alienating force. Unlike Thoreau's essay, however, *De Profundis* does not suggest either that it or its author can help to create 'a still more perfect and glorious State' ('Civil,' 90), or that its author has moved completely above the realm of his neighbours' existence: Wilde's representation of this individual does not become a constrictive code of conduct dictated from 'on high.' Rather, Wilde's letter notes its own inconsistencies and the dangers of its paradoxes, 'its changing, uncertain moods ... its aspirations and its failure to realise those aspirations' (511), acknowledgments which, as Andersen writes, create 'the impression that equilibrium has been only partly restored,'[58] just as Jacobs's freedom is only partially realized in the North. As Wilde himself wrote earlier, 'paradoxes are always dangerous things.'[59] Given this recognition and the potential theoretical difficulties involved in the very act of writing *De Profundis*, Robbie Ross's decision to seal the letter away in the British Museum until all of the primary figures involved would be dead takes on a particularly appropriate resonance. *De Profundis* becomes a defence from within the silence of the prison, and from beyond death, at once asserting its own authority and denying its applicability.[60] In the end, what Wilde says of the courtroom 'denunciation' of him could be applied to any of the discourses surrounding the trial, and Wilde's response to them with *De Profundis*: 'Suddenly it occurred to me, "*How splendid it would be, if I was saying all this about myself!*"' (502). Reworking the ineffability Jacobs attempts to create, Wilde asserts the power of privacy, and the degradation of the discursive, carceral matrix of the public. Through its reworking of the newspaper accounts and of the penological discourse of religious conversion, *De Profundis* constructs an understanding of the omnipresence of the disciplinary mechanisms of society. This construction not only explicates other prison authors' critiques of free society, but also still permits an understanding of how a prison author's construction of identity can be used to critique such discipline. Continuing with my larger argument that prison texts engage in a myriad of diverse yet related attacks on the carceral city, the next chapter shows that resisting such a powerful, oppressive system can also be done in a more active and social manner.

CHAPTER FOUR

Positioning Discourse:
Martin Luther King Jr's
'Letter from Birmingham City Jail'

Over half a century after Wilde's letter was written, another, very different letter was written from prison – Martin Luther King Jr's 'Letter from Birmingham City Jail.' Like Wilde's letter, King's is addressed specifically but is intended for a larger public audience. King was arrested on Good Friday, 1963, during non-violent protests against Birmingham's – and Alabama's – refusal to obey the 1954 US Supreme Court decision outlawing racial segregation. While in solitary confinement, he wrote 'Letter from Birmingham City Jail,' which was subsequently published in national forums, including *Time* magazine. Indeed, the centrality of the 'Letter' is pointed to by the level of academic attention it has received, including a recent book-length study by S. Jonathan Bass. This letter became a central text in the American Civil Rights Movement, continuing the tradition of the use of prison texts to further calls for social and political change. Specifically, King's work engages in the ongoing critique, originating in slave narratives and continuing in African American prison writings, of the racism of American society – a textual practice which I discuss in chapter 2, and which H. Bruce Franklin expertly details in his book. King's arrest occurred within a racialized socio-judicial matrix in which African Americans were not only denied legal access to certain jobs, to private and public organizations, to meeting places, and so on, but were thereby effectively refused entrance into dominant constructions of identity, namely, the self-governing individuality which Thoreau, among others, espoused. Arising from the racism of antebellum America – in which, as Jacobs shows, African Americans were explicitly relegated to non-human status in legal and constitutional forums – the racist subjugation of African Americans in the middle decades of the twentieth century was similarly based on legal, social, and ontological exclusion. Indeed, as Michael Bennett argues, legalized racial segregation and other social policies have led to what he calls, in one essay's title, a 'spatialization of race,' because black people have, throughout the twentieth century, become increasingly identified with ghettos and inner cities that, in turn, have become increasingly vilified and identified with crime.[1] It was in part this locational practice which King and other civil rights activists aimed to stop through their protests concerning segregation.[2]

Within this racialized social matrix, the prison and legal systems were not in practice means of reconstituting the identity of the condemned person into that of a 'proper' or even productive subject, but were instead used as means of enforcing racist hierarchies and social order – a split between theory and practice that I have detailed in the previous chapters. The twentieth-century American prison continues the oppressive identificatory practices of its nineteenth-century precursors while, as I mapped out earlier, it simultaneously takes over the racist social role previously filled by the institution of slavery. Sloop writes that, in the 1950s, as before, 'the pervasiveness of the cultural belief in the nature of human subjects as redeemable requires the omission of non-Caucasians in discourse about the prisoner because people of color are apparently viewed culturally as morally different from Caucasians.'[3] Sloop further argues that, in this period and moving through the 1960s and beyond, 'African-American and other "minority" male prisoners increasingly become constituted as violent, and irrationally so.'[4] Whereas Thoreau can reinterpret his imprisonment as a reaffirmation of his inviolable, transcendental freedom, the imprisonment of black people after the abolition of slavery is pursued, according to Davis, 'not so much to affirm the rights and liberties of the freedmen and women ..., nor to discipline a potential labor force; rather it symbolically emphasized that black people's social status continued to be that of slaves.'[5]

The 'Letter' responds to the criminalization of blackness, simultaneously claiming full and unfettered citizenship for black people while resisting the racism of the dominant society's identity constructions. Cementing this larger framework, King's text, like the other works discussed thus far, portrays the oppression resulting from these constructions as arising not only from the judicial and penological systems, but also from other social institutions. King's piece responds specifically to another open letter, published by eight Birmingham clergymen, in which they called for an end to the demonstrations. The clergymen's text can be read as an attempt to retain and to reproduce the status quo of local race relations by, in part, recreating racist social positions for blacks, and by reinforcing the authoritative positions of the police force and the courts as the keepers of 'law and order.'[6] Just as sentimental fiction was used by abolitionists in Jacobs's and Thoreau's time with the intent of improving the conditions of African Americans while in fact engaging in other forms of discrimination, the clergymen's letter calls for peace but in effect supports the officials who deny the legitimacy of the Supreme Court decision. As such, this open letter is framed within the prejudiced racial discourse of certain segments of white America, or what Karen Ho and Wende Elizabeth Marshall call the 'White Nation,' referring to 'policy makers and legislators' – and their supporters – who engage in 'thinly veiled attempts ... to maintain white power.'[7] Like the newspapers that condemn Wilde, and falling more generally within the functions of the carceral society as discussed in the earlier chapters, such discourse constructs and reproduces a series of differently valued, hierarchized social strata. The structure thus created is enforced and reproduced by the disciplinary and surveillance functions of a variety of social institutions, including the prison and the Church.

King's 'Letter' attempts to exploit the power dynamics of this structure in order to disrupt the deterministic subject positions that are created by the racist ideology that lies behind the language of the clergymen's letter and that informs the motivation behind King's arrest and imprisonment. Moreover, King uses the 'Letter' to open up the possibility of a discourse of racial harmony and to construct subject positions that exist beyond racism, in the hope of helping to instigate a world of 'Peace and Brotherhood.'[8] Like Jacobs and Wilde, King denies the authoritative, disciplinary identity that Thoreau creates, although he does situate himself within the dominant structures of American society. Unlike the critiques that Jacobs and Wilde offer, however, King does not situate his critique within a silent or unknowable identity, opting instead to rely on a forward-looking, dynamic agency that negotiates both dominant and dominated identifications, which I will demonstrate by analysing King's textual construction of his own position. Within the context of my larger study, King's letter offers another entrance point into a sustained attack on the practices of the prison, as well as on the disciplinary and oppressive structures of society as a whole. I will examine King's strategy using, in part, a more structural-

ist approach then I have used thus far, in order to help outline his rhetorical negotiations of identity. Unlike the texts studied so far, however,
King's letter generates a vision that exists beyond the carceral matrix,
while still avoiding the danger of constructing an individual, transcendental rebellion.

1. The Clergymen's Letter

King's 'Letter' works against the racist ideology lying behind the clergymen's letter. As Althusser says, 'State institutions like the Church'
teach '"know-how," but in forms which ensure *subjection to the ruling
ideology* or the mastery of its "practice."'[9] Norman Fairclough refigures
this theoretical structure in more active terms: 'Occupying a subject
position is essentially a matter of doing (or not doing) certain things, in
line with the discoursal rights and obligations' of that position.[10] In
order to understand King's 'Letter' and its attempted construction of
new identity categories, it is necessary to define the specific instantiation of racist discourse to which King is responding.

The clergymen's letter interpellates its readership into two large categories: those who have the authority to deal with 'racial matters' and
those who do not. As one would expect given the racist power structure of Birmingham at the time, people falling within the grouping of
'authority' are generally white and those without are black.[11] Within
the actions available to these different groups defined by the clergymen, certain venues are foregrounded as the best settings in which to
deal with 'racial matters':

> We the undersigned clergymen are among those who, in January, issued
> 'An Appeal for Law and Order and Common Sense,' in dealing with
> racial problems in Alabama. We expressed understanding that honest
> convictions in racial matters could properly be pursued in the courts, but
> urged that decisions of those courts should in the meantime be peacefully
> obeyed. (1)

In this opening paragraph, the clergymen set themselves up in a position of authority, not only as religious leaders, but also as men who
have had previous experiences dealing with civil unrest, as cued by the
reference to their previous text. This authority is doubly enforced since
that previous letter 'took exception to [Alabama governor] George
Wallace's ringing declaration for "segregation now, segregation tomor-

row, and segregation forever"':[12] they wrote that defying the desegregation order was 'neither the right answer nor the solution.'[13] While relying on their past authority as anti-segregationists (to whatever degree), the clergymen's emphasis on the need to 'obey' the dictates of what King calls 'the power structure' now works against that earlier position ('Letter,' 299). The ambiguity of the reference to court decisions (does it refer to the desegregation decision, or to the decision that the demonstrations were illegal and to King's subsequent arrest?) highlights the contradiction in the clergymen's stated position: on the one hand, they urge that the desegregation decision be obeyed, while on the other they state that people should obey the police and government who flagrantly disobey that decision. Even though, as King points out in his 'Letter,' the legal system and related institutions in Alabama and Birmingham are skewed against blacks, the clergymen restate the authority of those structures, thereby reproducing it and cementing their place within the matrix of the carceral society. Mimicking sentimental abolitionist discourse about the 'obedient slave,' the clergymen imply that blacks could gain 'true' freedom only by bowing to the very social structures that oppress them. William L. Andrews argues that this 'myth' of spiritual advancement, as exemplified by Stowe's Uncle Tom, helped to reconcile 'black progress with black alienation without threatening the white status quo.'[14] Using their letter for similar ends, the clergymen 'urge' that legal and social authorities, which are tied to their own, be obeyed, thus allowing the status quo to remain unchallenged, even if only 'in the meantime.'

The clergymen's letter is rife with euphemisms that sublimate the 'undesirable' associations attached to events that are directed against the status quo. Obvious examples of this are the phrases 'racial problems' and 'racial matters' in the opening paragraph. These 'matters' include not only segregation, demonstrations, and church bombings (which would eventually lead to the infamous bombing of the 16th Street Baptist Church that killed four young girls), but also riots in which several people were injured (and later two young black men were shot and killed, at least one by a policeman as the youth was running away).[15] The Commissioner of Police, Eugene 'Bull' Connor, had 'bragged that all he needed to solve the racial problem was "two policeman and a dog."'[16] To rephrase these acts of extreme violence and prejudice as 'matters' or mere 'problems' is to deny the deadly nature of the city's and state's race relations at the time. The effect of this denial within the letter is to remove the justification for the demonstrations in which King and his associates were engaged, thereby removing the right to self-determination and action from the African American community. Conversely, the clergymen refer to the actions and attitudes of the police as 'the calm manner in which these demonstrations have been handled.' The phrase 'calm manner' is apparently a description of not only the police violence, but also the fact that the police turned guard dogs loose on unarmed demonstrators. Thus, for the clergymen's letter, actions that take place through the 'proper channels' are always already justified, while those that take place outside of the power structure's authority, such as the demonstrations, can in no way be justified.

The reproduction of the dominant culture's racism, and the subject positions available therein, are apparent in the clergymen's use of pronouns, as well. As we saw in Jacobs's narrative, pronouns can be used both to create a bond between author and audience and to emphasize the distance between them.[17] In the clergymen's letter, the racism of the power structure that the authors are enacting is readily apparent in the dynamic existing between first- and third-person pronouns: 'However, we are now confronted by a series of demonstrations by some of our Negro citizens, directed and led in part by outsiders. We recognize the natural impatience of people who feel that their hopes are slow in being realized. But we are convinced that these demonstrations are unwise and untimely' (3). Mimicking Janet Gurkin Altman's assertion that epistolary discourse exists 'halfway between the possibility of total communication and the risk of no communication at all,'[18] the 'we' in the first sentence functions both inclusively and exclusively. Recalling Jacobs's use of second-person address within a sentimental construction of sympathy, the first-person plural here contains not only the eight clergymen, but also the larger society of Birmingham, since the entire population is being confronted by demonstrations. With the use of 'our' in that same sentence, however, the clergymen exclude the black population of Birmingham from inclusion in the plurality of *their* society. In other words, the clergymen represent the white population, while African Americans are constructed as being the property of that population – *they* are *our* Negro citizens – thus effectively continuing the liberal, paternalist discourse of some nineteenth-century abolitionists, many of whom, as Carolyn Williams writes, 'regarded blacks not as equals, but as wards.'[19] Indeed, Bass writes that while the older clergymen – specifically Charles Carpenter and Nolan Harmon – were more heavily paternalist in their view of blacks, the younger of the eight men, '[l]ike their older associates,' were at least influenced by this attitude.[20]

Some uses of plural pronouns in the letter are inclusive in the larger sense. These instances, however, occur only at points where the authors invoke the necessity of obeying the power structure, especially as incarnated in the police and legal systems: '[W]e believe this kind of facing of issues can best be accomplished by citizens of our own metropolitan area, white and Negro, meeting with their knowledge and experience of the local situation. All of us need to face that responsibility and find proper channels for its accomplishment' (4). The clergymen use pronouns similarly a few paragraphs later: 'When rights are consistently denied, a cause should be pressed in the courts and in negotiations among local leaders, and not in the streets. We appeal to both our white and Negro citizenry to observe the principles of law and order and common sense' (7). In both of these passages the white and black populations are joined together, but only under the auspices of the 'proper channels' of 'law and order' as perpetrated by the police and courts, which, as demonstrated in the earlier chapters, generally function as alienating and oppressive forces rather than as creators of any communal feeling. This distinction between perception and deed highlights the ideological effectiveness and social centrality of the carceral project: even as it is used to alienate communities from each other and reinforce the power of the dominant class, it is seen and portrayed as maintaining social harmony. As I will argue below, King rejects the possibility of this form of commonality in his letter, pointing out that the legal system and the power structure it represents are infested with racism and prejudice.

Homer Hawkins and Richard Thomas trace this institutionalized racism to the inflation of 'the policing systems' set up during slavery: 'After slavery, white southerners felt a greater need for policing the emancipated blacks, since to their minds slavery itself had been the most effective means of controlling and civilizing a "barbarous people."'[21] As detailed in chapter 2, slavery's abolition, the rise of the penitentiary, and concurrent changes in legal practice converged in a paradigm of punishment in which the cultivation and maintenance of the 'proper' social order was in part enacted through the brutalization and alienation of those who fell on the wrong end of the social hierarchies, who did not have access to Thoreau's implicitly racist 'universal' subject. Within the racialized construction of criminality and the practices of punishment, the clergymen's letter becomes another cog in the process of maintaining and hiding the racist status quo.[22] The authors deny the racialized nature of the carceral system by simply omitting any mention of racism or corruption. This supposed 'race blindness' is also transferred to their own authority: in the last sentence of the letter, quoted above, the clergymen assert their own paternalistic authority over the entire population of Birmingham. The pronoun 'We' possesses 'both *our* white *and* Negro citizenry.' Thus, the letter is framed by the authors' construction of positions of authority for themselves. Despite their stated aims and, in some cases, their personal beliefs, the clergymen's open letter is very much informed by and a reproduction of the racist ideology lying behind the authority of the state and the white church – the latter of which, as King writes in his letter and stated many times throughout his career, functioned in part as a means of retaining the status quo of race relations in the South. As demonstrated by the clergymen's statement, all of the 'legitimate' and 'proper' functions of positions of authority within the power structure tend to retain the cohesion of that structure. All positions of authority within the power structure necessarily function to retain the cohesion of that structure, so as 'to transmit [themselves] unimpaired to posterity' (Thoreau, 'Civil,' 63).

2. The Status Quo in 'Letter from Birmingham City Jail'

In his response to the clergymen, King highlights the racist ideology lying behind the previous epistle by redefining the limiting subject positions that the clergymen reproduce. In his 'Letter,' King rejects the concept that returning to the status quo is the only way to 'reach honest convictions in racial matters.' As Keith D. Miller suggests, the arrest of King and his colleagues highlighted the racism of the existing situation – as clearly seen in Alabama's continued and illegal racial segregation – and its reflection in the history of American penology: 'As they presented themselves for jail, African Americans in effect argued that jail symbolized racism.'[23] To foreground this relationship, King redefines the social groupings delineated by the clergymen's letter and opens up the possibility of new subjectivities available in a future era of racial harmony.

Richard P. Fulkerson notes in his influential article that King's 'Letter' addresses two audiences – the 'ostensible audience' of the eight clergymen and a larger audience of white liberals: 'Little, if anything, was to be gained in addressing white segregationists, black revolutionists, or people indifferent to civil rights. The situation called instead for an address to as wide a range of moderate-to-liberal, involved readers

White	Black
clergymen / Church	middle class / 'force of complacency'
State / police	
KKK	Nation of Islam
general, silent liberal populace	general and oppressed populace

as possible; so much the better if a substantial number of them were also leaders of public opinion.'[24] Like the ostensible audience, the broader audience is white, as implied by Fulkerson's comment on the 'leaders of public opinion.' Miller further defines this readership, explaining: 'Given that King wrote "Letter" for *Christian Century* and other left-of-center outlets, one can say that its original and primary audience was not the ostensible audience of eight moderate clergy,' but was instead 'liberal Protestants.'[25] Thus, while King is writing for two distinct audiences, both are still firmly within the ruling class.

Following this social paradigm, the dominant racial discourse interpellates people into 'proper' subject positions, which are constituted for whites in terms of action and power, and for blacks, passivity and subjugation to the (white) carceral city (courts, police, etc.). King describes – rather than attempt to recreate, as the previous letter does – the same racist state of affairs, but goes into much more detail than the clergy. The table above maps out his construction of the subject positions available within the controlling discourse. The general scheme found in King's 'Letter' can also be read as a description of the larger conditions of America, especially as indicated by the blank space opposite 'State/police,' as these forums were largely limited to whites. Indeed, the employment of 'members of the Ku Klux Klan' by Birmingham's police department[26] fully cemented the relationship between the disciplinary social function served by the legal system and the violent functions of extreme racism. To represent this situation structurally in an even more detailed manner,[27] the black grouping should be placed in a hierarchically subordinate position to the other category in order to show the ontological and social construction of blackness in its relation to that of whiteness – a construction that is played out in the attempted forced passivity or general social censure placed upon black people and organizations. This censure is especially obvious in the case of the largely vilified Nation of Islam, which King himself characterizes very negatively in the 'Letter' as a violent group whose black nationalism expresses 'bitterness and hatred,' further writing that if the white population refuses to work with King and his associates, 'millions of Negroes, out of frustration and despair, will seek solace and security in black nationalist ideologies, a development that will lead inevitably to a frightening racial nightmare' (296–7).[28]

King textually transforms this structure in order to engage in what could be called a resistant interpellation, creating new discursive or otherwise social possibilities for whites and blacks within a discourse of peace, focusing especially on the positions for whites at the top and bottom of the column – the 'clergymen/Church' and the 'general (silent) liberal populace,' or the ostensible and broader audiences, respectively, of the 'Letter.' The collective identity of the clergymen is to a large extent already defined by their own text, and is ultimately delineated by the fact that they have placed themselves in opposition to the beliefs and actions of King and his followers. As King writes, they have ensconced themselves in the role of 'criticism' (289), which the clergymen construct as a positive force designed to help foster peace by exhorting people to obey the power structure that they represent. King restructures the role of this criticism at the outset of his 'Letter,' stating that if he 'sought to answer all of the criticisms that cross my desk ... I would have no time for constructive work' (289). Writing that the clergymen's criticisms of the demonstrations – and therefore their implicit critique of King's attempt to force Birmingham to accept desegregation – interfere with 'constructive work,' King redefines the clergymen's position in the race struggle as unconstructive and negative. For King, their appeal is not for peace or 'Common Sense,' but rather for unjust social structures. While the clergymen take advantage of the epistolary form's ability to disguise 'relationships of power, politics, and economics,'[29] King, like Wilde, foregrounds these relationships in order to critique them.

King finds the same hidden racism configured as tradition or common sense within the institution of the white Church from which the clergymen derive their authority. To expose the bigotry within the Church, as a figure of the larger institutionalized racism of the carceral state, King first postulates an ideal Church, and then contrasts it to the actuality:

> I came to Birmingham with the hope that the white religious leadership of this community would see the justice of our cause, and with deep moral

concern, serve as the channel through which our just grievances would get to the power structure. I had hoped that each of you would understand. But again I have been disappointed. I have heard numerous religious leaders of the South call upon their worshippers to comply with a desegregation decision because it is the *law*, but I have longed to hear white ministers say, 'Follow this decree because integration is morally *right* and the Negro is your brother.' (299)

King's definition of the white Church is a negation of its claimed position and of the clergymen's foundation of authority. This religious structure supposedly has this authority due to a certain moral rectitude and its accordance to God's will, but King denies this connection, arguing instead that the institution is acting in opposition to its own religious and social traditions. An ideal Church would lead the populace towards a moral high ground, while the contemporary white Church in the South stands 'as a taillight behind other community agencies rather than a headlight leading men to higher levels of justice' (299). King redefines the clergymen's own construction of their subject position, not only by showing the racism hidden behind their 'common sense,' but also by showing that this racism in fact rests at the core of their authority, and that even their earlier call to obey the desegregation ruling was not based on a 'morally right' footing.

Further evidence that King restructures the clergymen's definition of the white power structure into a negative force can be seen in his responses to their specific criticisms: 'You deplore the demonstrations that are presently taking place in Birmingham. But I am sorry that your statement did not express a similar concern for the conditions that brought the demonstrations into being. I am sure that each of you would want to go beyond the superficial social analyst who looks merely at effects, and does not grapple with underlying causes.' (290). There are three separate but related movements in this passage. First, King highlights the racist silence of the clergymen's statement which, under the guise of concern for 'our' Negro population, attempts to erase the physical violence being perpetrated on the black population. Second, King subtly answers the charge that the demonstrations are being instigated by 'outsiders' by placing the blame on the 'conditions' of society. King transposes the blame that the clergyman try to ascribe for the demonstrations from himself onto the state of race relations in Birmingham, and therefore implicitly condemns the clergymen.

In the third movement of this passage, however, King works against the negative limitations of the clergymen's subject position, as he defines it. By writing, 'I'm sure each of you would want to go beyond ...,' King opens a space for the clergymen to change their position in relation to the race problem. He writes, 'You may well ask, "Why direct action? Why sit-ins, marches, etc.? Isn't negotiation a better path?" You are exactly right in your call for negotiation. Indeed, this is the purpose of direct action' (291). King not only interpellates the clergymen by placing words in their mouths, but also reformulates these questions into a call for 'negotiation,' thereby constructing a common ground between himself and his opposition. This leaves the clergymen with the possibility of agreeing with King in his call for direct action, while at the same time keeping a semblance of their original position. This move towards constructing a common ground is not simply a gesture on King's part so as not to offend men in power; it is a method of leaving the definition of this audience's position open and free to change.[30] In contrast to Althusser's narrative of interpellation, in which a policeman hails someone on the street, identifying them within the law of the authoritative structure, what I'm calling King's resistant interpellation, originating from *within* a prison cell, rearticulates the dominant hail, turning it back on itself in order to pry open the dominant determinations of identity, and allowing for new definitions to be made. Such a possibility for change is crucial for King's project as a whole, as the attempt to open up new identities and beliefs within the field of race relations is the substance of the civil rights movement.

Taking full advantage of the epistle's ability to address multiple audiences,[31] King uses the same redefinition of subject positions in his attempt to convert the larger audience and, as Keith D. Miller writes, to 'reinforce [the] earlier support' of the already converted.[32] Unlike the address to the clergymen, the sections of the 'Letter' aimed at the larger audience are mostly indirect, while other passages are directed at both the ostensible and general audiences. As Fulkerson writes, King addresses this larger readership 'in terms of the clerical audience,' as a means of focusing his argument.[33] There are also passages where King refers to the broader group in the third person, in order to delineate what he sees as their place within the discourse of race:

> I have almost reached the regrettable conclusion that the Negro's great stumbling block in the stride toward freedom is not the White Citizen's Counciler or the Ku Klux Klanner, but the white moderate who is more devoted to 'order' than to justice; who prefers a negative peace which is

the absence of tension to a positive peace which is the presence of justice
... I had hoped that the white moderate would understand that law and
order exist for the purpose of establishing justice, and that when they fail
to do this they become dangerously structured dams that block the flow
of social progress. I had hoped that the white moderate would understand that the present tension of the South is merely a necessary phase of
the transition from an obnoxious negative peace, where the Negro passively accepted his unjust plight, to a substance-filled positive peace,
where all men will respect the dignity and worth of human personality.
(295)

The subject position that King describes here as being that of the white
moderate is one that is outside the realm of justice and positive peace.
The metaphors 'stumbling block' and 'dam' contradict the traditional
white liberals' concept of themselves as socially progressive, which
King himself hoped to be the case. He redefines this identity as one of
'[s]hallow understanding' (295). The strength of this particular passage
(as well as the converse strength of the silencing forces of racism) is
evidenced by the fact that when the 'Letter' was published in *Time*
magazine in January 1964, the above passage was one of the sections
left out.[34] As he does for the clergymen, however, King notes a space
within the larger audience that could be expanded to allow room for
these positions to change into what he sees as more 'positive' ones, as
can be seen in the simple fact that he still writes of this group as 'people of good will' (295). This indeterminate interpellation works in
direct opposition to the overly determining, brutalizing forces of the
disciplinary mechanisms of the carceral city, as evidenced by the reinforcement of the racist status quo in the clergymen's letter. The ambig-
uously determinative definition of subjectivity is necessary for King's
project, as he goes on in the 'Letter' to construct subject positions
within a discourse of racial harmony.

3. Tension Building

In order to get to this space, King must form a bridge between the
existing socio-political discourse of racial discord and the ideal situation of racial harmony. He does this through his self-construction in the
'Letter.' Having been defined, if not specifically named, in the clergymen's letter as an 'outsider,' and in the courts as a criminal, King necessarily sets his self-construction in opposition to that previous letter,

in what can be seen as a structural and thematic echo of Wilde's response to his 'public infamy.' King rejects the notion of being an outsider on the immediate level by writing that he was invited by Birmingham's local black leaders, and also by writing that no American can be an outsider anywhere within the country (289–90). King also rejects the idea that he is an outsider in any sense of the word. He defines himself as the epitome of all things American and Judeo-Christian, placing himself in a seat of power over the white populace, whom he writes of as acting irreligiously and as being anti-American. King's positioning of himself within both the religious and secular American traditions is the crucial step in constructing himself as a dynamic bridge between the discourses of racial discord and racial harmony, between the status quo and the 'Promised Land' of his famous later speech.

Within the religious and specifically Christian tradition, King constructs his identity against that of the clergymen. In so doing, he writes of himself as the tradition's natural inheritor:

> I must honestly reiterate that I have been disappointed with the church. I do not say that as one of the negative critics who can always find something wrong with the church. I say it as a minister of the gospel, who loves the church; who was nurtured in its bosom; who has been sustained by its spiritual blessings and who will remain true to it as long as the cord of life shall lengthen ... Yes, I love the church; I love her sacred walls. How could I do otherwise? I am in the rather unique position of being the son, the grandson and the great-grandson of preachers. (298, 299)

King not only shows himself to be part of the same religious tradition as the clergymen, but he also implies that he is the true inheritor and interpreter of that tradition. The conjunction of the birth and mothering metaphors and the construction of church as family (and vice versa), when combined with his shoring up of the church's social power as 'sacred,' serves to naturalize King's authority within what was, in the clergy's letter, part of the segregated power structure.

Another of the methods King uses to show his affinity with the clergymen is to remind them of his ties to the active Christian community. Relying on the biblical tradition that underscores much African American resistance literature (as evidenced by Jacobs's and other slaves' narratives),[35] King places his actions solidly within Christian discourse:

I am in Birmingham because injustice is here. Just as the eighth century prophets left their little villages and carried their 'thus saith the Lord' far beyond the boundaries of their hometowns; and just as the Apostle Paul left his little village of Tarsus and carried the gospel of Jesus Christ to practically every hamlet and city of the Graeco-Roman world, I too am compelled to carry the gospel of freedom beyond my particular hometown. Like Paul, I must constantly respond to the Macedonian call for aid. (290)

These lines are written to remind the specific audience of the eight clergymen that King is also a religious leader, with all of the special influence and knowledge that this connotes, placing him on the same religious level as his critics. As David Lewis writes, the average lay reader may be 'astounded by the apparent immodesty of these opening sentences,' but to the clergymen these comparisons 'were meant to have the special impact redolent of the divinity-school seminar.'[36] King is also here picking up on the long history of African American spiritual autobiography that, as Andrews writes, drew on a tradition which 'spoke profoundly of the telos of life as liberation from bondage,' and that 'admitted Afro-American spiritual experience into literature on a footing apparently equal to that of whites.'[37]

King's letter moves beyond this creation of an equal footing, however, offering a subtle condemnation of these specific opponents. King argues that he is on a religious mission, one that presumably any religious leader would undertake. By writing that his sojourn to Birmingham is one of religious necessity, he is silently questioning the sincerity of the clergymen's convictions and actions. This critique of the dominant culture on its own terms places King firmly in the tradition of the African American pulpit. John Ernest writes that within this tradition, there is a tendency to highlight 'a fundamental discrepancy between United States social order and that of God's moral government.'[38] Even on a basic level, King's more adept handling of this mutually shared religious discourse is readily noticeable. His 'Letter' is rife with religious allusions, while the clergymen's lacks any such references. This comparison is especially damning when one considers that the foundation for the clergymen's authority is their privileged place within the world of religious discourse.

Moreover, as Malinda Snow has demonstrated, King adds to his religious authority by casting the 'Letter' in the form of a Pauline epistle: 'like Paul, King declared his own apostleship so that he might present himself as one possessed of religious truth and able to define moral action in light of that truth.'[39] Relying on Paul's position as both the founder of the Church and as a 'prisoner of the Lord' (Ephesians 4:1), and as, for King, the foundational prison-letter writer, King undermines the clergymen's authority by showing his own more powerful grasp of their common heritage and religion; this undermining is still more effective since it occurs under a tone of Christian 'Peace and Brotherhood.'[40] The only recourse for the clergymen, if they want to retain their authority, would be either to show a still stronger hold on the religious discourse or to acquiesce to King's point of view.

King also subverts the authority of the broader white audience by showing his own mastery of general American and Western literary and philosophical discourses, and then by showing how that mastery is more thorough than theirs. Erwin Smith elaborates on King's use of citations, writing that King 'variously referred to Kant, Aquinas, Whitehead, Mill, Nietzsche, Plato, and Heidegger.'[41] He makes further allusions to such foundational figures as Socrates, John Bunyan, Abraham Lincoln, and Thomas Jefferson. The reference to Lincoln is redoubled in the opening of the 'Letter,' specifically the passage, mentioned earlier, in which King echoes Lincoln's sentiment about critics, which King mentioned again in an interview with Alex Haley: 'As Lincoln said, "If I answered all criticism, I'd have little time for anything else."'[42]

In addition to Paul's prison writings, Thoreau's 'Civil Disobedience' also lies in the background of the 'Letter.' King knew Thoreau's essay both from his personal reading and through Gandhi's interpretation of Thoreau's notion of non-violent resistance.[43] In *Stride Toward Freedom*, King writes, 'During my student days at Morehouse I read Thoreau's *Essay on Civil Disobedience* [sic] for the first time. Fascinated by the idea of refusing to coöperate with an evil system, I was so deeply moved that I reread the work several times.'[44] The relationship between King's 'Letter' and Thoreau's essay is especially evident when King states that 'an individual who breaks a law that conscience tells him is unjust, and willingly accepts the penalty by staying in jail to arouse the conscience of the community over its injustice, is in reality expressing the very highest respect for law' (294). When placed next to the following passage from Thoreau's text, the influence becomes apparent: 'Under a government which imprisons any unjustly, the true place for a just man is also a prison ... If any think that their influence would be lost there, and their voices no longer afflict the ear of the State, that they would not be as an enemy within its walls, they do not know by how much truth is stronger than error' ('Civil,' 76). Strategically using Thoreau's essay, King incarnates and specifies Thoreau's 'higher laws' as the anti-segregation decision and the potential for racial harmony that it represents. King also turns the general social alienation – as perpetuated by the State's disciplinary institutions – that Thoreau discusses into a specific form of alienation between racial groups. King thus picks up the 'happy prison' motif used in Thoreau's text in order to highlight the specific forms of social discipline and punishment that King is trying to combat. This intertextuality of prison letters (King's, Thoreau's, and even Paul's) is, moreover, an attempt to force his contemporary educated and liberal reader into reversing the valuation of the criminalization of African Americans – King's presence in jail does not negate what he has to say. In fact, it might, through the association with a founding American author like Thoreau, place King's 'Letter' into a prominent, privileged mode of discourse within that reader's mind. The connection to Thoreau and the other figures, as well as the more specifically religious allusions, act as cues to the larger white audience, establishing King as an authoritative figure within the dominant culture.

We can now see the intricate ways in which King writes himself into the intertwined discourses and traditions of both of the audiences that Fulkerson identifies.[45] Some of King's contemporaries, and specifically some other imprisoned activists, criticized his use of white forms and traditions, seeing in it a reproduction of the dominant culture rather than an attempt to alter the culture's racist practices. In a letter written from Soledad prison shortly after King's assassination, Black Panther and militant activist George Jackson writes that while he respected King 'as a man,' he disagreed with him 'as a leader of black thought,' specifically because King's method 'presupposes the existence of compassion and a sense of justice on the part of one's adversary. When this adversary has everything to lose and nothing to gain by exercising justice and compassion, his reaction can only be negative.'[46] Eldridge Cleaver, another massively influential African American prison author and the Panther's Minister of Information, goes further than this, equating King with Booker T. Washington, who, Cleaver writes, supported the racialized doctrine of 'separate-but-equal,' which 'was enforced by day by agencies of the law, and by the KKK & Co. under cover of night.'[47] Cleaver critiques King's strategies as being in keeping with the dominant culture and its most racist carceral and disciplinary practices.

Despite statements like Cleaver's, however, King does not solely reproduce the dominant discourse of white America; nor does he reproduce Thoreau's emphasis on the Enlightenment individual, which carries with it the same racism King is trying to combat. In addition to his use of 'white' traditions, King also engages in the more communal mode of signification associated with African American resistance, closely parallelling Jacobs's representation, in the graveyard passage, of the voices of a rebellious black community. King uses traditional African American sources and forms of discourse as partial means of celebrating his cultural heritage and of bolstering his position with his colleagues and followers. As Baldwin reminds his readers, 'Though King was deeply influenced by his training at Crozer Theological Seminary and Boston University, it is a mistake to conclude that his revolt was rooted in white political and theological sources.'[48] Indeed, as some critics have noted, the entire structure and content of the 'Letter' is infused with African American religious traditions.[49]

Beyond defining his identity in terms of the dominant culture, therefore, King also constructs it as part of a communal African American identity, what Philip Page calls the 'powerful intersubjective web that characterizes African American culture.'[50] Dolan Hubbard writes that the black church helped to create this community through the use of dominant texts: 'Black religion served as an organized way to perfect the rhetorical modes by focussing on the oratory of the black preacher, which was placed in the context of oral Western texts – the prime example being the Bible. Using the church as a forum for organizing black social reality, the preacher thus kept alive the African continuum.'[51] As Hubbard goes on to argue, part of the vivacity of the black sermon, and its coincident creation of community, arises from the use of a call-and-response technique that allows for active participation by all of the members of the congregation. Within this tradition, King's use of particularly African American religious tropes and images can be seen as part of a continuous, ongoing, and communal creation of identity, in which each participant both adds to and gains from the larger discussion. Defining call and response in terms of 'testifying' and 'witnessing,' Page writes that the transmission of this oral tradition into written form allows texts to 'enhance the interplay among multiple speaking and listening minds, including characters, narrators, readers, and authors. As they do so, they reproduce and further create the invisible threads of African-American culture.'[52] King's use in the 'Letter' of African American theology and style needs to be viewed, then, not simply as a recognition of his influences and culture, but as an active participation in the creation of a communal African American identity.

By negotiating different forms of discourse, King constructs an identity for himself that is at once within and without the dominant white society: inside, because he is a master of the literary, religious, and general discourses that form the foundations of the dominant class; outside, because he is black and therefore part of a communal identity that works against European notions of individuality, and specifically because he is disrupting the racialized practices that form a large part of the audiences' identities and the carceral matrix surrounding them.[53] King is in an unstable dual position, therefore, within both the dominant and dominated worlds. Unlike Thoreau's formation of a transcendental individual, King's construction of subjectivity is not one that presents a coherent model that can hold in all situations, nor does King want it to hold. He uses this place of 'tension' to try to form a bridge to a new world. As he writes, either society moves to the 'Promised Land' of racial harmony or the tension will tear society apart: 'I have tried to stand between these two forces, saying that we need not follow the "do-nothingism" of the complacent or the hatred and despair of the black nationalist ... If this philosophy [of non-violent action] had not emerged, I am convinced that by now many streets of the South would be flowing with floods of blood' (297). King's construction of a dual subject position for himself strongly resonates with W.E.B. Du Bois's concept in *The Souls of Black Folk* (1903) of the African American's 'double-consciousness':

It is a peculiar sensation, this double-consciousness, this sense of always looking at one's self through the eyes of others ... One ever feels his two-ness, – an American, a Negro; two souls, two thoughts, two unreconciled strivings; two warring ideals in one dark body, whose dogged strength alone keeps it from being torn asunder. The history of the American Negro is the history of this strife, – this longing to attain self-conscious manhood, to merge his double self into a better and truer self.[54]

Both King and Du Bois form an identity that is at once inside and outside of white America, and is torn by the resultant tension. Both writers also picture this strife as a temporary step on the way to a better self.

Many years before the 'Letter,' in 1956, King clarified his understanding of tension in a sermon entitled 'When Peace Becomes Obnoxious,' which he delivered before facing an earlier trial. He states:

> I had a long talk with a man the other day about this bus situation. He discussed the peace being destroyed in the community, the destroying of good race relations. I agree that it is more tension now. But peace is not merely the absence of this tension, but the presence of justice. And even if we didn't have this tension, we still wouldn't have positive peace. Yes, it is true that if the Negro accepts his place, accepts exploitation and injustice, there will be peace. But it would be a peace boiled down to stagnant complacency, deadening passivity, and if peace means this, I don't want peace.[55]

King's refusal of this form of peace is a refusal of the type of complacency he critiques in the white liberal community of his audience. Tension is not an ideal in itself, but is a necessary part of the struggle, without which 'positive peace' can never come into being. As he and others said in a statement to President Eisenhower, 'Frequently tension is an inherent element of basic social change ... The nation can adopt forthrightly a bold program which moves through tension to a democratic solution; or it can depend upon evasion and compromise which purport to avoid tension, but which in reality lead the entire society toward economic, social and moral frustration.'[56]

The tension is not only part of King's construction of himself and of the black community, but also a difficulty of white identity. Clark defines this particular problem as follows: 'The moral distance between creed (all men are created equal) and deed (segregation) created a dissonance or what Martin Luther King Jr, called 'tension,' that could be resolved only by progressively moving toward an extension of human rights.'[57] Whereas the tension of African American identity is created by the necessity of negotiating two separate cultural paradigms at once, and by combatting the racist structures enforced by the disciplinary society, the tension of white identity is created through the dominant group's own incongruous action. However, both tensions are portrayed as merely a step on the march towards a harmonious society. This point is reinforced in a story related by Clark, who refers to a conversation between King and Stanley Levison in which King 'complained ... about having to cut whole sections from his Birmingham letter, he noted particularly "a section – strong – [that the] whole idea [of the] struggle was not just something for the Negro but how it also frees the white man.'"[58] Positive peace equals a freedom for all parts of society, from both the imposition and exercise of oppression.

Before moving on to how King textually formulates the new, undifferentiated subject position available within a discourse of racial harmony, it is necessary to show how he highlights the tenuous nature of all the subject positions heretofore constructed within the status quo of the differentiated discourse of race. In a society as culturally, racially, and economically split as was the American South, all subjectivities can only be envisioned as temporary. This is to a large extent due to the unstable definition of 'race' itself – when it is a mythical 'one drop of blood' that results in a person's inclusion in one race and not another, racialized subjectivities are necessarily unstable. Henry Louis Gates Jr's now classic formation of this instability argues that '[r]ace is the ultimate trope of difference because it is so very arbitrary in its application.'[59] One result of this instability is the inevitability of a black rebellion, whatever form it takes. As King writes, 'Oppressed people cannot remain oppressed forever. The urge for freedom will eventually come' (297).

King shows the instability and 'two-ness' of the structure of dominant and dominated subjects through constantly changing his use of pronouns. In a letter, generically, it is safe to assume that the audience will be referred to in the second person, and the author(s) will be referred to in the first person. This may change somewhat in an open letter, where the authors could use the first-person plural to refer to the group they represent or to which they belong, but generally the use of pronouns will remain the same. We saw this type of structure for the most part in the clergymen's letter and in Wilde's text. While it remains true for sections of King's 'Letter,' it is by no means a guiding principle.[60] In the opening three paragraphs of the 'Letter,' the first person does refer to the author and his affiliates, while the second person is used for the audiences. In the fourth paragraph, however, 'we' refers inclusively to 'all communities' and every American, white or black. In the eighth paragraph, the use of pronouns changes once again: 'we were confronted with blasted hopes, and the dark shadow of a deep disappointment settled upon us. So we had no alternative except that of preparing for direct action, whereby we would present our very bodies as a means of laying our case before the conscience of the local and national community' (291). Here, 'we,' 'us,' and 'our' refer only to the activists, excluding all others. In the tenth paragraph, the ambiguity surrounding the pronouns is expressed within two sentences: 'We, therefore, concur with you in your call for negotiation. Too long has our beloved Southland been bogged down in the tragic attempt to live in monologue rather than dialogue' (292). Due to the specificity and exclusiveness of the prior pronouns, the 'our' in the second sentence becomes ambiguous – is it an inclusive term again, meaning all people, or does it mean only one group? This ambiguity, and there are several examples (including more than one in which African Americans are referred to in the third person), arises from the fact that King is trying to form a new type of racial discourse in which all subject positions are equal. As Mary L. Bogumil and Michael R. Molino write, 'King wants his audience to see the overall goals of his organization and to recognize that his position and theirs should be the same.'[61] King is constructing a discourse that is a dialogue rather than a monologue, where all pronouns are collectively included in one 'us.'

Not only is the overall ambiguity of pronoun usage socio-linguistically powerful, but each instance of the shift in pronouns is also potentially transformative. The best example begins with King writing, 'I guess it is easy for those who have never felt the stinging darts of segregation to say, "Wait,"' and then continues in the longest sentence of the 'Letter,' which reads in part:

> But when you have seen vicious mobs lynch your mothers and fathers at will and drown your sisters and brothers at whim; when you have seen hate-filled policemen curse, kick, brutalize and even kill your black brothers and sisters with impunity; when you see the vast majority of your twenty million Negro brothers smothering in an airtight cage of poverty in the midst of an affluent society ... when you have to concoct an answer for a five-year-old son asking in agonizing pathos: 'Daddy, why do white people treat colored people so mean?' ... then you will understand why we find it difficult to wait. (292–3)

In her discourse analysis of prisoners' spoken narratives, Patricia E. O'Connor writes that this form of shift from first-to second-person address functions in part to invite 'the listener, as it would a reader, to participate in the experience,'[62] thus shrinking the distance between the narrating prisoner and the free auditor in a manner similar to that of call and response. Similarly, starting with the sentence that begins 'I guess it is easy ...,' and moving directly to the second-person address with 'But when you ...,' King linguistically shifts the white reader into a textually constructed black subject position in order to create a sympathetic bond through suffering, bridging the formal epistolary 'gulf between presence and absence' that Altman discusses.[63] The white reader is also thrown momentarily into a new subject position, filling in what Greg Moses refers to as the 'gap that persists between those who live on the receiving end of a structure and those who don't.'[64] Issuing from within King's constrictive cell, his 'Letter' puts the white reader in 'an airtight cage.' In other words, King's 'you' is not a straightforward call to the reader, but is, as O'Connor notes of other prisoners' use of this technique, 'inclusive of both the speaker, the addressee, and a generalized other,' whereby the prisoner 'is also subtly getting his audience to accept and to agree with his assessment of what he experienced.'[65] After this textual transformation of identity, this resistant interpellation or hailing, King emphasizes his point by reverting to the common 'you' and 'we' of the audience's and author's groups.

In order to prove the viability of the discourse that he is constructing, King uses examples of white people who have themselves entered into a new space within the general picture of racial discourse:

> I am thankful, however, that some of our white brothers have grasped the meaning of this social revolution and committed themselves to it. They are still all too small in quantity, but they are big in quality. Some like Ralph McGill, Lillian Smith, Harry Golden and James Dabbs have written about our struggle in eloquent, prophetic and understanding terms. Others have marched with us down nameless streets of the South. They have languished in filthy roach-infested jails, suffering the abuse and brutality of angry policemen who see them as 'dirty nigger-lovers.' They, unlike so many of their moderate brothers and sisters, have recognized the urgency of the moment and sensed the need for powerful 'action' antidotes to combat the disease of segregation.[66] (298)

King shows by example the new identifications that are available and possible for his white readers. These are not attractive positions at the moment, as they involve brutality and prison (again de-emphasizing the relation of prison to crime, replacing it instead with an image of criminally violent police), but nowhere does King suggest that the road to freedom is a simple or unperilous one.

In the end, what the 'Letter' does, through the construction of subject positions within a discourse of racial harmony, is bridge the current segregated social system – in which whites are accorded privilege and blacks are subjected to a disciplinary regime which criminalizes blackness itself and brutalizes people – and the future system of 'Peace and Brotherhood.'[67] King ends the 'Letter' by stating:

> I also hope that circumstances will soon make it possible for me to meet each of you, not as an integrationist or a civil rights leader, but as a fellow clergyman and a Christian brother. Let us all hope that the dark clouds of racial prejudice will soon pass away and the deep fog of misunderstanding will be lifted from our fear-drenched communities and in some not too distant tomorrow the radiant stars of love and brotherhood will shine over our great nation with all of their scintillating beauty.
> Yours for the cause of Peace and Brotherhood,
> Martin Luther King Jr (302)

King writes that he hopes that, after the chaos of the fight for freedom, all subjectivities will be equal and undifferentiated in their relationships within power relations, so that all people live as 'Brothers' in 'our great nation,' in an attempt to remove the separation of groups pictured earlier through the diagram. Rather than assume that everyone has equal access to the courts and occupies the universalized individuality that would allow such access – an implicitly racist assumption in which the clergymen engage, which ignores actual social and institutional biases – King constructs a view in which people must fight for such an equality of treatment. King thinks that '[h]istorical change comes about by human responsiveness to the *Zeitgeist*,' a sense of agency within historical change that is represented in the way in which King constructs himself in the 'Letter.'[68] Thus, moving beyond the structural rigidity of either Hegelian or Althusserian theory, King textually enacts Fairclough's assertions that '[s]ocial agents [can be] active and *creative*' and that discourse types can be combined 'in ways that meet the ever-changing demands and contradictions of real social situations.'[69] From inside his *solitary* confinement, King proposes a creative and *communal* reformation of the subject positions in the racialized carceral systems of American discourse and society. Rather than simply assert himself as an image of the 'still more perfect and glorious State,' as Thoreau implicitly does ('Civil,' 90), King uses himself as an embodiment of the process towards change. He thereby avoids reproducing the dominating authority that Thoreau courts and in which the clergy engage. He also offers a more agential vision of identity than that of either Wilde or Jacobs, who, due to their specific circumstances, try to create spaces outside of discourse. Page discusses the emphasis on potential, as opposed to enacted, change as a general structure for African American theology: 'Envisioning an alternative future creates a meaningful space and time for African Americans and has the potential of revitalizing American culture.'[70] King's text permits a creative identity that can actively combat oppression. But, by emphasizing the tenuous nature of this identity, he also attempts to avoid its reification as an authoritative ideal. Adding to the diverse ways in which prison authors can use reconstructions of identity in order to critique the dominant culture that imprisons them, King's negotiation of the carceral city's determinations of identity offers the possibility of seeing how a multiply identified, forward-looking construction of self can serve to frustrate disciplinary oppression. In the following section of this study, I elaborate on this structural indeterminacy of subjectivity, showing how it is further exploited and expanded upon by two authors who occupy privileged positions in their societies. These prison writers build on the concept of tension, using widely fragmented portrayals of identity, in order to examine and critique the ways in which their privilege can duplicate and reinforce carceral authority.

PART THREE

Prisons, Privilege, and Complicity

CHAPTER FIVE

Being Jane Warton: Lady Constance Lytton and the Disruption of Privilege

The texts analysed in the previous sections have discussed the difficulties that prison authors face in avoiding – in their redefinitions of identity as social commentaries – the reproduction of the carceral forces of dominant discourses and cultures. With the exception of Thoreau, the authors themselves have been isolated from the ruling culture due to its racialized, gendered, sexualized, or classed character, among other classificatory categories. So King, for example, may use the language of the dominant class to assert his own authority, but this is more a means of accessing his white reader than it is a repetition of that reader's norms, since King is raced as 'other' within the contemporary paradigms of US culture. Similarly Wilde, while he could be seen to a degree as a member of the dominant class, is actively othered in terms of his sexuality by the trials and newspapers, as well as in terms of his nationality. In this final section, two authors deal with their imprisonments and their direct and acknowledged membership in the governing class that controls that imprisonment. In order to engage in the form of social critique that underlies the prison works being studied here, these two authors must present their readers with a series of complex redefinitions of identity, undermining the Enlightenment ontology that gives rise to their different forms of privilege, to the prison, and to the carceral society of which both are a part.

Like Wilde's *De Profundis*, Lady Constance Lytton's *Prisons and Prisoners* details experiences in the modern prison system of late Victorian and Edwardian England.[1] As the prison system moved into the twentieth century, the emphasis on the moral rehabilitation of the criminal began to shift into principles of a 'welfarist administration' that was geared towards a 'therapeutic rationale' that focused on the sociological causes of crime – a change that resulted in more explicitly socio-ideological methods of redemption.[2] Nevertheless, as Sloop argues about later American prisons, the redeemable nature of the inmate was still discussed in terms of the inmate's relationship to the dominant society. Ontological assumptions about the nature of certain groups – members of the lower classes, for example, or women – alter their relationship to the category of 'redeemable' simply because their natures are seen as differing from, or in some cases as simply being removed from, the category of the Enlightenment individual. Thus, the early-twentieth-century prison's emphasis on 'build[ing] up force of character'[3] coexists with revised methods of further classifying and separating 'types' of prisoners, including children, the mentally ill, and women. These people, then, become subject to severe and stringent forms of prison discipline, as a means of supposedly transforming them into 'useful' objects for the dominant society, rather than giving them access to dominant forms of subjectivity.

As Lytton shows, for women the typing and disciplining of prisoners was a means of reinforcing gender roles, which are tied up with other identity constructions within the disciplinary practices of the larger society.[4] Lytton describes how women's activities in prison focus on cleaning and sewing; in one of her prison stays, a few books are provided, including a bible, a devotional text, and 'an instructive book on domestic hygiene, "A Perfect Home and How to Keep It."'[5] The emphasis on rehabilitating women as proper domestic subjects reaches its height in the prison's role in attempting to break down the women's suffrage movement, just as the American penological structures would be used half a century later to attempt to break up the civil rights movement.

In a manner similar to that of the texts of Thoreau and Jacobs, and looking forward to King, Lytton's narrative examines the socio-political ramifications of the oppression of both individuals and groups through the socially sanctioned and institutionalized methods of punishment and oppression. Lytton was arrested several times for her activities as a member of one of the major (if not *the* major) suffragette organizations, the Women's Social and Political Union (WSPU). While the upper-class Lytton was disguised as the working-class 'Jane Warton' during her third imprisonment, she was forcibly fed several times while on a hunger strike. This violent act, which was visited on numerous suffrage activists (both men and women), resulted in a stroke that partially paralysed Lytton, forcing her to write *Prisons and Prisoners* 'laboriously, with her left hand.'[6] Lytton's class passing not only exposes the prison system's unequal treatment of people from different economic positions, but also highlights the larger social connections between class and gender oppression.[7] The narrative demonstrates how a person can be conflictingly identified within different but contiguous ideological frameworks. Depicting her class privilege as something that should be viewed as a part of the same ideological matrix that results in gender oppression, Lytton struggles in her text to remove herself from her class position, while at the same time making her unprivileged position as a woman visible and active. By portraying her existence as both Jane Warton and Lady Constance Lytton, neither of which can be the authentic or complete Enlightenment individual, Lytton's text forces one to go beyond readings of suffragette prison writings that foreground either their engagement in the collective voice of resistance to the patriarchy or their reproduction of the silencing of the working-class woman.[8] Lytton attempts to create a position for herself in which she is disempowered as a member of the upper class but empowered as a member of the collective voice of the parallel communities of women and prisoners, and she does so in order to offer a powerful critique of the interconnections of identity construction and class and gender oppression within both prison and the social structure that it supports.

1. The Role of the Prison Narrative in the Suffragette Movement

Lytton's imprisonments occurred within the context of political action for the enfranchisement of women, and specifically concerned her activities as a member of the WSPU.[9] Concerted militant action started with marches through cities to political sites such as the House of Commons, which led to arrests for disturbing the peace. Organized mostly by the WSPU and its offshoot, the Women's Freedom League (WFL), these campaigns eventually escalated to mass window-breaking events and arson, and to hunger strikes by those who had been imprisoned. The WSPU's militant campaigns largely came to a halt with the beginning of the First World War, when many, though by no means all, suffragettes rallied behind the government. The vote was given to propertied women after the war in the Representation of the People Act of 1918 and was extended to all women in 1928.

The militant campaigns were extraordinarily well documented by both the popular press and the suffragettes themselves. The suffragettes were invested in publicizing their movement as much as possible through both the spectacle (to appropriate a term used by both Green and Lisa Tickner) of their demonstrations and the representation of themselves in newspapers, pamphlets, and literary and other artistic works.[10] These publications served to offset the negative portrayal of the movement by the popular press and through other media. Maroula Joannou writes that the suffragettes' depictions of themselves and other positive portrayals 'were welcomed and read avidly by women who had become habituated to seeing the behaviour and motives of the suffragette maligned in public elsewhere.'[11]

Among the suffragette materials, prison narratives and the related accounts of forcible feeding hold a prominent place, in part because they undermine the effects of the silencing that imprisonment imposed. As Green writes, '[I]n moving from street to prison, [the suffragettes] left the realm of the exhibit ... and arrived at a realm of surveillance, voyeurism, and invisibility. They countered that invisibility with autobiography, bringing life-writing to the service of feminist activism.'[12] The goals of the suffragette prison narrative thus mimic those of the movement: to replace enforced silence with active voices, and oppression with agency.

Lytton's *Prisons and Prisoners*, and the experiences on which it was based, were among the best known and most publicized accounts of imprisonment and forcible feeding. Because of Lytton's family's fame, and its social status as part of the aristocracy (her brother, Victor, was an outspoken and pro-suffragette member of the House of Lords, while her grandfather was Edward Bulwer-Lytton, the famous novelist), her story was repeated *ad infinitum* in the press, in parliamentary speeches, and in suffragette-controlled media. Lytton's own work transforms the general content of such suffragette texts, however, in order to deal not only with gender oppression, but also with the implications of her class and its privileges.

Glenda Norquay writes that women's suffrage writing is constructed as 'a direct intervention in public and political debate' and is 'aimed at altering the structures of society.'[13] This being the case, the manner in which these texts construct the society that they wish to change takes on a certain primacy. The representation of the patriarchal system of late Victorian and Edwardian England forms the discursive ground to which suffragette authors respond. In addition to displaying the overt manner in which their society oppressed women, through depictions of scenes such as domestic abuse and forced feeding, many of the texts show the ways in which their authors were made to realize more subtle forms of oppression. These realizations generally culminate in the depiction of the author's conversion to the feminist cause.[14] Lytton's work is no exception to these generic conventions. These moments in her autobiography both provide the reasons for her suffragette action and encourage the reader's sympathy, while at the same time offering a conceptual matrix for understanding the patriarchy's system of oppression. Through these formulations, Lytton textually reconstructs the ideological underpinnings of the definitions of women's subjectivity, including her own.[15]

2. Class Privilege and Patriarchy

In the second chapter of the text 'My Conversion,' Lytton describes her lengthy stay with a group of suffragettes that included two of the leaders of the movement, Emmeline Pethick-Lawrence and Annie Kenney. Once she is made aware of their militant allegiances, she tells them that 'although I shared their wish for the enfranchisement of women, I did not at all sympathise with the measures they adopted for bringing about that reform' (10). Lytton goes on to describe the logical arguments used by Pethick-Lawrence and Kenney to attempt to sway her opinion.[16] Her conversion is only achieved, however, through her sympathetic identification with an animal:

> All kinds of people were forming a ring round a sheep which had escaped as it was being taken to the slaughter-house. It looked old and misshapen. A vision suddenly rose in my mind of what it should have been on its native mountain-side with all its forces rightly developed, vigorous and independent. There was a hideous contrast between that vision and the thing in the crowd. With growing fear and distress the sheep ran about more clumsily and became a source of amusement to the onlookers, who laughed and jeered at it. At last it was caught by its two gaolers, and as they carried it away one of them, resenting its struggles, gave it a great cuff in the face. At that I felt exasperated. I went up to the men and said, 'Don't you know your own business? You have this creature absolutely in your power. If you were holding it properly it would be still. You are taking it to be killed, you are doing your job badly to hurt and insult it besides.' The men seemed ashamed, they adjusted their hold more efficiently and the crowd slunk away. (12–13)

After this passage, Lytton explicitly compares the treatment of the sheep to that of women: 'But on seeing this sheep it seemed to reveal to me for the first time the position of women throughout the world. I realised how often women are held in contempt as beings outside the pale of human dignity, excluded or confined, laughed at and insulted ... I was ashamed to remember that ... I had been blind to the sufferings peculiar to women as such' (13–14). Lytton's epiphany about the status of women is echoed by later feminist writers who, as Susan Hekman summarizes, argue that women, through the way in which they are defined, do not have discursive access to the normative, transcendent identity such as that described by Thoreau, since this identity 'is defined in exclusively masculine terms.'[17] On the one hand, this masculine identity, as Sidonie Smith argues, 'suggests the certitudes of stable boundaries around a singular, unified, and irreducible core';[18] on the other hand, women's identities, as Lytton makes explicit, are portrayed as existing 'outside the pale of human dignity' (13). Looking forward to Smith's conclusion that 'the woman who would reason like a man becomes "unwomanly," a kind of monstrous creature or *lusus naturae*,'[19] Lytton states that any woman who fights against sexist definitions of women's identity is treated as 'a distortion, an abnormality, an untidiness of creation' (41). Man is free to define himself; woman is 'confined' by definitions placed on her.

If the sheep in the above scene is to be read as a metaphor for the position of women in Lytton's society, then the portrayal of the sheep's handlers and of the crowd inform her depiction of the structures of that society. The passage relates the two sheep handlers to the policemen or gaolers who, later in the text, violently enforce the patriarchal decisions of the Liberal government. The more informative section of the scene in terms of Lytton's construction of general society involves the representation of the crowd encircling the sheep. Functioning as both spectators and imprisoning fence, the crowd's gawking does not just reconfigure the handlers' violence as entertainment, but in fact enables that violence, cutting off the sheep's means of escape. Lytton here turns around contemporary anti-suffragette depictions of the 'unruly feminine crowd.'[20] This 'specter,' as Green calls it, was used by the popular press not only in order to discount the suffragettes' demonstrations and the reasons for them, but also to remove any suggestion that the violent suppression of those demonstrations by the police was unjustified, or to remove that violence altogether.[21] Lytton's metaphorical depiction of a crowd being entertained by violence against women thus serves to counteract anti-suffrage propaganda by turning the 'unruly crowd' into an image of a society that enables such violence through its silent gaze and subsequent slinking support of the patriarchy.

Lytton explicates the populace's support of the oppression of women by referencing Thoreau's prison essay. Cementing the relationship between these two prison authors, Lytton begins the chapter 'Jane Warton' with a quotation from 'Civil Disobedience,' which she alters to make it gender non-specific: 'Under a Government which imprisons any unjustly, the true place for a just man (or woman) is also a prison' (234; Thoreau, 76). In the following chapter, 'Walton Gaol, Liverpool,' she recounts that while imprisoned as Jane Warton she wrote the same phrase, along with 'Votes for Women' and a biblical passage, on her cell wall (264).[22] This relationship informs Lytton's portrayal of the general populace in a passage that could allude to Thoreau's statement 'There are thousands who are *in opinion* opposed to slavery and to the war, who yet in effect do nothing to put an end to them' ('Civil,' 69), a passage King would also later echo. She writes that, early in the process of her conversion, she

> was much concerned with the arguments of Anti-Suffragists. I wrote a pamphlet to refute their points of view, as generally presented in newspapers and magazines. I was always, as it were, stopping on my road to combat their attitude. It was only after considerably longer experience that I realised the waste of energy entailed by this process, since the practical opposition which blocks the way to the legal removal of sex disability is not due to those men or women who have courage to publicly record their opposition, but to those who take shelter in verbally advocating the cause, while at the same time opposing any effective move for its achievement.[23] (15)

The oppression of women is not enabled solely due to the robustious (to resurrect an appropriate archaism) support of patriarchal institutions and social practices, but also through the silent, hypocritical consent of the generalized crowd, which renders its engagement in oppression invisible by mimicking the suffragettes.

Lytton demonstrates that this silent consent by the public to the subjugation of women and to the violent suppression of suffragettes makes itself visible, however, in everyday acts committed by 'average' people across society. Writing of her first involvement in a WSPU Deputation, in a march to the prime minister, she again depicts violence in the gaze and taunts of a crowd:

> I heard for the first time with my own ears the well worn taunt 'Go home and do your washing' ... From the moment I heard that 'washing' taunt in the street, I have had eyes for the work of the washers. If there is one single industry highly deserving of recognition throughout the world of human existence and of representation under parliamentary systems, it surely is that of the washers, the renewers week by week, the makers clean. I determined, if I should find myself the solitary representative of the Deputation and its untrained spokeswoman, I should point to the collars and shirt fronts of the gentlemen who received me and claim the freedom of citizenship for the washers. (42–3)

Followed by a description of the violent force used by the police against the Deputation, this passage illuminates the relationship between everyday oppression and the actions taken against the suffragettes. Not only do the sexist taunts of the crowd serve to highlight the means through which women are oppressed on a daily basis, but the very apparel of the men in the crowd and in the government serves a similar function. Lytton realizes that the 'proper' social appearance of the men who control the State is made possible by the politically unrepresented labour of women.

The passage concerning the washers also points to one of the central tensions in Lytton's text. Her worry about speaking to the government, she suggests, is due to a feeling that she is 'not equipped to represent' working-class women (42). In questioning the legitimacy of her representational ability, Lytton challenges her own position within the suffrage movement, which to her, if not all suffragettes (as I discuss below), is ultimately concerned with the complete political representation of all women. Lytton thus perceives her class privilege in terms of its reinforcement of gender hierarchies: if the men in parliament illegitimately 'represent' the women of the nation, Lytton wants to avoid replicating this illegitimacy, to avoid participating in the oppressive milieu because, as a 'member of a prominent aristocratic family, sister of a peer, and a "chronic invalid,"' she was, in the words of Mary Jean Corbett, 'wary of special treatment from the authorities.'[24]

Despite her appreciation of this situation, Lytton's class consistently frustrates her attempts to be a representative feminist figure. This is especially apparent during her first imprisonment, when the prison authorities consistently accorded her better treatment than the other prisoners. At one point, Lytton is approached by one of the women wardens, who asks, 'What have you been complaining about?' Lytton replies, 'I haven't been complaining,' but the wardress responds, 'Yes you have – you complained of something to a visitor':

> I then remembered that, when reassuring my sister as to my health and to prove to her the genuineness of my statements as to prison conditions being in no way harmful to me, I had mentioned two things which proved rather trying, viz., that my underclothes and stockings were too short to cover my knees, and the fact that one small towel had to do service for all purposes during a week. I reported this to the wardress, but explained that I had mentioned these not in complaint but to prove to my sister that my discomforts were insignificant. 'Well,' she retorted, 'next time you have anything to complain of come to me with it – if not I shall get into trouble.' This seemed the very reverse of prison regulations, for usually the trouble was caused by anything out of the ordinary being granted to a prisoner. From that time forward I was supplied with two towels, one of them renewed every week, and two rolls of flannel bandages were brought to me to cover my knees. (112–13)

Lytton learns after her release that these privileges were accorded to her because her brother 'had interviewed the head of the Prison Commissioners Department' (113). The social position of Lytton's family seems to disrupt the prison's specific mechanisms of power, forcing the officials to treat her differently, and therefore partially reverses the power dynamic between Lytton and her gaolers – but this reversal could in turn result in the punishment of yet another woman, the wardress.[25]

Nonetheless, such privileges highlight for Lytton the mistreatment of lower-class prisoners. She describes the prison chaplain who, during this same period of imprisonment, made the distinction between her and the other prisoners explicit:

> He instanced how wrong it would be if, when we were hungry, we yielded to the temptation of stealing bread. At this remark an old woman stood up. She was tall and gaunt, her face seamed with life, her hands gnarled and worn with work. One saw that whatever her crimes might have been she had evidently toiled incessantly ... The tears streamed down her furrowed cheeks as she said in a pleading, reverent voice, 'Oh,

sir, don't be so hard on us.' The wardresses immediately came up to her took her by the shoulders and hustled her out of the ward; we never saw her again. The Chaplain did not answer nor even look at her, and continued his address as if nothing had happened. (120–1)

Despite his callous indifference towards the woman, he treats Lytton with deference and respect, referring to her as 'your ladyship' (121). This leads Lytton and others to compare 'the attitude of the Chaplain towards the prisoner who had appealed to him during his address and towards myself. It was on this occasion I first noticed that the dress-jacket I wore was different from those of my companions' (122). Afterwards, 'it became a sort of game to watch for the privileges that were accorded to me' (122). This situation, in which an upper-class prisoner was consistently treated with more respect than others, was common in the late Victorian and Edwardian prison. As Wiener writes, 'The very drive to subject all criminals to uniform discipline made prisoners who, for whatever reason, did not fit the criminal stereotype for which that discipline had been devised into a problem requiring new and special measures.'[26] Recognizing the special care taken in her own case, Lytton uses it to highlight the improper treatment of the other prisoners, as a means of making a larger social point about class distinctions.

At the same time, Lytton's membership in the generalized group of prisoners in the chapel, evidenced by her use of 'we' in the chapel scene, is invalidated by the Chaplain's deference to her, and by the prison's definition of her as a person who exists outside of the stereotype of the common criminal. Her recognition of this invalidation creates a division in Lytton's perception between her prison experience and that of other suffragettes. Even though she was arrested as a militant, and even though she serves her prison time with other members of the cause, she feels that she is not 'shar[ing] the lot of the bulk of my Suffragette companions' (123). This split is reinforced at the trial for her second arrest, where she and another well-known figure are given special consideration: 'The whole "trial" was unworthy of the name – it was a device whereby Mrs. Brailsford and I should be separated from the others and treated with more respect, I having been the only one to do a glaring act and an, apparently, harmful or greatly risky one' (225). Despite Lytton's 'harmful' act of throwing a rock at a moving car (she writes that she 'threw the stone low down, so that it should not hit the chauffeur or anyone' [223]), she is separated from the majority of the women who share her beliefs. This separation is indicative for Lytton of the interdependent relationship between class structures and gender divisions, in that both effectively silence the majority of women.

Lytton's portrayal of her arrest and imprisonment is one in which class prevents her from having an 'authentic' suffragette prison experience, which further keeps her from being representative of the movement and from being able to have any lasting effects. She makes this problem explicit when she describes a group of prisoners marching in the yard, and compares them to an upper-class social gathering:

> As I had watched the prisoners I saw before me a counter-procession of women of this leisured class, herded as I have so often seen them at ballrooms and parties, enduring the labours, the penalties, of futile, superficial, sordidly useless lives, quarrelling in their marriage market, revelling in their petty triumphs, concerned continually with money, yielding all opinion to social exigencies, grovelling to those they consider above them, despising and crushing those they think beneath them, pretending to be lovers of art and intellect, but concerned at heart only with the appearance of being so ... And immediately the procession of Holloway yard seemed human, dignified, almost enviable by the side of that other ... Whether or not the women alive to-day in the ruling class can be cured is of comparatively little importance, but clearly the causes which have brought them forth must be altered at the root. (135–6)

For Lytton, the women of the leisured class may be equally creations of the patriarchal system as the lower class, but their active involvement in the social processes of their own privilege not only makes them ill equipped to engage themselves in the feminist movement, but also renders them contemptible. Somewhat working against what Marie Mulvey-Roberts sees, in her critical-biographical essay about Lytton, as the latter's understanding of 'the constraints of the feminine role imposed upon aristocratic women,'[27] Lytton portrays these women as also actively participating in (re)creating their own social position at the expense of the members of the lower classes. And it must be remembered that, despite Lytton's distancing of herself from these women through the use of the third person, she herself is a member of their order, one of the group that forms 'the weakest link in the chain of womanhood' (135). Despite Green's assertion that '[i]n the prison Lytton gained access to those disenfranchised women from whom she had been separated,'[28] at this point in her imprisonment Lytton can only attempt to understand those disenfranchised women through a comparison to women of her own class. Even the privileged women's preoccupation with appearance is a mimicry of 'how much appearances were respected by officials' of the prison (164). Lytton's concern, then, with representation and participation within the suffrage movement as a whole, but more specifically in suffragette prison experiences, replicates the women's larger concern with representation and participation in the political process. Adding to the definition of the carceral society offered by the other authors discussed in this study, Lytton thus demonstrates how privilege, patriarchy, and prison all function as divisory forces that alienate people from each other and reinforce the ruling group's power through that alienation.

3. Being Jane Warton

As Green notes, the models upon which Lytton bases her text could result in another reinforcement of some of the oppressive functions of the carceral matrix. Using 'the gaze of the social investigator' (58) to validate her readings of inmates and of the prison system, Lytton occasionally constructs the 'common prisoner' within a set of stylized and often silent types instead of dealing with particulars. Quoting an early passage in Lytton's text (33), Green writes: 'Throughout, Lytton is the protector of other imprisoned women – through activism the "superfluous spinster" finds a way of exercising a maternal instinct after all. This model of womanly reform, however, threatens to infantilize and silence the "common criminal."'[29] Indeed, some contemporary observers also criticized Lytton in this way: an editorial in *The Egoist* (unattributed, but likely written by Dora Marsden) tries to 'make clear' to Lytton and others who are 'Saviours' that they 'are misguided more than willingly by erring; that their avocation is futile and distressful; that they in concrete fact actually spoil the landscape for those whom they believe they serve.'[30] As these critics point out, such activities (as in the conjoining of 'true womanhood' and abolitionism) necessitate an objectification and infantilization of those whom they would help.[31] Therefore, to be effective, Lytton must attack class privilege in order to attack the patriarchy, just as Jacobs must attack the construction of 'true womanhood,' even as she exploits it, in order to fully critique the racism surrounding her. Lytton must decry the class structure not only as it appears in favours given to her, but also as it exists in her own gaze and perception. In her early attempts to disrupt the system of privilege that favours her, she focuses on changing people's perception of her. For example, when she notices that her prison dress is better than others, she switches jackets with another suffragette prisoner (122). Yet, she realizes that this early and superficial cross-class-dressing does not have much affect on her status as *Lady* Lytton. In order to attack fully the image of her privilege, she must attack the embodied image of that privilege – herself.

Her first such attack is a physical attempt to rewrite the text of her classed body. In an effort to ensure her movement from the relatively undisciplined infirmary to the more rigorous 'other side' (173) of the prison, Lytton decides to carve the words 'Votes for Women' onto her body, 'beginning over the heart and ending it on [her] face' (164). She only manages to cut a deep 'V' into her chest before she is discovered, but this is enough to effect her transfer. Green writes: 'Knowing that the physicians employed a medical gaze to limit hers (as an "observation case" Lytton, with her heart condition, could not join the other prisoners in the general cells), Lytton exaggerated her position as spectacle, literally engraving her body's secrets onto her skin so that medical inspection was made moot.'[32] In fact, the oppressive medical gaze was strongly directed at the suffragettes as a whole. The movement itself was occasionally figured as the result of vaguely worded medical problems in the women's bodies.[33] Lytton's attack on her own body can be read as an attempt to subvert not only the medical gaze directed at her, but also that directed at all suffragettes since, as Foucault argues, the medical gaze is part of the larger institutional matrix of society.[34] Lytton's actions not only disrupt the medical gaze (which functions as one of the prison's regulatory systems), but also rewrite the status of her body within the classificatory regimes of her society (regimes which the prison serves to protect and produce).

Since the specific phrase 'Votes for Women' is associated with the WSPU and other such organizations, it also carries with it some resonance of the non-aristocratic classes.[35] Lytton's attempt to carve this phrase into her flesh, then, functions both to attack her embodied upper-class femininity and to rewrite that femininity into the larger community of suffragette activists. This victorious 'V' (unintentionally mimicked years later by Liberal prime minister, and friend of Lord Lytton, Winston Churchill) places Lytton in opposition to the culture from which her privilege arises. This rebellious or contrary position is even evidenced typographically, with Lytton's 'V' appearing as the inverse of the phalanx of police that attacked the suffragette deputation, inscribed in Lytton's text as 'a ∧ shaped avenue of police' (44). The act of cutting herself is, in Lytton's words, a direct 'analogy' for the entire women's movement. Discussing the Senior Medical Officer's decision to allow her transfer, she writes:

> With him it was a real temptation to say, 'If now, why not before?' to point out how effective had been the behaviour which two days previously he had professed to find so incomprehensible, also to draw the analogy between this little prison episode and the women's fight for the vote – a reasonable demand, continuously pressed in a reasonable way and with great patience; result, blank refusal on the part of responsible powers. Militant action, by means of strike and protest; result, anger, condemnation, and the request is granted. (174)

Lytton's violence against her own body, which takes the form of the act of writing, repeats in miniature the actions of the group from which she has been separated by her status and, in so doing, allows her more visibly and actively to join that community. Her secondary textual portrayal of the act in turn allows her to direct the reader's attention away from herself and onto the aims of the group.

Lytton's attempts to deny her class position and to become a full member of the suffragette society are most forcibly portrayed in her class passing as a working woman named Jane Warton. After another imprisonment, this time in Newcastle, Lytton decides that the only way to remove herself from the privileges of her class is to dissociate herself from her name. This decision is made in large part due to the onset of suffragette hunger strikes and the resulting forcible feeding ordered by the government. Suffragettes began these strikes as a means of protesting the government's refusal to treat them as political prisoners who, after the influx of Irish nationalist and other political and gentleman prisoners in the late nineteenth century, were accorded different status in the prison.[36] The first such strike was committed in February 1909 by Marion Wallace Dunlop, who was released early, as were several subsequent hunger strikers. In September of the same year, however, the government ordered the forced feeding of all hunger strikers. The first woman to be forcibly fed was Mary Leigh. The government justified this action by assuring members of parliament and the public that it was the only way to save the striking prisoners' lives. Howlett describes the way in which the bill for forcible feeding was introduced:

> On September 29 Herbert Gladstone (the home secretary) informed the House of Commons of his decision to introduce forcible feeding. It was, he declared, his duty to do so: forcible feeding was the only way the women's lives, which were 'sacred,' could be preserved (without releasing them and thus making a mockery of the law). However, as the Liberal journalists Brailsford and Nevinson argued in a letter to the *Times*, Gladstone was thus discounting the alternative option of granting the WSPU's demand and officially recognizing the suffragettes as political prisoners.[37]

Indeed, in a December 1909 statement concerning the 'Suffragist Women Prisoners,' the Home Secretary provided statements from doctors testifying to the safety and necessity of forcible feeding, while also going to great lengths to explain why the women could not be considered political prisoners.[38] Howlett, however, discusses how the Home Secretary's reasoning is further flawed by the fact that, rather than being a life-saving measure, forcible feeding was 'a brutal and life-threatening procedure' which was used 'as a deterrent ...; its value to the government was not that it saved life but that it inflicted pain and had a perceived ability to decimate the movement.'[39] As I have shown, this masking language is characteristic of prison discourse: the violent and brutalizing effects of the prison are housed within statements of benevolence and, more importantly, of discipline geared towards the 'proper' reconstitution of the subject.

It is in this context that Lytton decides to pass as Jane Warton. Following some discussion of the brutal treatment of the strikers, and of the horrors of forcible feeding, she writes: 'The altogether shameless way I had been preferred against the others at Newcastle ... made me determine to try whether they would recognise my need for exceptional favours without my name' (235). In order to do this, she engages in an extended and effective masquerade. Lytton reconceives her outward appearance, beginning by rejoining the WSPU as Jane Warton, and by buying new apparel: 'I accomplished my disguise in Manchester, going to a different shop for every part of it, for safety's sake. I had noticed several times while I was in prison that prisoners of unprepossessing appearance obtained least favour, so I was determined to put ugliness to the test' (239). By putting her costume together in piecemeal fashion, and by scouring Manchester to do so, Lytton becomes what she depicts as an amalgamation of all the working-class women of the area. She writes: 'On inquiry for a "cheap" draper, three different people recommended me to a certain shop named "Lewis" ... So many Miss Wartons were of the same mind that the street was blocked with customers for some distance down' (241). Lytton turns the sociologist's gaze (which Green discusses) upon herself, using the same patronizing language, but this time in order to transform herself into a spectacle for others. She writes that, upon entering the house where she is to stay as Jane, the daughters, who were 'zealots,' 'welcomed Jane without a sign of criticism. I saw the mother gasp a little when I entered her drawing-room, but she was nevertheless most courteous and kind' (242). Performing working-class 'ugliness,' the opposite of her previous fashionable appearance, Lytton effectively removes the social barriers of privilege that protect her from the judgmental gaze of others.

This removal causes a split in Lytton's depiction of herself. As the social reformer who had 'always been interested in prisons and ... prison reform' (10), Lytton objectifies her new identity as Jane Warton much as she does the 'common criminal,' resulting in a depersonalized, third-person account of her shopping trip to the aforementioned shop: 'A sale was on there and Jane found that it was the very place for her ... The hat was a special difficulty; every article of millinery was of the fashionable order, warranted to cover half the body as well as the head. This did not suit Jane. Finally she succeeded in getting the right one of stitched cloth, with a plait of cloth round the crown' (241). Jane, as a woman with no social barriers between her and the rest of society, is always already open to the derogatory gaze of those around her. Thus, even Lytton can classify her alter-ego in the third person, and note Jane's divergence from acceptable norms (in this case those of fashion). Jane's dress embodies this openness; whereas fashionable women (such as Lytton, presumably) can cover themselves with their hats, such shielding does 'not suit Jane.'

Yet such an easy distinction between Constance and Jane is untenable. The passage above concludes: 'Before leaving Manchester I realised that my ugly disguise was a success. I was an object of the greatest derision to street-boys, and shop-girls could hardly keep their countenances while serving me' (241). The sudden shift from the third-person description of Jane to a first-person account of Lytton's treatment by street-boys and shop-girls demonstrates that Jane's ugliness also exposes Lytton to the gaze from which her privilege had protected her. The success of the disguise does not lie in its ability to fool others, but in the performative function of turning Lytton into an object of derision. The abuse hurled at working-class Jane is received by the upper-class Constance.

The instability of identity created by Lytton's performance continues after Jane's arrest.[40] Jane is again described in the third person in a lengthy passage, and again treated as an object open for abuse, but this time she functions as a synecdoche for all suffragettes. Lytton describes the booking in process, writing,

> It was the turn of Jane Warton ... Her standing out in the room was the signal for a convulsed titter from the other prisoners. 'It's a shame to laugh at one of your fellow-prisoners,' said the policeman behind the desk, and the tittering was hushed. It was all I could do not to laugh, and I thought to myself 'Is the *Punch* version of a Suffragette overdone?' As I got back to my companions they too were laughing, but I thought it won-derfully kind of the policeman to have spoken on my behalf. (249)

In analysing the 'status of Lytton's (suppressed) laughter' in this pas-sage, Howlett writes that it does not matter whether she is laughing 'at the success of her mimicry' or 'at the sheer ridiculousness of Jane's appearance,' and thus whether she identifies with the other suffragette prisoners or with the common prisoners. 'In either case,' argues Howlett, 'what Lytton is clearly *not* doing is identifying herself, the subject of the laughter, with Jane, the object of the prisoners' contempt and the policeman's pity.'[41] This point is in fact emphasized by Lyt-ton's reference to Jane as a *Punch* version of a suffragette. The cartoons of suffrage activists, regularly published in *Punch*, were heavily stereo-typed and negative, so Lytton's reference to her version of the work-ing-class suffragette as a *Punch* image could work to reproduce the magazine's 'comic' dismissal. While I agree with Howlett that Lytton's subjectivity is ambiguous here, I believe that this is due precisely to the fact that Lytton recognizes herself *both* as Constance and as Jane. Thus, Lytton can write of Jane in the third person at the beginning of the pas-sage, and at the end write that the policeman spoke 'on my behalf.' This shifting use of pronouns is not so much a transformation in her understanding of herself as it is a signal of the problems raised by her class passing. She alternates between the subject laughing and the object of laughter. Like the pronoun shifts in King's letter, which serve to highlight the tension created by the oppressive society while also engaging the reader's sympathy, the pronoun shifts in this passage serve to signal the problems of subjectivity created by the class distinctions of her society, but they also point towards the problematic nature of her masquerade. As in the description of the taunting she received when buying her outfit, Lytton's text struggles at the moment of public scrutiny between depicting Jane as object or as subject.

The ostensible reason for her class passing is to effect the removal of privilege in her treatment as a prisoner. As Constance Lytton, she is told that the official justification for these privileges was the diagnosis of a pre-existing heart condition. The Home Office's report, 'Suffragist Women Prisoners,' quoting its own letter to the Fabian Society, stated that Lytton 'was released solely because she was suffering from serious heart disease, and because violent resistance on her part to the medical treatment appropriate to her case would have involved some risk to her life,' and that any 'statement that Lady Constance Lytton's release had anything to do with her rank or social position' was 'a wilful and deliberate misrepresentation.' That Lytton did have such a condition was not disputed; rather, she wanted to demonstrate that, without having the privilege of her name, this condition would not have any effect on her sentencing or treatment. This is proven to be true during Jane's second forcible feeding:

> I told him [the doctor] I should not faint, that I was not liable to this or any form of collapse; I did not mention the slight chronic debility of heart from which I suffered. He called in the junior medical officer, who happened to be passing at the time, to test my heart. The junior doctor, who was in a jovial mood, stooped down and listened to my heart through the stethoscope for barely the space of a second – he could not have heard two beats – and exclaimed, 'Oh, ripping, splendid heart! You can go on with her' ... (275)

When imprisoned as Constance Lytton, she is given thorough medical tests and treatment. As Jane Warton, she notes that a careless and superficial test is enough to prove her health. Going beyond what Mulvey-Roberts argues is a distinction between Jane's 'private' medical history and Constance's 'public' one,[42] this passage demonstrates that Lytton's disguise changes the very way in which she is embodied by changing her relationship to the prison through removing the signs of her privileged status. In other words, Jane Warton is, as far as Constance Lytton is concerned, as different on the inside as she is on the outside, despite their sharing of one body.

The dual subjectivity, which continues throughout Jane's imprisonment, reaches its apex during Jane's first forcible feeding, making the political effectiveness of Lytton's passing clear. Lytton ends her detailed description of the process of the feeding and the horrendous physical suffering it creates as follows:

> The horror of it was more than I can describe. I was sick over the doctor and wardresses, and it seemed a long time before they took the tube out. As the doctor left he gave me a slap on the cheek, not violently, but, as it were, to express his contemptuous disapproval, and he seemed to take for granted that my distress was assumed. At first it seemed such an utterly contemptible thing to have done that I could only laugh in my mind. Then suddenly I saw Jane Warton lying before me, and it seemed as if I were outside of her. She was the most despised, ignorant and helpless prisoner that I had seen. When she had served her time and was out of the prison, no one would believe anything she said, and the doctor when he had fed her by force and tortured her body, struck her on the cheek to show how he despised her! That was Jane Warton, and I had come to help her. (269–70)

Lytton refigures herself as the 'common woman' so well that the doctor presumes her suffering to be 'assumed' since, as an official of the prison and of the cultural structures it represents, he cannot accept the self-sacrifice in which the working-class Jane is engaging. Looking on his actions from her privileged position, Constance wants to laugh, as she does during Jane's booking in, but this time the inward laughter is directed at the doctor who is, even though a professional, also her social inferior. However, because Lytton refers to herself during the forcible feeding in the first person – the suffering happens to the 'I' that is both Jane and Constance – Lytton can reinterpret the doctor's slap as a direct and contemptible act upon Jane, in a direct parallel to her reaction to the treatment of the sheep, which is also hit in the face by a man who 'resent[s] its struggles' (13). Redirecting the reader to the ambiguity of her subjectivity, to the knowledge of the dual nature of the 'I,' by reverting to the third-person depiction of Jane in the above passage, Lytton creates a powerful political moment where, as the working-class woman, she experiences the full violence of the patriarchy and, as the upper-class woman, she can talk about it in public.[43] This section of *Prisons and Prisoners* looks forward to Shoshana Felman's figuration of women's autobiography, wherein the author can only have access to her own 'story' through an act of reading. Felman writes: 'Trained to see ourselves as objects and to be positioned as the Other, estranged to ourselves, we have a story that by definition cannot be self-present to us, a story that, in other words, is not a story, but *must become* a story. And it cannot *become* a story except through the *story of the Other.*'[44] While this structure would be problematic for Jacobs, whose otherness is forced upon her and thereby threatens to silence her suffering, Lytton does gain 'access,' to use Felman's term, to her own autobiography and to her voice as representative only at the moment when she can read herself as other.[45] By placing Jane and Constance in a cell together, Lytton uses her dual identity as a privileged suffragette to disrupt the prison's attempt to isolate the prisoner from the public and thereby silence her outraged voice, while also disrupting the patriarchy's attempt to isolate the upper-class woman from the larger community of women and thereby silence her potential political force. Through an effective denial of her privilege, Lytton joins the suffragette community and can speak on their behalf.

This politically effective moment, where a community is formed despite the oppressive forces arrayed against it, is solidified by the writing of *Prisons and Prisoners* itself. According to Howlett, the generic duplication of narratives of forcible feeding demonstrates that 'the ordeal is not an isolated and isolating bodily experience but a point of identification and union between many women.'[46] Corbett takes this further; citing Michael Sandel, she argues that suffragettes refigure the self-contained individual as a more communal, 'intersubjective' construction, leading 'beyond an individualist paradigm for identity and toward a collectivist model.'[47] The production of texts becomes one of the central means of creating this collectivist suffragette identity. The repetition of the 'formulae' of narratives of imprisonment and forcible feeding, which Howlett discusses,[48] is a space for the construction of this multiple, fully participatory subjectivity.

With this use of text in mind, one can read Lytton's description of her attempted carving of 'Votes for Women' on her body as an intradiegetic representation of the act of writing *Prisons and Prisoners* itself. Lytton recognizes that the act of writing does more than allow her to join her fellow prisoners, and is more than a symbol for the movement. Her act reconstructs her own being as a function of the larger collective identity. This reconstruction of the ostensible autobiographer is emphasized by the author's signature – or rather the authors' signatures, for the book is co-authored by 'Constance Lytton and Jane Warton, Spinster.' The splitting of the author into both Constance and Jane serves the dual purpose of giving Jane a voice and of allowing Constance to speak as a member of the collective (while also removing both from a direct male influence, since 'Spinster' could describe either 'Constance Lytton' or 'Jane Warton'). This retooling of the traditional signature of the single author is also indicative of Lytton's and other suffragettes' communal reworking of the traditional autobiography. Comparing women's autobiographies in general to the male-dominated genre as a whole, Mary G. Mason makes the general case that

> the egoistic secular archetype that Rousseau handed down to his romantic brethren in his *Confessions*, shifting the dramatic presentation to an unfolding self-discovery where characters and events are little more than aspects of the author's evolving consciousness, finds no echo in women's writing about their lives. On the contrary ..., the self-discovery of female identity seems to acknowledge the real presence and recognition of another consciousness, and the disclosure of female self is linked to the identification of some 'other.' This recognition of another consciousness – and I emphasize recognition of rather than deference to – this grounding of identity through relation to the chosen other, seems ... to enable women to write openly about themselves.[49]

Somewhat revising the foundations of this argument, Lytton paradoxically embodies Mason's paradigm of a referential subjectivity by attempting to become the other through and, more importantly, *with* whom she identifies herself. In a way, Lytton's text can be seen as a reversal of Boethius's seminal prison autobiography, *The Consolation of Philosophy*. Rather than intellectually or spiritually renewing herself through reference to an ephemeral Lady Philosophy, Lytton instead secularly renews herself as a member of the suffragette collective through an identification with the embodied and tortured Jane Warton. Taking both Lytton's renewal and the repetitive nature of suffragette textual practice into account, Caren Kaplan's general reading (which relies on Harlow's discussion of women's prison writing) of this type of identification is especially pertinent. Writing that this identification is a subversion of the 'institution of literature,' she argues that '[o]ne form of subversion can be identified as the deconstruction of the individual bourgeois author (the sacred subject of autobiographical narrative) and the construction of a collective authorial entity – a kind of collective consciousness that "authorizes" and validates the identity of the individual writer.'[50] Lytton's passing and the dual authorship of the text can be seen as an engagement in the communal critique of the patriarchy and its tradition of autobiography, a tradition which, as Sidonie Smith and Rita Felski argue, is engaged in the reproduction of the type of individual which Thoreau lauds.[51] Lytton's text is a rewriting of Thoreau's prison transcendence, which recognizes others only in terms of their deference to him. Lytton's acts of writing on her body, of passing as Jane Warton, and of writing *Prisons and Prisoners* are means through which she attempts to transmute her privileged individual identity into membership in the suffragette collective identity.

4. Working Silence

Notwithstanding her text's potential for dissidence, however, the repetition of suffragette narrative in which Lytton engages – and the communal subjectivity that it represents – can reproduce the system of privilege, and the silencing of the voices of working-class suffragettes, that Lytton is attempting to escape. Drawing on the contemporary critiques of the WSPU by ex-member Teresa Billington-Grieg and others, Corbett states that dissidents 'charged that WSPU leaders exploited willing women by subjecting them to violence at the hands of the government, and then capitalized on their victimization for publicity's sake.'[52] Portraying the Pankhursts as commercially minded autocrats, Billington-Grieg complained that 'the WSPU had taken up revolution as a performance and appropriated the methodology of advertising culture ... thus mechanizing feminism.'[53] Billington-Grieg argues that such a reproduction of dominant forms of discourse may create a communal identity, but that identity is ultimately still subjugated to the ruling culture. In the process of this subjugation it is only the middle- and upper-class leaders of the WSPU autocracy who are allowed to speak.[54] Corbett writes that some working-class activists desired to have the opportunities of the middle-class women given 'to other women of their class, and not to promote a political ethic that would reinscribe women's cultural disposition to self-sacrifice.'[55] Within this reading of the suffragette movement, the mass reproduction of narratives of imprisonment and forced feeding, representative as they are of the violent acts perpetrated against the bodies of women, serve only to recreate that very violence for the benefit of those in positions of privilege, thus working against the members of the community that it purports to create and represent. The emphasis on similarity can fall into the trap of generalization and essentialism which underpins the discourse supporting the oppression of women and prisoners.

Despite her attempt to engage in a communal critique of patriarchy and privilege, Lytton's masquerade as a working-class woman, when combined with her stylized portrayal of forced feeding, may only succeed in further silencing the people whom she is attempting to represent. The scene of her first feeding, in which a disembodied Constance looks at the 'tortured,' embodied Jane Warton, could be interpreted as a duplication of the Enlightenment ontological hierarchy discussed by Sidonie Smith, in which the privileged members of society gain access to the 'universal,' disembodied transcendent self, while the unprivileged are embodied. Sue Thomas, indeed, reads this particular scene in exactly this way, using language that closely echoes Brombert's 'happy prison' motif, wherein prison authors portray the prison as a space that strengthens the authors' individual, transcendent freedom. Thomas writes that Lytton occupies the space of 'spectator of the violence,' which is here also the space 'of the transcendent spirit,' arguing that when 'Lytton tak[es] up the position of spectator of Warton's person there is a distancing of narcissistic libido from the body image and a refusal of the spirit to submit.'[56] Constance may read Jane in Felman's terms, but she is also writing her, subjecting the image of the working class to the violence that the upper-class woman literally stands above. Corbett does not take her argument this far, instead stating that Lytton's masquerade 'made her own point of view more authentically if not wholly representative.'[57] Such a reading of the representative nature of Lytton's passing can be supported by the fact that Lytton's book became an authoritative text that lower-class women used in their subsequent depictions of prison,[58] a conclusion further supported by the fact that Olive Schreiner dedicated *Woman and Labour* (1911) to Lytton.[59] Still, as Thomas's reading shows, such a representation can cut two ways, for the authenticity that Corbett lauds is tied to Lytton, thereby belying the 'representative' nature of her text by making it an authority that suppresses, rather than enables, the voices of working-class suffragettes and prisoners. Indeed, Regenia Gagnier sees such a suppression as a generic figure of working-class autobiographies that deal closely with gender. Writing about nineteenth-century British examples of these texts, Gagnier argues that, while their authors 'extensively adopted middle-class ideology' and '[a]lthough they attempt self-analysis,' still 'their experience cannot be analysed in the terms of their acculturation. This gap between ideology and experience leads not only to the disintegration of the narrative' but also 'to the disintegration of personality itself.'[60] The use of Lytton's text as a model by working-class suffragette prison authors could, according to Gagnier's theory of textual production, lead to the disintegration of the working-class voice.

There is a further tension created through the use of what Green refers to as 'spectacular feminism,' that is, the textual and visual displays – including parades – that the suffragettes used for their political ends. While the elision of difference by the autocracy of the Pankhursts and the authority of Lytton's text may reinscribe the silencing of working-class women, the emphasis on difference, which Billington-Grieg espouses, could have equally damaging effects, since prisons function along lines of alienation and isolation, denying any form of prison community or even communication. In this context, Howlett notes, '[d]ifference was deadly; to be different was to be isolated, both experientially and politically.'[61] Sidonie Smith sees such a dangerous difference as a possible result of the autobiographical strategy of 'self-fragmentation': '[S]hattering the old notion of the unitary individual in favor of the split and multiply fragmented subject may not always serve emancipatory objectives; rather it may serve further oppressive agendas.'[62] Suffragette prison writing, including Lytton's text, is locked into a conundrum where the elision of difference threatens to silence many women, but the emphasis on difference allows the continued destruction of feminist community, both of which, therefore, reproduce the ideological effects of the prison and the carceral city as a whole.

Lytton's prison narrative, I argue, is an attempt to discuss and effectively remove this difficulty. Her effort to do so does not lie in her ability to make her voice authentic but, rather, relies on a decentring of her own authenticity and on a construction of her identity in which 'Constance' is as equally an act as is 'Jane.' In order to make Jane representative of the working-class suffragette, *Prisons and Prisoners* must wash out the taint of privilege by erasing the identity of Constance. Mulvey-Roberts points to a similar movement throughout Lytton's life, in which she 'react[ed] against being a member of a family whose conspicuous display of wealth epitomised colonialism and aristocracy.'[63] However, rather than allowing Lytton, in Mulvey-Roberts's words, 'to go beyond empathy to an identification' with working-class women,[64] and rather than solely reproduce 'class difference through discriminatory gazes,'[65] *Prisons and Prisoners* instead lends Jane a voice by trying to remove that of Constance. Her inscription of the 'V' on her body was an early attempt at such an erasure, because this act of rewriting herself as a member of the larger suffragette community is, in some ways, a 'violent splitting of the subject of her autobiography,' which 'can better be read as violence against herself than against the object(s) of her mimicry,' the members of the working class.[66]

I would take this splitting one step further. In opposition to Mulvey-Roberts's Thoreauvian assertion that '[t]hrough incarceration the image [Lytton] held of her own imprisoned self could eventually be released,' I argue that Jane's ordeal gives her a voice, but results in the erasure of Constance.[67] The final three chapters of the text function to remove Lytton's claim to authorship and, indeed, to any form of action. Chapters XIV and XV, 'The Home Office' and 'The Conciliation Bill,' are composed primarily of quotations from newspapers, letters, and medical and governmental reports, with a large portion of the original text serving solely to introduce the other material. The last chapter, 'Holloway Prison Revisited: My Fourth Imprisonment,' offers much less detailed descriptions than the earlier prison chapters and ends with depictions of the actions of others. In addition, we learn that Lytton suffers a stroke and is partially paralysed, resulting in her inability to serve the WSPU physically: 'From that day to this I have been incapacitated for working for the Women's Social and Political Union, but I am with them still with my whole soul' (335). Lytton's emphasis on the words and actions of others and her portrayal of her stroke are placed at the end of the narrative not only for reasons of chronology, but also for the purpose of removing Constance Lytton's voice from the authoritative prominence of the narrative's conclusion. *Prisons and Prisoners* does engage in the communal project, but does not allow Constance's voice to become fully representative or determinative of that community. As Susan Stanford Friedman argues, 'In taking the power of words, of representation, into their own hands, women project onto history an identity that is not purely individualistic. Nor is it purely collective. Instead, this new identity merges the shared and the unique.'[68] Rather than reproducing through her class the ontological dominance and oppression of the masculine Enlightenment identity and the disciplinary practices involved with it, as Thoreau does, and rather that engaging in the removal from discourse that characterizes Wilde's and Jacobs's texts, Lytton uses *Prisons and Prisoners* to enact a dual movement of self-silencing and self-creation that allows for an engagement with a communal statement that works against the imprisoning discourses of the patriarchy. Lytton's shifting identity, then, provides my study of prison writing with another space of tension and instability, in turn providing an entry point for a critical analysis of the ontological basis of the carceral matrix. In so doing, she creates a political statement that attacks two of the visible oppressions of her society.

CHAPTER SIX

Frustrating Complicity in Breyten Breytenbach's *The True Confessions of an Albino Terrorist*

Breyten Breytenbach ends *The True Confessions of an Albino Terrorist* in a traditional way, by inscribing at the bottom of the last page the date and place of the composition of the work. While the text was physically composed after his release from the South African prisons where he was sent for his activities against the apartheid state, it draws on material and experiences from the period of his incarceration. The placement marker at the end of the text tells us that it was written in *'Pretoria / Pollsmoor / Palermo / Paris,'* and gives the date *'29 December 1983,'* Pretoria and Pollsmoor being locations of two prisons in which he was confined, and Paris his home both before and after prison.[1] The third place name, Palermo, needs a more detailed explication.

In a chapter of the *Confessions* entitled 'A Separate Section,' Breytenbach outlines and classifies those whom he calls 'the various tourists one meets in prison' (179). The first person he describes is Colonel Huntingdon, the chief investigator and interrogator involved with Breytenbach's case. In detailing the interrogations conducted by Huntingdon, Breytenbach writes:

> I am reminded of that Company of Whites which came into being in 1541 in Palermo, during the Inquisition, consisting of 'gentlemen and honourable persons,' who had the noble task of preparing the victim for the Great Step, convincing him by subtle or not so subtle (but infinitely absorbing) means of persuasion (or perversion) to willingly and liberatingly participate in the 'spectacle of justice.' For the just man to use base methods is an act of abnegation and purification, of becoming a blind tool in the hands of God. To preserve our security ...[2] (180)

Palermo, the third site of composition listed at the end of the *Confessions*, is constructed as the exemplary site of coercive interrogation and of a willing complicity, both of which are used to further the 'security' of the self-anointed divine state.[3] The interrogator *forces* the subject of the interrogation to comply *willingly*; thus, the security preserved by the interrogation is referred to with the plural and possessive first person, thereby embracing the interrogator, the interrogated, the readership, and society at large. This forced willingness is an oxymoron used ironically by Breytenbach at several points in the text. As J.M. Coetzee writes about a similar technique in some of Breytenbach's prison poems, 'Breytenbach the writer takes possession of the enemy's discourse for a purpose of his own, ... a grimly satiric one.'[4] However, the text also complicates the idea of a willing complicity with the oppressive forces that demand that cooperation. Like Lytton, Breytenbach shifts and decentres his identity in order to divest it of its connection to positions of privilege and to interrupt the social power structures based on that privilege. His consistently self-reflexive comments on this ungrounded and fragmented identity is the postmodern refraction of Thoreau's transcendent individual. Breytenbach's text goes even further than Lytton's in highlighting the dangers of such a decentring, which can lead to a duplication of the ontological basis of the alienating dominant culture. By examining the power dynamic between the investigator/interrogator and the investigated/interrogated, Breytenbach attempts to deconstruct the hierarchical assumptions lying behind the apartheid state. His work also calls into question, explicitly and otherwise, the concepts of individual will and of uncomplicated resistance in the face of oppressive force, providing another detailed analysis of the difficulties involved in attempting to work against the carceral functions of society – an analysis that, as I will argue, is, while rich and complex, not an unproblematic one. This effort adds another perspective on the reading of the relationship between Enlightenment constructions of the individual and the oppressive identificatory practices of the modern prison, while also detailing how those practices are enmeshed within the social framework, even existing within the relationships between author and reader.[5]

1. Classifying Prison

Breytenbach was born in 1939 in the small, predominantly Afrikaner town of Bonnievale in the Western Cape, an area that was generally strong in its support of the Nationalist government which instituted apartheid in 1948, a legalized and expanded version of the already extant racist segregation in all sectors of South African society, including the disenfranchisement of all non-whites.[6] Becoming one of the best known Afrikaner poets of his generation, Breytenbach moved to France in 1959 and was later married to a woman of Vietnamese descent. In part because such a 'mixed' marriage was a violation of South African law, Breytenbach was required to continue living in exile. In collusion with other white exiles, Breytenbach formed the resistance group Okhela, which may or may not have had ties to the African National Congress (ANC) – shortly after his release Breytenbach referred to Okhela as 'an unofficial offshoot of the ANC.'[7] During an illegal Okhela recruiting trip back to South Africa in 1975, Breytenbach was arrested under the Terrorism Act, and later sentenced to nine years in prison with no possibility of remission. He served seven years before being released by the government, which was under pressure from the French government to do so. His first few years in prison were served in solitary confinement. Hand in hand with his revolutionary attitude to the South African power structure, Breytenbach's politics were also at odds with his immediate family: in the *Confessions*, we are told that Breytenbach's eldest brother, Jan, was 'the commander of his country's crack anti-guerilla special unit, a brigadier-general, a trained (and enthusiastic) killer, be it with knife or gun, a "dirty tricks" expert for Military Intelligence'; his other brother was 'a reporter, fellow traveller of the Greys, with decidedly fascist sympathies' (67–8).[8]

Breytenbach's *Confessions* is an account of his life from the moment of his imprisonment through to his release in 1983. In an afterword to the *Confessions*, he states that the text, composed immediately after his release, 'took shape from the obsessive urge I experienced during the first weeks and months of my release to talk talk talk, to tell my story and all the other stories. It must have been rather horrible for him or her who happened to be victim to my vomiting' (337). He also writes here that '[i]t was my intention to produce a political text' (339). Like many of the other texts I have examined, his *Confessions* are designed to function in terms of both his personal life and the larger socio-political dynamic surrounding the author's imprisonment. Breytenbach's comment on his text states baldly the argument I put forward in relation to the other texts: that the personal and the political cannot be separated, that, as Wilde says of his letter, the prison narrative is written 'as much for your sake as for mine' (152). The *Confessions* explores the way in which the representation of personal identity can be used polit-ically. Breytenbach's text goes beyond the depiction of a rebellious identity to show how one who is either actively or passively *complicit* in the oppressive power structure represented by the prison can use that complicity to undermine and deconstruct the structures support-ing that oppression. Breytenbach's analysis of his own status as an Afrikaner, when paired to his status as a convicted traitor, is an attempt to frustrate the taxonomies which the apartheid regime used in order to 'transmit itself unimpaired to posterity' (Thoreau, 'Civil,' 63).

Much of the text is dedicated to describing or defining the power structure of the South African state as it existed during Breytenbach's time in prison. For him, the structure of the prison system itself is a synecdoche for the state: 'At the heart of the South African prison sys-tem is the denial of the humanity of "the other," and in that it is only a reflection of the larger South African cosmos' (273). An examination of the structures of South African prisons brings to the surface one of the aspects of the bigoted ontological assumptions of those in other coun-tries – that of race. As in the United States, prisons were used in apart-heid South Africa not only as a means of attempting to silence political dissent, but also to criminalize and demonize those who do not 'belong' to the dominant culture. Describing the horror of the ritualis-tic violence of prison society, Breytenbach states, 'I'm telling you that what I'm describing is *typical* of that mirror which the South African penal universe holds up to the Apartheid society – and that it is *inevita-ble*' (273). Sloop makes a connection between larger cultural assump-tions about race and the segregation-era American prison's place within them that echoes Breytenbach's depiction: 'When a majority of redeemable males are depicted as Caucasian and a majority of im-moral and irrational inmates are represented as "other," we have a subtle cultural morality in which particular prisoners ... are considered naturally, and perhaps permanently, inhuman. Indeed, one can per-haps safely assume that such identifying characteristics were wide-spread throughout the culture during this period.'[9] While the dominant cultural morality of apartheid South Africa functioned on less than subtle levels, Sloop's equation of the criminalization and irre-deemability of the racial 'other' and the larger cultural paradigms holds true. Not only do the systemic horrors of prison exist as reflec-tions of the larger system of oppression, but that oppression also inexo-rably leads to those horrors.

The penal and apartheid systems are defined by Breytenbach in terms of the oppressive hierarchies and taxonomies that they create and through which they function. Both apartheid and the legal-penological system supporting it function by classifying people and placing them in relation to the power structure according to those classifications. As Oliver Lovesay notes in reference to the *Confessions*, 'Prison language emphasizes abusive categories ... Breytenbach ... demonstrates how this penchant for categories ... mimics the structure of apartheid.'[10] Like the apartheid state, the prisons were set up along white and non-white lines, with the non-whites being further split formally into Africans, Coloureds, and Asians (or Indians), and the whites being informally divided, according to Breytenbach, into those who speak Afrikaans as their first language and those who speak primarily English. These divisions are then accorded certain power and privilege within the system, with Afrikaners being the most privileged, and Africans being the least privileged. Taking the classification of prisoners which began in the early twentieth century to its absurd, violent, and racist extreme, the South African prisons and the apartheid system bluntly highlight the ideological use of punishment as a means of reinforcing the cultural assumptions about, and maintaining the material distinctions between, groups of people.[11]

Breytenbach points out, though, that this racial division is only the most obvious of the classificatory divisions of the prison system. The individual prisoner is also divided into various parts, of which race is one. At various points in the *Confessions*, Breytenbach describes the process as one through which his outside identity is stripped away and replaced with a highly ordered prison identity. At the end of the first section of the book, for example, he writes of his entering into the prison in Pretoria:

> My hosts weren't violent in any way. Why should they be? I was dead. All they had to do was to process the dead, to pick over the bones. They weren't particularly interested. Again I had to go through the procedure of stripping and then I was counted: that is, all my possessions were itemized and these were then carefully noted in red ink on a large sheet of paper ... [A]s we arrive at the end of this first talk, permit me to give you a brief extract of what I consisted of as written down on this sheet of paper. (21)

Breytenbach then goes on to give a list over a page-and-a-half long, consisting of fifty-seven items (some with additional commentary), ranging from airline tickets to coins to such inconsequential objects as a box of matches and three glass bangles. After reproducing this list, Breytenbach writes: 'There you see me, Mr. Investigator, in all my naked glory, with all my possessions around me, as I stand that first evening. *Ecce homo*' (23). Addressing himself to the quasi-mythical 'Mr. Investigator,' whom the author figures in the second person (a strategy I further discuss below), in the place of the reader, Breytenbach equates the reader's perusal of the list with a vision of Breytenbach himself – '*There* you see me.' Breytenbach becomes, or rather is forced to become, a being identified solely by his position within the taxonomies of the prison and the totalitarian state.

That this reformulation of Breytenbach's identity is more than a simple bureaucratic utility is made apparent in the first of what are called 'inserts' in the *Confessions*. These inserts are usually written as post-prison, philosophical reflections or tangential meditations on Breytenbach's period of imprisonment and how it affects his newfound freedom. In the first insert, Breytenbach details the effects of his taxonomical redefinition. He describes his need to buy a pipe when he was in South Africa 'undercover,' even though it may give away his 'true' identity:

> I thought I'd be clever, I thought I'd leave it in my suitcase to smoke it only in the secret of my hotel room. And of course they dug it up at the airport and they had me hold it and they recognized my way of fondling the pipe as someone else might have recognized my way of handling a pen or my way of stuttering into a tape recorder ... What fastidious workers they are, how obsessed they must be! Look how they dig into one's past, how they project one's future, how they alter one's present. I have no private lives: it's all in their hands; they know the I better than I do, they are far more interested in it than I am. They have the files, they have the computer. Or they know all about my ways, my preferences, my accretions, my little secrets – my gardens – be they political or sexual. And they are fascinated by it. They smell it like freshly mixed tobacco. They knead it. They manipulate it, they slobber over it. (25)

Seemingly inconsequential objects, such as the pipe and tobacco, are used by the security police as clues to re-identify 'Christian Galaska' as Breyten Breytenbach. These objects are perceived to be attached solely to Breytenbach, to be almost a priori parts of his being. The items are then used, along with a plethora of other objects and characterizations, as a way of forcing the person now identified as Breytenbach into being a creature defined solely by his relationship with the security forces and the prison. He becomes the list of items that the authorities write under his name, as symbolized by his metaphorical identification with – or to state it more strongly, his *becoming* – the pipe tobacco in the final lines of the passage. Breytenbach's description highlights the continuation of Thoreau's connection between property, alienation, and prison. As in the process Thoreau describes, Breytenbach's identity is erased, replaced instead solely by his relation to society as figured in his possessions. Breytenbach concedes this reformation of his identity when he states that he has 'no private lives: it's all in their hands; they know the I better than I do,' and that 'There is no "I," there is no name, there is no identity' (25), echoing Wilde's statement in his prison text that he 'had no name at all' while incarcerated (182–3). This statement about an absence of identity is emphasized by Breytenbach's reference to himself as being 'dead' (21). His attempted construction of an absent identity is not, here, the positive space away from public determinations that Wilde tries to create. Rather, his supposed lack of an 'I' is bemoaned as the loss of privacy, of a self-referential identification in the face of a public knowledge of his habits. His identity becomes subject to the police, and the reader, who not only seem to 'knead' it into the shape they desire, but who also 'need' to reform it for their own purposes, since, in turn, '[i]t justifies their lives ...' (25).

Breytenbach also uses the image of his own death as a means of portraying an endlessly fragmented subject in *A Season in Paradise*, first published while he was in prison. The book opens with a description of his childhood, a time during which he 'had the annoying habit of dropping dead now and then.'[12] The rendering of all of these deaths, sometimes given in horrific detail, can be read as an earlier representation of the multiple and un-self-referential subjectivity that Breytenbach continues to describe in the *Confessions* and elsewhere. His most recent autobiographical prose work, *Dog Heart: A Memoir*, begins with the sentence 'To cut a long story short: I am dead,' and continues with a description of the author's lack of control over his identity: 'Do you think I'm joking? Am I not lurking behind these rustling words – perhaps a little thicker around the waist, a little darker in the mind? ... But no, when I look into the mirror I know that the child born here is dead.'[13] The self-referential text, the supposed mirror that the writer holds up to himself, represents only a cancellation of the identity it purports to represent. Writing becomes 'an after-death activity.'[14] As Reckwitz notes about *A Season in Paradise*, 'The grotesquely bizarre childhood reminiscence ... becomes an indexical sign pointing ... to a fragmented, deeply disturbed memory of the I speaking. Breytenbach, when looking at himself in the mirror of his reminiscences, is unable to experience childhood as an intact, meaningful whole.'[15] In the *Confessions*, the use of this trope of fragmentation demonstrates, I argue, that for Breytenbach there can be no self-contained, or even self-knowledgeable, individual in the police state. The 'I' becomes completely subject to the panoptic surveillance of the regime's classificatory system, in a reversal of Thoreau's meditations on the futility of imprisonment. The passages about death and fragmentation in Breytenbach's texts can lead to the conclusion that he sees no space of transcendence, privacy, or tension that can be used against the carceral forces, as, to varying degrees, do the other authors studied here. In Breytenbach's work, however, it seems as if there is only a death of the individual self in the face of panoptic scrutiny and determination.

This rather bleak vision is reinforced at several points in the *Confessions*, specifically in the sections that deal with daily prison life. In a chapter entitled 'I am the Plague,' Breytenbach describes his immediately pre-prison position in terms of a puzzle: 'Everything was coming to a close; the various pieces of the jigsaw puzzle were being fitted together and, perhaps fatalistically, I felt that it was no longer possible to fit the odd-shaped blank piece that I am into any other hole than the one that seemed to be preordained for it' (117). Breytenbach's identity as fragmented *tabula rasa* is, under the strict surveillance of the police, rapidly being re-formed and filled in by others, outside of his control. Further examples of the way in which Breytenbach is redefined by the state are more blunt: in prison '[y]ou forget perhaps that you were then [in the past] a different person, that you have become that entity which inhabits this time which consists of clearly defined patterns, repetitions, the same again and again and again. You yourself are purified or reduced to some other personality' (143). Rather than allow the prisoner to reconstitute a more 'proper' identity through self-reflection, prison, as portrayed here, changes the identity of the prisoner through the constant repetition of patterns, just as in Wilde's depiction of prison the archetypical prisoner becomes an embodiment of repetition itself. Breytenbach elaborates on this subjugation in the following passages describing his 'booking in':

You are issued now with your prison identity. In normal circumstances your booking in takes place in the reception office ... The initiation consists of one being fingerprinted and one's complete physical description being entered in a really gigantic book looking like the ledger one imagines St Peter – or whoever keeps the records in Heaven – has ready for all us sinners on earth. Literally every birthmark or scar must be written down ...

These books then – because there also has to be one for your private possessions – were dragged up to the office in C-Section, and I was born. As prisoner 436/75. (126, 128)

The lengthy description of this process refers to a change in identity forced on one by the system, a change that is intimately related to the taxonomical and inventory-like textual creation of the prisoner and his possessions. Breytenbach heightens the sense of alienation that is enacted in this recreation of identity by referring to his own experiences in the second and third person only until we are told, '*I* was born. As prisoner 436/75.' The experiences he describes himself going through, both when he enters the prison and when he becomes acclimatized to its rhythms, are displaced into the second and third person because of the creation of the second self that is not 'Breytenbach' or even 'Galaska,' but is instead '436/75' – a number that only has meaning within the categories and walls of the prison. O'Connor describes a similar use of the second person by prisoners which, unlike King's use of second-person address, is not so much an attempt to create a solidarity with the reader as it is a prison narrator's attempt to distance him- or herself 'by dropping the "I" and using a "you" that indicates the self as generically or commonly like others in that position.'[16]

Mouroir: Mirrornotes of a Novel, a series of loosely interconnected stories and fragments that Breytenbach wrote while in prison, contains a piece that satirizes the fragmented subjection that is recreated through the prison and the carceral society as a whole (indeed, the fragmented nature of this collection/novel/anti-novel mimics the fracturing of the self). 'The Man with the Head' begins like a fairy tale by describing a nameless protagonist: 'There was a man, whether from Japhet or from Novgorod I do not know; and he was very sad. *Pee-too-wee! Pee-too-wee!* the man said out of sadness ... and *pee-too-wee* he groaned again dejectedly for there was no gaol in his country. That is why he was so sad.'[17] The silence surrounding the name of the man would seem, as Hans-Georg Golz suggests, to fulfil a fairy-tale function of creating an everyman, lending to the work an 'aspect of universality.'[18] The confusion about the name of his country, however, points to another function of the silence. Without a jail, the man and, indeed, the whole country lack cohesive identity. This lack is emphasized in the story immediately following the above introduction:

> There were old people and there was no prison to put them in; there were fat people and clever people and people with glasses and knotty veins and half dead people and some all humid with cancer and property owners and people with skirts and corns and real people and nowhere a gaol to lock them up. There weren't any black people in his country but nevertheless not even the smallest or cheapest little old gaol or boop or slammer or *calabuso* or *ballon* or clink or *taule* or cooler wherever and however to keep them separated. *Pee-too-wee* the man sighed ...[19]

The lack of a prison results in the country's inability to separate and therefore distinguish between groups of people and even individuals. The commentary on apartheid is clear: rather than keep pre-existing classifications of people apart, apartheid (and the legal and penological systems supporting it) is the force that creates the hierarchical social distinctions. Echoing Wilde's statement in 'The Soul of Man Under Socialism' that '[w]hen there is no punishment at all, crime will either cease to exist, or, if it occurs, will be treated by physicians as a very distressing form of dementia, to be cured by care and kindness,'[20] Breytenbach implies that without the institutions and apparatuses in place that enforce social distinctions, such classifications would seem ridiculous (as they do in this story). The function of the prison as codifier is also highlighted in the satiric representation of its own codification, through the multiple names ascribed to it. 'The Man with the Head' takes this social critique to its satiric limit when the man's own face falls off and starts arguing with the rest of his body, resulting in the man's misrecognition around town.

2. Breaking Down the Prison

The panicked nature of this hyper-classification and re-identification exists, as Judith Butler says about heterosexuality, to hide the fact that the power of the state 'is perpetually at risk, that is, that it "knows" its own possibility of becoming undone.'[21] The ongoing necessity to re-classify, re-identify, and re-categorize each person that is perceived as some form of social threat belies the fear of the possibility that those people may in and of themselves, aside from any act associated with them, point out some weakness inherent in the power structure. Jolly notes the first stage of this dynamic, stating that in the *Confessions* 'Breytenbach points out that, paradoxically in view of their overwhelming power, the interrogators are dependent upon the prisoner to justify their existence. More specifically, they are dependent upon the success of their efforts to force the prisoner to conform to their image of who he is' (63). Beyond this, Breytenbach demonstrates at several points in the text precisely how the state's oppressive structure begins to fall apart on its own terms, showing what happens when the prisoner does not or will not 'conform to their image of who he is.'

One of the allusions Breytenbach uses to portray the sense of collapse arising from the prison's dependence on the prisoner is to the tale of the labyrinth and the Minotaur. Recurring throughout the *Confessions* and *Mouroir*, this allusion highlights the prison officials' paradoxical reliance on the prisoner for their existence and power. The story of the Minotaur, as it is told in Ovid's *Metamorphoses*, is threefold: Pasiphae, the wife of Minos, the king of Crete, has sex with a bull and gives birth to a half-bull/half-man; Minos, in order to hide the fact of his wife's infidelity, has Daedalus construct a labyrinth in which the Minotaur is hidden; after several others fail, Theseus negotiates the labyrinth and kills the Minotaur.[22] For Breytenbach, the story of the nearly non-negotiable maze and the despised creature in it parallels the experience of the prisoner. Breytenbach reinterprets the myth, however, emphasizing the prisoner's power over the officials who inhabit the maze with him. In the section of *Mouroir* titled 'The Double Dying of an Ordinary Criminal,' the site of execution is described in terms of the Minotaur story: 'In our time the place of execution is a privileged one, where it is dark, behind walls, in the heart of the labyrinth. Few people know when the seeker has found it. It is there like some bashful god, like the blind and deaf and self-satisfied idol of a tiny group of initiates, for the satisfaction of an obscure tradition.'[23] In this description, the Minotaur is not the prisoner, but the gallows itself, which functions only in terms of the 'traditions' of the officials who worship it. The gallows is both the space of ignorance for the officials and the space of freedom for the prisoner. The 'last route' for the prisoner, we are told, is 'secure and actually no longer part of the personal hell' of the deadening routine of prison life.[24]

This 'gallows freedom' is obviously problematic: like Harriet Jacobs's use of suffering as a means of removing herself from the judgment of others, finding freedom in death is bittersweet at best, and claiming that to be executed is really a form of gaining such freedom conjures the spectre of a justification of the prison methods or an unwitting acceptance of the prison state's methods of brutalization. In the *Confessions*, Breytenbach highlights the complexity of this space by again using the figure of the Minotaur:

> When first I came out of prison I was thrown into emptiness and I found all space around me cluttered. For so long had I been conditioned to the simplification of four walls, the square of a barred window, a double square door, a square bed, emptiness, nowhere to hide the smallest illegal object, ... nowhere to hide your anguish: all these had been erased by being apparent. So that when I found myself ejected into what *you* would consider to be the normal world, I found it terribly confusing ... Freedom is the minotaur outside the walls. (26–7)

The space of freedom, the 'normal world,' is depicted as cluttered and confusing. Nothing seems to be in the 'proper' relation to anything else. Summarizing this confusion in the phrase 'Freedom is the minotaur outside the walls,' Breytenbach, as in 'The Man with the Head,' defines the social world in terms of its own use of definitions. The 'minotaur outside the walls' is an ironic oxymoron, since the Minotaur and the labyrinth surrounding it only exist in terms of each other – when Theseus completes the maze, the Minotaur dies, and vice versa. And it must be remembered that the freedom Breytenbach is describing here is not only that of the 'ex-prisoner,' but also that of '*you*,' the reader; it is the 'normal world.' Freedom, Breytenbach suggests, relies upon its removal, through the means of prison. Davis defines a similar function of incarceration in the racialized matrix of US society, writing that 'white men acquired the privilege to be punished in ways that acknowledged their equality and the racialized universality of liberty.'[25] The parallel between Davis's and Breytenbach's conception of freedom as reliant on its opposite (with both writers arguing in terms of a heavily racialized society) could mean that Breytenbach inadvertently emphasizes the supposedly positive function of the prison as a means of teaching members of the dominant society the 'true' meaning of freedom, as it does for Thoreau. However, in opposition to the normative perception of this relationship, which Davis describes and Thoreau enacts, Breytenbach does not use the negative valuation of incarceration to highlight the positive aspects of freedom, but instead uses the prison to show the illusory nature of freedom. Thus, the distinction that the power structure draws between prisoners and non-prisoners, the non-normative and the normative, is at best overstated. This does not only mean, however, that the status quo power relations are even textually or personally threatened or reversed, because Breytenbach's own long-awaited freedom becomes confused and 'cluttered' as well. The danger of the justification of prison methods is turned in on itself, becoming instead a damnation of the supposed freedom of the outside world.

This perpetually enacted and repressed collapse of the social structure is, of course, especially apparent in the categories that the apartheid state imposes on racial identity. In discussing the effects of apartheid on South African literature, André Brink writes that 'contextually the binarities persisted in the tendency to reduce the world to predictable patterns of us and them, black and white, good and bad, male and female.'[26] Breytenbach's portrayal of the penal system's attempt to inscribe forcibly the racial binary of 'black and white' shows how such 'reductions' seem always to be under threat. Again, during a discussion of the cataloguing and categorizing that takes place upon one's entrance into prison, Breytenbach notes:

> Sometimes there is confusion, particularly in the Cape, over whether a prisoner should be considered as White or Brown. I've known people who've done time both as Brown prisoners and as Whites ... There was also the case of one man being booked and nobody being able to make out where he should be shunted off to. Until the sergeant in charge shouted in his frustration, 'Now tell us what the hell you are – Black or White?' And the man answered, 'But of course I'm White, my *baas*.' (127)

As Nelson Mandela writes in his autobiography detailing the anti-apartheid struggle, *baas* is 'the Afrikaans word for boss or master, [and] signifies subservience,'[27] so claiming the status of whiteness while simultaneously using the word '*baas*' is a linguistic mimicry of the slippage between black and white (as those categories are figured through power differentials), pointing to the differences in power between the two. Seen from outside of the hegemonic control of the state, difficulties in classification like this would seem to call for the abandonment of the taxonomical structure. But such a removal of vision is impossible for the prisoner and, seen as part of the larger system of racial and social oppression, these difficulties can only form a 'frustration' that opens up the possibility for the violent silencing of that particular problem. While these moments of discord may provide a chance for positive transformation, then, they go for the most part unheard. Breytenbach writes:

> The danger then comes from the internal conflicts they [the security police] have to struggle with. The dichotomy is between doing what they have been conditioned to do unquestioningly and the leftover feelings of humane compassion, and – as they are not mentally or culturally equipped to resolve these contradictions or even to recognize them – they tend to become very violent in an unconscious effort to blot out and perhaps to surpass the uneasiness. However strange it may sound ... I am convinced that some of the people they have killed in detention probably died when the interrogator was in a paroxysm of unresolved frustrations, even that the interrogator killed in an awkward expression of love and sympathy for a fellow human being. (50)

The moment when the system begins to break down around its enforcers is also the moment of its ultimate reinforcement through the final silencing of the dissenting, problematic being; again, we are confronted with the problem of 'gallows freedom.' The guard silences at the moment when his *own* identity is threatened by the contradictions surrounding him. His frustration arises, according to Breytenbach, from 'the internal conflict' that in turn arises from the state-sanctioned external situation. In order to resolve his own conflict, he ends the external one, by killing.

Not all South African prison writers feel that 'internal conflicts' were the reason behind any of the violence of the Security Police. Prisoners of all races in South Africa have described their torture at the hands of uncaring and simply sadistic police officers. Ruth First, a leader in the South African Communist Party who was killed in 1982, wrote of the Security Branch's officers: '[T]hey tell themselves, they are only doing their duty. They all talked like little Eichmanns. There was rarely a Security Branch detective who did not say: "It's the law, we're only doing our job." This is the danger. Like Eichmann they will do anything in the name of their job. They will be answerable for nothing. Torture itself becomes no more than the pursuit of their daily routine.'[28] Likewise, Molefe Pheto goes to great lengths to document his own torture during interrogation, dedicating much of his *And Night Fell: Memoirs of a Political Prisoner in South Africa* to describing the cruelty of the Security Branch, regular police, and prison guards, writing that one torture session stopped only because the man who beat him 'was tired.'[29] Hugh Lewin recounts his own severe beatings, and the sounds of other prisoners being tortured and killed. At one point, while describing his own torture, he writes that a Security Branch officer 'came in, looking for the towel hanging behind the door. He needed it to wipe his hands; his fists were full of blood ..., he said, "that Harris – another one who said he wouldn't talk without a lawyer." Wiping the blood off his fist, and laughing. The other two laughed too.'[30] Indres Naidoo similarly describes police laughter during his own and others' brutal torture.[31]

In these accounts and others too numerous to list, the internally conflicted interrogator which Breytenbach describes is absent, replaced instead with willing and energetic torturers, who are sadistic even to the point of, in Dingake's words, 'foaming at the mouth.'[32] Breytenbach's account simultaneously seems to rationalize the brutality of the interrogators, while trying to show the impossible position in which their oppressive system has put them. This could be dismissed as an attempt, conscious or not, by Breytenbach as a white South African and an Afrikaner to explain away the brutality of members of his own community. But such a rash dismissal would ignore Breytenbach's own actions against the apartheid regime and would risk denying his own suffering at their hands while in prison. In order for one to understand this portrayal, Breytenbach's own depiction of his conflicted identity as an 'albino terrorist,' as a privileged prisoner, needs to be examined.

3. Frustrating Complicity

It is the moment of frustration, of the simultaneous collapse and rebuilding of the oppressive situation, that Breytenbach portrays through his self-description in *The True Confessions of An Albino Terrorist*. Breytenbach, as he constructs himself in the text, exists in the blind spot of apartheid South African society: the anti-apartheid Afrikaner, the 'albino terrorist.' He becomes a hyper-classified subject who cannot be slotted into any one of the categories supplied by the prison state. As David Schalkwyk writes, 'To be a self-acknowledged "terrorist" is both to distance oneself from the values of white South Africa and to accept its pejorative categorizations: to call oneself an "albino" terrorist is to forgo inclusion within the affirmative community of struggle politics, to insist on an intrinsic abnormality.'[33] Breytenbach was not without models for this tense position, though; indeed, he was not the only, or even best known, Afrikaner to fight against the bigoted state. Bram Fischer, the lawyer who defended Nelson Mandela and others at the Rivonia trial, who was himself later sentenced to life imprisonment and died while under house arrest, also recognized the difficulty of being both an Afrikaner and an anti-apartheid activist. In his statement from the dock, Fischer noted: 'It was to keep faith with all those dispossessed by apartheid that I broke my undertaking to the court, separated myself from my family, pretended I was someone else, and accepted the life of a fugitive.'[34] Mandela expands on the alienation from his own community that Fischer endured because of his political beliefs: 'No matter what I suffered in my pursuit of freedom, I always took strength from the fact that I was fighting with and for my own people. Bram was a free man who fought against his own people for the freedom of others.'[35]

Demonstrating the ways in which this disparity between cultural and political identification can result in a split perception of a person's identity, Breytenbach's text shows how his affiliations are too multiple to allow a simple reduction to 'enemy of the state,' despite the attempts to categorize him within the existing system. Jolly writes:

> Breytenbach represents a failure in the discursive politics of 'self' and 'other,' because the Afrikaner nationalist rhetoric structured around those poles fails to account for his subjectivity as it is demonstrated by his actions. According to this rhetoric's definition of self and other, he represents the impossible, for he represents both 'self' and 'other'; he is Afrikaner by 'virtue' of his birth and poetic talent; yet his political allegiances render him a traitor.[36]

Jolly reads this impossible definition of self as an attempt by Breytenbach to limit or halt 'the violation' of his identity by others. He does so, she writes, through his constant denial of complete self-knowledge, and through a denial of the possibility of objectively knowing the truth or truths behind his experiences, leading to her conclusion that his writings constitute 'a complex and vital act of self-defense.'[37] In discussing *Mouroir*, Jolly quotes Cixous: '"Being several and insubordinable, the subject can resist subjugation" ... Paradoxically, then, the autonomy of the subject – its power to resist violation – lies in the destabilization, not the assertion, of the concept of the unified subject.'[38]

The 'both/and' nature of Breytenbach's identity as an 'albino terrorist' is more complex than even Jolly's excellent reading allows. The entirety of the *Confessions* is addressed to an ephemeral figure who is named, variously, 'Mr. Investigator,' 'Mr. Interrogator,' 'Mr. Investerrogator,' 'Mr. Confessor,' 'Mr. Eye,' and 'Mr. I.' This multiple naming reflects the multiple identities ascribed to this figure, who shifts between races, between political allegiances, and, since the book is sometimes addressed to Breytenbach's wife, between genders. Schalkwyk makes this explicit, stating that the addressee is 'a continually displaced confessor, who is constituted variously (if we follow the grammar of the address where it leads) as the reader, Breytenbach's wife, his alter ego, his Security Police interrogators, a Supreme Court Judge, and the black South African activists who dismiss Breytenbach for being a naive and expedient sell-out.'[39] All of these categories lead back to Schalkwyk's first construction, that the Mr Investigator figure functions to represent Breytenbach's unseen reader.

That the *Confessions* is addressed to this figure functions both to undermine the interrogator/interrogated relationship that structures Breytenbach's life in prison and to replicate it. In reproducing that relationship, he not only illustrates its complexity and its centrality to everyday life; he also represents it as inescapable.[40] In fact, his attempt to undermine this particular power dynamic is intimately tied to his reproduction of it. Like Thoreau's text, the *Confessions* is caught in a matrix of rebelling against and reproducing the basic ontology lying behind the oppressive State. The attempted undermining takes place through the portrayal of the moment of frustration that arises when the system is confronted by its own 'internal conflicts' of identity, the moment when the system's categorizations appear to begin to break down around themselves. Breytenbach demonstrates how the police and the interrogators went to great lengths to classify him, to make him fit into their world view as an enemy. One final example of this, from near the beginning of the book, highlights it well:

> Indeed, it's clear that the political police were making me out to be a terrorist in the minds of those with whom I had been in contact. You feel like laughing, Mr. Investigator? You splatter. What? Am I not a terrorist then? No, no, no, don't get me wrong, I'm not denying that. I've accepted it. *Mea culpa*. (I am guilty in any event. All that's still lacking is the crime to fit the guilt. I'm sure you can help me there, Mr. Eye.) I was accused of being a terrorist, I was brought before the courts in terms of the Terrorism Act, I was convicted of being one, I was sentenced as a terrorist, on my jail ticket where it asked 'sentence or crime' it was written, carefully, 'terror-

ism'; therefore, because this is the way we do things in No Man's Land, therefore I am indeed a terrorist. (38)

Mr Investigator, supported by his mirror image, the all-seeing, panoptic Mr Eye, laughs when Breytenbach suggests that he is not a terrorist because, within the classification system of the apartheid state, Breytenbach is a terrorist whether he committed acts of terrorism or not. This function of the police and judiciary systems can be read in general, as Jeremy Tambling notes of inquisition and confession, as a 'desire to close the gap between law and Law – to give an absolute status to standards otherwise arbitrarily held and believed in and enforced.'[41] Breytenbach is inscribed, therefore he is.

Breytenbach goes to great lengths, however, to show how he is complicit in this categorization of himself, how he and Mr Investigator are one, and how the moment of frustration for the system is also a moment where he himself is frustrated. As he says in the appendix to the text, 'It was not my intention to take revenge on a system or on certain people – at least, I don't think it was. We are too closely linked for that' (339). And, at the beginning of the text, Breytenbach describes the manner in which the *Confessions* was composed (basically, he spoke the text into a tape recorder):

> Isn't that the whole process of our being, this looking for a name? And then, this same process is an open-ended one; I can hear the echoes. As it continues – this jumbletalk, this trial – I can go on searching, and I can hear the reverberation of my own voice. I'm sitting here – I have this little instrument in my hand; I have the earphones on my head and I speak to you and I listen to the voice coming back. And I learn from these words the reality as it is being presented at the moment of emitting the sounds. That is perhaps as close as I can come to what the identity is considered to be. That is as close as I come to the truth. Here I am. Here the truth is also. I hope, Mr. Investigator, that that is what you expect of me. (13)

The intimate tie that Breytenbach talks about in the appendix is here, at the very beginning of the text, an impossible knot of frustrating utterances – Breytenbach is speaking to Mr Investigator and hearing the words himself, begging the observation that he and this Mr I are one and the same. Indeed, as a white South African, Breytenbach *is* Mr Investigator (as an image of the *investigating* power structure at the time of Breytenbach's imprisonment and at the time of the text's composition). The self-directed nature of his discussion also mimics the arbitrary nature of the Nationalists' justification of apartheid, which creates the distinctions between races by enacting them. As a 'terrorist,' however, he is the non-I, the 'Other' that the Afrikaner Investigator must silence. For Breytenbach, the moment of complete identification, of ultimate complicity, is also the moment that Mr Investigator and the apartheid state's taxonomical system breaks down. He writes: '[T]he System is historically defined and conditioned, and the people come like words from the belly of the System. It cannot change by itself. It is structurally impossible for those who are bred from it to modify the System significantly from within. The *structure* must be shattered by violence. And violence will be blind' (239). The violence needed to tear down the structures of oppression must come from the outside – it must be the 'other' which forces itself into the system in order to disrupt it. By showing how the 'other' is at the same time the 'self,' and how absolute truth and a definable identity are always deferred, Breytenbach attempts to undermine the assumptions that support the deterministic system.

The Mr Investigator figure, however, is at times referred to as being black. The most prominent example of this occurs at the end of the chapter entitled 'Up, Up and Away': 'We must launch a dialogue. I must warn you that the system by which we're trying to replace the present one will grind us down, *me and you*, as inexorably. I must tell you that I cannot hold my criticism, my disaffection, in abeyance; that I cannot condone your (our) agreements and compromises – not even tactically. I love you too bitterly for that. I hear you chuckling, you who are Black' (260). By positing a black person in the reader's / Mr Investigator's position, Breytenbach envisions a post-apartheid social structure. He does not construct this as an ideal social existence, as the completely positive end to the search for justice in South Africa. Breytenbach states instead that the future state must also avoid falling into dichotomies and biased taxonomical structures – a statement he once again supports through the use of the Minotaur: 'I have seen you as the Minotaur, which is the I, which does not exist since it is a myth ... I see you now as my dark mirror-brother. We need to talk, brother I' (260). Breytenbach again uses notions of both identification and complicity (through the Minotaur, yes, and also through '*me and you*' combined with 'which is the I, which does not exist'), this time in order to point out possible future injustice. Notably, both during and after the ANC's rise to power, Breytenbach retained what he called a position of 'principled criticism'[42] – that is, a critical position balanced with obvious joy at the overthrow of the apartheid state and by a respect for Mandela and his aspirations for South Africa.[43]

The systemic collapse of totalitarian structures that Breytenbach attempts to portray comes at a price, for he must give up the illusion of being the completely non-complicit, non-frustrated revolutionary. This renunciation disrupts the traditional position of the confessing figure who attempts 'to stand as an authoritative producer of "truth,"'[44] as Thoreau does. Breytenbach calls his own authority and abilities into question as the passage about the violent disruption of the system continues:

> And violence will be blind because its eyes will be useless from the despair of having seen too much ... of never having truly seen anything at all ... The land shall belong to no one. Not even to the deads. What then? You must go on, even if you lose yourself along the way. I do not know whether what I aim for will be any better but I do know that this is unacceptable and that it will have to be destroyed to make it possible for the *other* – maybe better – to take its place. And I know I am lazy ... my knees are weak ... I genuflect so easily ... The temptation is to remain in the labyrinth which finally offers the security of the known. I have unceasingly to pull myself up by the bootstraps. My arms get tired from pretending to be wings. (239–40)

While trying to retain a recognition of the necessity to overthrow the oppressive police state that was the Nationalist government, Breytenbach simultaneously creates a position for himself that denies his very ability to revolt. As he says later, with a note more of despair than of aggrieved humbleness, 'I had to purge myself ... If I say "purge" it may imply that there are events – that I myself have done things – which are improper, which I ought to be ashamed of. It is true: I am not a hero; I am not even a revolutionary' (337). While I agree with Jolly that the *Confessions* 'depends upon a representation of subjectivity that dislocates, rather than locates, identity,'[45] I believe that she does not fully address the problematic nature of the rebellion/complicity relationship when she writes:, 'The narrative attempts to represent the intersubjective relationships that it investigates – the alignments of subjectivity around the poles of self and other – as reflections, not complete identifications, of one another.'[46] Despite seeing the identity Breytenbach constructs in his text as a 'dislocation' of autonomous notions of individuality, Jolly still reads that identity as, to a certain degree, self-contained and whole. She writes: 'The structural features of [the *Confessions*] represent intersubjective relationships as playing reflexive or mutually independent, rather than complementary, roles in the constitution of subjectivity.'[47] That there is an important degree of complementarity and complete identification, rather than any form of independence, is apparent in the existence of the figure 'Mr I,' which contains and describes Breytenbach, his Interrogator, and his reader. This identification allows the space for all participants to engage in both complicity and rebellion. Lovesay notes part of this cycle of complicity, stating: 'The nature of this figure's construction indicates the reader's complicity produced by the act of reading Breytenbach's revelations.'[48] The double motion of complicity/rebellion and rebellion/complicity forms the contradictory political action that is *The True Confessions of an Albino Terrorist*.

The relation between complicity and rebellion is also portrayed in Breytenbach's transformation of the traditional autobiographical form. By constructing the confessions as a text he tells to himself, Breytenbach formally emphasizes the contradiction of his position. Such a contradiction is summed up by Derrida, in a lecture entitled 'Otobiographies,' originally published the year of Breytenbach's release from prison and the year before *Confessions* was released. Discussing Nietzsche's *Ecce Homo*, an autobiography which the narrator says he tells to himself, Derrida argues that '[t]he contradiction of the "double" thus goes beyond whatever declining negativity might accompany a dialectical opposition. What counts in the final accounting and beyond what can be counted is a certain step beyond,' where 'step beyond,' we are told by the translator, can also be translated as 'not beyond.'[49] Although different than Lytton's text, Breytenbach's *Confessions* can also be read as a subversion which can be 'identified as the deconstruction of the individual bourgeois author (the sacred subject of autobiographical narrative).'[50] While not engaging in the collective authorship that Kaplan describes, Breytenbach's complication and fracturing of his identity can be read as an attack on the bourgeois author and the privilege which that figure represents. Harlow reads this attack as one committed by all authors of prison memoirs, because such texts present 'a serious threat to the authorities' control over the "power of writing,"' and, with the import of writings from the 'outside,' help to form a 'political fraternity inside the prison' that resonates with, for example, the collective authorship of the suffragettes.[51]

At the same time, though, Breytenbach seems to work against such a fraternity, creating a textual identity that is unique in its complete lack of collective identification – rather than '*an* albino terrorist,' he seems to become '*the* albino terrorist.' Such a uniqueness would reproduce the individuality of the bourgeois author, and Breytenbach's text would therefore walk a thin line between rebellion against the dominant society and the reproduction of it. Like Lytton's class passing, which could fall into a further silencing of the working-class activist, Breytenbach's rejection of 'the old notion of the unitary individual in favor of the split and multiply fragmented subject may not always serve emancipatory objectives; rather it may serve further oppressive agendas,' as Sidonie Smith writes generally of post-modern 'contestatory autobiographical practice.'[52] In Derrida's words, Breytenbach's undermining of the interrogator/interrogated, oppressor/oppressed power relationship is at once a 'step beyond' and an existence 'not beyond.'[53]

Breytenbach elaborates on this double motion in the final paragraphs of *Mouroir*'s 'The Double Dying of an Ordinary Criminal.' After the central narrative of execution, there is a second section, separated from the main story by the roman numeral 'ii' (a doubling of an 'I'). This section functions in much the same way as the 'inserts' of the *Confessions* do: it is an addendum which, constructed as if it was written chronologically after the events of the main body of the text, offers commentary on the central storyline:

> Mirrors have a life too and that which gets caught in them continues existing there. Reality is a version of the mirror image. It is a literary phenomenon I'd like to point out to my colleagues: the ritual must be completed in us also. Before death points? Does death depend on us? ... This is the result: the eye and the hand (the description) embroider the version of an event, the anti-reality without which reality never could exist – description is experiencing – I am part of the ritual. The pen twists the rope. From the pen he is hanged ... He hangs in the mirror.[54]

Writers, in composing a narrative of violence, actually create the violence that they supposedly only describe. The 'literary phenomenon' is part of the cycle of violence itself. This movement is even visible in the title of *Mouroir* which, as Egan notes, 'conflates the concepts of self-reflection and death, or self-discovery in confrontation with death, [and] it also describes life writing as a death sentence.'[55] The mirror image that is the narrative becomes the violence which it would seek to combat, just as Breytenbach sees the violence of Mr Investigator mirrored in himself, thus creating Mr I.

As in the *Confessions*, however, 'The Double Dying of an Ordinary Criminal' attempts to show how this complicity can be reworked into an anti-hegemonic force:

> And the writer just as the reader (because the reader is a mirror to the writer) can seemingly make nothing undone. He cannot reopen the earth, cannot set the snapped neck, cannot stuff the spirit back into the flesh and the light of life in the lustreless eyes full of sand, cannot straighten the mother's back, cannot raise the assassinated, cannot reduce the man to a seed in the woman's loins while a hot wind blows over the Coast.
>
> Or can he?
>
> Is that the second death?
>
> (Shiva, as Nutaraya – King of the Dancers – has in his one right hand a drum which indicates sound as the first element of the unfolding / budding universe; the uppermost left hand holds a fire-tongue, element of the world's final destruction ... The other arms represent the eternal rhythmical balance between life and death. The one foot rests on the devil of 'Forgetfulness,' the other treads in the void, as is usual when dancing, and depicts, according to Heinrich Zimmer, 'the never-ending flow of consciousness in and out of the state of ignorance.' Shiva, god of destruction, god of creation, et cetera. The heart is a mirror / The mirror is a heart.)[56]

What starts as a contemplation of the writer's and reader's complicity in the ritual of execution becomes, in the parenthetical passage, a religious and philosophical examination of the complete interdependence of both poles of all binaries. Incarnated in the multiply armed Shiva, this construction of the interdependence of opposites seems to be a reply to the question, 'Is that the second death?' Jolly, examining this story without referring to the parenthetical statements, sees 'the second death' in the above passage as an 'alternative,' an escape from the writer's and reader's repetition of the violence of the hanging.[57] She goes on to explicate this alternative in some of Breytenbach's other works, stating that 'the relentless logic of determinism may be "broken"' through '[t]he metaphysics of absence.'[58] Rather than cleanly escape the violence inherent in textual representations, however, Breytenbach instead shows how those representations always contain the possibility of the undoing of their violence. At the same time, however, it is implied that representations that claim to escape the repetition of violence often in fact reproduce it. Paul de Man's description of autobiography parallels Breytenbach's notion of representation: both are 'caught in this double motion, the necessity to escape from the tropology of the subject and the equally inevitable reinscription of this necessity within a specular model of cognition.'[59] For Breytenbach, though, such a circular model is not as fracture-proof as de Man's description would make it seem. What must be done in order to interrupt (as opposed to escape) the flow of violence is to try to recognize one's own 'ignorance' and actively work against 'Forgetfulness,' while all the time recognizing the possibility (or *fait accompli*) of one's own complicity. One must 'entertain the idea of a permanent revolution' despite the fact that 'it is so horribly difficult to do so.'[60]

Breytenbach constructs this 'permanent revolution' as a positive force, but the ability to engage in it, to be able to recognize one's own ignorance, may not be as self-evident as his text suggests. When the positive portrayal of the permanent revolution is paired to his construction of identity in the text – an identity which seems to be conceived at least as a movement towards such a revolution – the complicitous nature of Breytenbach's rebellion risks becoming, like Thoreau's self-construction, exemplary and an image of 'proper' and universal action. Thus, Breytenbach's identity risks becoming an heterogenous image of the ideal, which can be tied to 'dominating one's fellows,' to use Georges Bataille's words.[61] Breytenbach's identity as constructed in the *Confessions* can be read as an idealization of a permanent revolution, which risks slipping into a romanticization of his acts of complicity, which, in turn, can lead to a reproduction of the forces he is attempting to combat. This concern becomes especially troublesome when Breytenbach's portrayal of his identification with Mr Investigator is paired with the accounts of the other South African prison writers mentioned earlier, who see any form of cooperation with interrogators as either a betrayal of their cause or as the inevitable result of the brutal violence used against them. Breytenbach indeed recognizes and writes against such oppressive violence, but leaves his most direct statements for an appendix to the central text. His construct of a complicitous rebellion could be seen to operate directly against the depictions by these other prison authors. His shifting subjectivity functions against the background of the seemingly less problematized, more unitary subjectivities of the other revolutionaries, the majority of whom were non-white. Indeed, other South African writers note the problematic connection that exists between Breytenbach and the oppressive dominant culture despite his battles against it. Pheto writes of Breytenbach that 'my political freedom was not dependent on White friends ... [I]t depended on me and on Black people.'[62] Dingake notes that even Breytenbach's ability to write in prison can itself be seen as an act that separates him from the struggle: 'The demand for permission to write creatively [in prison] was a ticklish issue at the time, because a precedent had already been created with Breyten Breytenbach ... Breytenbach had been obviously favoured, whether because he was a "son of the soil" or for some more obscure reason, we did not know.'[63] Dingake does not suggest that Breytenbach was aware of this favouritism, but this passing reference does note the problematic position that Breytenbach and his writings occupy. Breytenbach's critique of the Enlightenment individual through his shifting identity may be just as dependant on the privilege of his white identity as Thoreau's transcendent individualism is. Within the context of my larger argument, Breytenbach's textual creation of a non-unitary identity can be read as a further bolstering of the carceral identificatory practices – re-emphasizing the oppressive results of dominant ontological structures – rather than as an attack on those practices. The act of constant rebellion in Breytenbach's text – as well as my own engagement with Breytenbach's theoretical debate – risks becoming an objective and easy formulation that denies the dangers of situating a rebellion within complicity.

However, pointing out such dangers similarly risks being seen as an *ad hominem* attack on Breytenbach and as a denial of his own prison experience, which I certainly do not want to do. Instead, my aim is to suggest that Breytenbach's text can remind us of the necessity for questioning even the most seemingly well thought out or well intended acts or theories. It can also remind us that nothing should be taken for granted – not even the act of questioning itself. The importance of Breytenbach's text lies not, I think, in its mutually dependant positioning of complicity and rebellion, but in its attempted complication of the two poles. Whether or not Breytenbach's text or his personal battle are successful is not the question I would ask; what we can take from his text is a recognition of the need to constantly examine and question positions, not just those of others, but also our own.

I would like now to return to the signature at the end of the *Confessions*, '*Pretoria / Pollsmoor / Palermo / Paris, 29 December 1983.*' Breytenbach is not just equating the South African prisons at Pretoria and

Pollsmoor with the Inquisition and Palermo. He is also implicating Paris, the 'civilized' Western world. Palermo did not just lead to Pretoria and Pollsmoor, but also to Paris, to the Revolution, and to the reader – who, you'll remember, is *always* in the position of Breytenbach's 'Interrogator.' 'Paris' and the date of composition, the supposedly 'free' present (for Breytenbach), appear at the end of the alliterative oppressive sequence of 'Pretoria / Pollsmoor / Palermo' not just as the end (death) of the sequence, but also as its end (goal). Paris becomes a textual or cognitive space in which we can recognize our own ability to function like Shiva – to hold down forgetfulness and combat ignorance, in an endless battle to recognize oneself and others. More importantly, it also becomes a reminder not to romanticize the act of rebellion. Breytenbach's prison writings offer a notion of a continuously ongoing struggle, where freedom must be consistently fought for from oppression, where we must recognize that the former can always become the latter. Breytenbach's text reminds us of the danger of trying to create Utopias, stating that 'there will *never* be a perfect society *anywhere*,' and that we must aim to create systemic ruptures, for 'ruptures can be flashes of comprehension' (360). One of his final statements can be used not only as a means of rebelling, but as a positive means of interpreting his own attempts, his frustrated complicity and complicitous frustration: 'Try to see it as a continuous *process*, not a rigid goal or structure' (360). In the following final statements to my study, I will examine some of the implications that this reading of Breytenbach's work has for my overall project.

Closing Statements /
Opening Arguments

I wish in closing to explore further the ramifications of the question- and process-oriented conclusion of the final chapter. I want to use this space not only as a formal closure to my statements on prison writing, but also to continue the process I began in my 'opening statements' of trying to 'open up' discussion. I will begin by raising some arguments and problems that are covered in this study, and which may compli- cate some of the previous conclusions I have offered; I do so not only with the explicit hope of engaging readers in continuing and energetic dialogue, but for two more specific reasons, as well. First, to end the last chapter by raising the necessity of questioning one's own position and then to go on to offer a firm and decisive conclusion would be, at best, contradictory. Second, an immersion in prison writing cannot come without a healthy disrespect toward overly authoritative uses of language, and toward the use of texts as part of a set of controlling mechanisms that first define and then assert the absolute necessity of their own views, especially within institutional settings, ranging from the prison itself to, say, the academy. As Harlow argues, prison writing 'challeng[es] the contemporary university structure and the institu- tions of state of which it is a part to rethink the social and cultural tra- ditions ... that the university has inherited and is engaged in reproducing.'[1] In order to fully engage in the social critique offered by the authors studied here, my own identity as 'scholarly authority' (if such, indeed, I can claim) as constructed through this study needs to be questioned.

There is a central problem to which I wish to direct the reader's attention, a problem raised by the thrust of the present work's overall argument. The study as a whole analyses prison authors' constructions of identity as general critiques of the Enlightenment individual and of the ontological and social frameworks involved with it. Thoreau's transcendental individual, as a subset or outcropping of the larger category, is thus held up as a potential means of discursively reinforcing the very oppression Thoreau fights against. The discussion that continues through all of the chapters shows a general shift away from notions of the individual to more post-structuralist understandings of the subject as a creation of a multitude of social forces. The argument arising from this discussion culminates in the final section of this work, which details both Lytton's and Breytenbach's attempts to 'ground' more just societies on a decentring of identity as well as their emphasis on the necessity of understanding the multiple ways in which people are constructed. The authors demonstrate how people engage in and are engaged by often contradictory forms of discourse, and are therefore constantly in the process of being reconstructed by social forces. This is not, however, construed as a permanent oppression, since, as Butler writes, 'agency begins where sovereignty wanes. The one who acts (who is not the same as the sovereign subject) acts precisely to the extent that he or she is constituted as an actor and, hence, operating within a linguistic field of enabling constraints from the outset.'[2] The prison authors studied here can thus use writing in order to creatively negotiate these 'constraints' and the identities constructed within them, giving rise thereby to Foucault's 'plurality of resistances, each of them a special case.'[3]

Notions of individuality as they arise from the Enlightenment, however, are not only consistent with the dominant values reinforced by oppressive carceral discipline (as we saw in chapter 1), but are also intricately tied to notions of equality, to the idea that each individual is essentially identified with 'inalienable rights and freedoms,' an idea that *all* of the authors here are arguably striving to assert in and through their texts, and one of the reasons that Thoreau's text has become so central to many of the social battles discussed here. Judicial and penological protocols are based on assertions of individual responsibility and culpability, and therefore call for a uniformity of procedure and punishment not as alienating and disciplinary forces, but as attempts to ensure equal treatment under the law, to legally disable arbitrary decisions based on bias or bigotry. Calls for a decentring of notions of the individual – to see each voice or resistance as the 'special case' – raise the ugly spectre of biased and arbitrary decisions about punishment, and give rise to the related spectre of violent (or more subtle) forms of oppression. This critique can also be levelled from another direction: is not Foucault's assertion of the 'special case,' and the contemporary theorist's call for plurality, simply a reworded version of democracy and, as such, would it not also carry with it the biases and bigotries of the ontological framework of contemporary so-called democracy, which have been discussed throughout this work? The 'special case' is damned from either of these directions, and can be seen to work against the uniformity and equality of treatment for which the authors studied here call.

But while these issues raise questions about my argument, they do not negate the value of its process, of the examination of the inherent bigotries of the Enlightenment subject and of the legal and penological structures founded upon it. Such critiques are necessary steps in the analysis and, hopefully, the dismantling of institutional oppression. So, we are stuck in a quandary between the need to critique our under-standings of identity and political-penological structures in order to discover their problems, and the need to retain a uniformity in struc-ture in order to disallow the unequal treatment of people based on, for example, racial or gender bigotries. A solution to this problem is beyond the scope of this project and, I would argue, a *permanent* solu-tion is perhaps beyond the scope of any one project. Still, some motions toward better understandings of the problem, and toward means of negotiating the theoretical and practical paradoxes raised, can be offered in the hopes of engaging conversation. To invoke Said again, the goal is 'to be critical of humanism' – characterized by him through the very form of Enlightenment individualism I discuss – but to do so precisely 'in the name of humanism.' He argues that this is possible because, 'schooled in its abuses by the experience of Eurocentrism and empire, one could fashion a different kind of humanism that was cos-mopolitan and text-and-language bound ... and still remain attuned to the emergent voices and currents of the present, many of them exilic, extraterritorial, and unhoused' – a list to which I would add 'impris-oned' because, while the other terms imply unfettered space, like imprisonment they also indicate and are the result of marginalization, dispossession, and disenfranchisement.[4] The critical practice to strive for, then, is one of an ongoing ethics not limited by the paradoxically material biases of the abstracted Enlightenment individual. The ques-tions that need to be raised in this project are centrally structural ones. Is it possible to retain a structure (e.g., legal, penological, educational, critical) based on a uniformity of process in order to ensure equal treatment, while simultaneously allowing for a plurality of resistance that can point out biases hidden behind the structure?

Some possibilities for the embodiment of such a structure have been made by the recent work of prison abolitionists. These latter-day abolitionists argue for a rejection both of what Davis refers to as the 'social-scientific and popular discourses that assume a necessary conjunction between crime and punishment' and of the 'philosophical literature on imprisonment' which argues 'that individuals are punished because of the crimes they commit.'[5] Using the criminalization of blackness as her example, and relying on the research of several penal abolitionists, Davis effectively demonstrates that 'crime' is not necessarily the determiner of punishment, but that other factors, including class, gender, and race, all play important roles: 'Thus a major theoretical and practical challenge of penal abolitionism is to disarticulate crime and punishment. In fact, many abolitionists deploy statistics that demonstrate how relatively few people who have broken a law are actually called upon by criminal justice systems to answer for their crimes.'[6] The realization of the disjoined nature of crime and punishment – that is, the recognition that being 'called upon' or interpellated as a criminal may in fact have little to do with the commission of crime – leads to a questioning of current disciplinary practices, and therefore can open arguments for ways of dealing with crime that are not centrally fixated on punishment.

Here, once again, we come to the problem of instituting changes, of forming structures which can avoid the authoritative and alienating powers of current penology, while not allowing arbitrary systems to dominate. Several ideas have been offered, and some have even been instituted on a small scale.[7] As Duff and Garland note in their collection, many of the abolitionist theories of responses to crime focus on concepts of conflict or dispute resolution, in which crime is perceived not 'as an individual's culpable disobedience to some supposedly shared moral norm' but is instead understood 'as a matter of "conflict" between members of the community.'[8] Within this conception of crime, legal structures would be geared towards an actively communal process of reparation, rather than punishment. The uniform structure offering equal treatment would be geared around the function of mediators or facilitators, rather than prosecutors, defenders, and judges. Herman Bianchi summarizes one way of looking at this general position:

Crime in abolitionist thought has to be defined in terms of *tort* ... Lawyers and jurists are the allies of abolitionists, since they are capable, and hopefully willing, to develop new concepts of tort which would be suitable for the regulation of crime conflicts, and rules for the settlement of disputes ... The new system would no longer be called criminal law but *reparative law*.[9]

Bianchi uses tort law to describe a potential replacement for criminal law since the former is concerned primarily with ensuring that the victim of a certain act is compensated by the perpetrator of that act. Rather than being centred on punishment, tort law is centred on recompense. In order to move more quickly towards the instantiation of such a system, critics like Bianchi and Davis call for, among other things, the decriminalization of certain acts (such as drug possession), and an immediate reworking of them into a different structure of community reparation and resolution between the disputing parties. It is important to remember, though, that prison abolitionists – as their self-identification implies – are finally not interested in prison reform, but are calling for an eradication in large part of the contemporary structures of penal servitude and for a revisioning of criminal law.

I should restate that I am not suggesting one particular solution, one strategy as a utopian structure. A system such as that discussed by Bianchi is also liable to problems concerning, for example, the processes involved in choosing mediators and in ensuring that they act fairly. What the abolitionists seek to do which current systems do not, however, is to emphasize communication not only as a way to derive 'facts' about a certain case, but also as a means of defining the various relationships between people and the ways in which those relationships alter and affect certain situations.[10] This understanding of social interaction as a dynamic situation has immediate echoes with my project in that it does not allow for simplistic or overly deterministic solutions to particular conflicts. Indeed, Mathiesen's foundational statements on prison abolition bear a remarkable resemblance to Breytenbach's 'permanent revolution' and Said's 'unending' critical task: '[T]here is no reason to expect any terminated condition of final abolition; for example, no country can count on attaining a terminated condition of final revolution; a retrospective "consolidation" of the abolition which has been attained ... is the same as finishing the abolition and in large measure returning to the old. The maintenance of an abolition implies that there is *constantly more to abolish.*'[11] Such a penological – or critical – system, and the dynamic understanding of identity involved with it, is perhaps doomed to feel unresolved, to be painful and expensive,[12] but it lessens the dangers of consistently silencing some groups while positioning others to make judgments. Relying on similar principles, abolitionist structures would allow us to listen to the person who is currently imprisoned, not only to hear their complaints or justifications, but also to listen for how they have negotiated the restraints of their own particular past, as a means of better understanding other situations. In many current systems, prisoners are not allowed to vote, let alone allowed to have their voices heard in more active manners.[13] And, perhaps just as importantly, these structures could also allow more active roles for the *victims* of crime, permitting them to be more involved in the reparative process than the current dehumanizing legal system does, thereby allowing for a more community-oriented system in which all involved parties may have the opportunity to provide meaningful input. A more open system may result in a feeling of a lack of closure, but perhaps that feeling is a positive one if it would replace the current assurance of the prison's failure to do anything but perpetuate itself – a failure perhaps most incisively summarized by well-known death-row prisoner, activist, and author Mumia Abu-Jamal. Writing of prison uprisings in Pennsylvania in the late 1980s, Abu-Jamal states: 'Perhaps there is a certain symmetry in the circumstance of a prison system in crisis in the very state where the world's first true penitentiary arose ... Two hundred years after initiation of this grim experiment, it is clear that it has failed ... Repression is not change; it's the same old stuff.'[14] The contribution I hope to have offered here is to provide an understanding that, in any attempt to move beyond 'the same old stuff,' the words of the prisoners need to be as actively listened to and interpreted as those of any other if we are to try to understand the functions of our prisons, our criticisms – and our societies: no one should ever make the mistake of inadvertently assuming or asserting that prisoners' viewpoints are limited to and delimited by the prison itself. Part of any answer must be to open a dynamic conversation – as opposed to one which is merely superficial and effectively one-sided – with the people who have been placed at a remove, who have been forced to 'cry out' from the 'Cold Places.'[15] In that conversation, we may all find ourselves fitting sentences.

Notes

Opening Statements

1 Garland, *Punishment and Modern Society,* 160. Similarly, prison literature has forerunners in seventeenth- and eighteenth-century criminal biographies, ballads, and novels, and its roots can be traced back further to such works as Boethius's *Consolation of Philosophy,* from the sixth century, and François Villon's fifteenth-century poetry. See my 'Criminal Autobiography' for a brief description of the historical connections between these genres and contemporary prison writing. W.B. Carnochan offers a quick history of the 'literature of confinement,' listing and briefly discussing fictional accounts of confinement as well as writings from prison (including some of the authors studied here). On medieval imprisonment, see Jean Dunbabin's recent study, *Captivity and Imprisonment in Medieval Europe 1000–1300.*
2 Harding and Ireland, 18–19.
3 Bender, 14.
4 Even the terminology describing non-prison punishment is telling in terms of the centrality of incarceration. John M. Sloop, in his in-depth analysis of prisons and American society and culture, discusses the discourse of 'alternative' punishments (172–9), while Michael Tonry analyses the judicial system's use of 'intermediate' punishments. Tonry explicitly points to the popular understanding of the prison as the central locus of punishment, despite what he describes as the growing use of other punishments in cases that would not require imprisonment, writing that 'new intermediate punishments are often conceived in large part for use *in lieu* of incarceration' (136; my emphasis). Marc Mauer and Meda Chesney-Lind, in the introduction to their volume of essays *Invisible Punishment,* further write that, in the US, imprisonment has become 'the predominant mode of crime control [in]

the past thirty years,' leading to 'a social policy that can be described only as mass imprisonment' (1).

5 Lauterbach, 140n54. According to Vivien Stern, US penological systems are still being used as a model for other nations' prisons: '[t]he unprecedented rise in the use of imprisonment in the United States in recent decades presents a model to the world of a society committed to the use of punishment as a primary mechanism of crime control.' While European nations have adopted these practices only to varying degrees, Stern goes on to state that 'these policies have begun to alter the political and cultural climate in which issues of crime and punishment are perceived in different nations' (279).

6 Rothman, 121.

7 P.Q. Hirst details the prison project's emphasis on the reconstruction of the prisoner's 'criminal' identity into a more 'proper' one, writing that '[p]rison regimes were intended ... to produce a self-governing and industrious' subject who exhibited 'orderly habits' (277). For discussions of the prison's connection to democracy, citizenship, and equal rights, see, for example, Foucault, *Discipline*, esp. 221–4; Orlando F. Lewis, 8; Sloop, 21–2; and Haslam and Wright's introduction to *Captivating Subjects*.

8 For a discussion of the contemporary debates over retributive and reformatory penal practices, see Sloop, 197–9. Sloop writes that '[t]oday, while explicit arguments for rehabilitation have fallen almost completely out of favor, a shade of the argument that prisoners not only need but deserve rehabilitation appears to be reemerging' (199).

9 Wiener, 185. Also see Marie-Christine Leps, 24.

10 Harding and Ireland, 186.

11 Foucault, 'Technologies,' 18.

12 Richard Jenkins, for example, in a brief overview of contemporary approaches to criminology, notes the interconnection of various social practices to the subjugating surveillance system of the prison. He writes that 'Stanley Cohen, adopting an explicitly Foucauldian perspective, makes a cognate point. The classificatory work of assessment done by licensed, authoritative specialists such as psychologists and social workers is central to the modern social control project and tends to lead, despite the stated objectives of the professionals and the policies they pursue, to the raising and strengthening of boundaries of exclusion' (157).

13 D.A. Miller, 60.

14 Bentham, 34.

15 Ibid.

16 Foucault, *Discipline*, 201.

17 Ibid.
18 Ibid., 204.
19 Ibid., 307–8.
20 Travis, 18.
21 Ransom, 40.
22 Garland, *Punishment and Modern Society*, 165.
23 Ibid., 170
24 Foucault, *History*, 96.
25 Garland, *Punishment and Modern Society*, 170.
26 Deleuze, 71, 82.
27 Gelfand, 19. Several critics fall into a middle space in this debate. Hirst, for example, discusses the opposing views of, on the one hand, the prison as an intended space for rehabilitation and, on the other, the disciplining nature of the rehabilitative techniques, and concludes that '[p]ainting a rosy future for supervision and "treatment" and denouncing a new "gulag" run by psychiatrists, social workers, etc., are parallel faults; both overestimate the effectiveness of the methods praised or damned' (278). Garland himself calls for a melding of Foucauldian notions of discipline and other, less power-oriented theories. Foucault's lack of discussion of the impact of slavery on the modern prison system was recently addressed by panellists in a session entitled 'The Imprisonment of American Culture,' organized by the MLA's Radical Caucus at the 116th MLA Convention in Washington, DC. I elaborate on this connection in the second chapter of the present study.
28 On the author function see, of course, Foucault, 'What Is an Author?'
29 See, for example, Foucault, *Discipline*; and Harding and Ireland.
30 Franklin, *Victim*, 235.
31 Paul Smith, xxxiii–xxxiv.
32 Ibid., xxxv.
33 For another discussion of Paul Smith's terminology as it relates to prison writing, see my 'Discovering Identity in James Tyman's *Inside Out: An Autobiography of a Native Canadian*.' Smith's terminology relies not only on autobiography studies, but also on a Lacanian and Althusserian framework, although one which emphasizes the creative discursive possibilities available to subjects (as 'agents'). See also Norman Fairclough, and my discussion of his work in chapter 4.
34 Bender, 50; my emphasis.
35 Haslam and Wright, 18. In a recently published article, Dylan Rodríguez makes a similar point, arguing, as his title puts it, 'Against the Discipline of "Prison Writing."' Based in part on prisoners' own discussions of 'prison writing,' Rodríguez states that

[t]he construction of prison writing as a literary genre is ... a discursive gesture toward order and coherence where, for the writer, there is generally neither. Structuring the order and coherence of imprisonment is the constant dis-integration of the writer's body, psyche, and subjectivity – the fundamental logic of the punitive carceral is the institutionalized killing of the subject ... This logic is precisely that which is obscured – and endorsed – by the inscription and incorporation of prison writing as a genre. (409)

36 Davies, 3.

37 See my discussion ('Discovering') of James Tyman's autobiography for a discussion of a political text by a 'common' criminal, and my brief definition of 'Criminal Autobiography' for a discussion of the difficulties in offering general definitions of criminality and criminals' writings. For discussions of George Jackson's life, see, for example, his own *Soledad Brother: The Prison Letters of George Jackson* and *Blood in My Eye*, and Davis, 'Trials,' 83–4. While there are several recent prison authors I could single out here for further exploration, for some brief selections of contemporary writings by 'common' prisoners see, for example, *Doing Time: 25 Years of Prison Writings*, edited by Bell Gale Chevigny, and Franklin's anthology, *Prison Writing in 20th-Century America*. Other recent anthologies include *Sentences and Paroles: A Prison Reader* (edited by P.J. Murphy and Jennifer Murphy) and the significant collection *Wall Tappings: Women's Prison Writings, 200 A.D. to the Present* (edited by Judith A. Scheffler, now in its second edition). *This Prison Where I Live: The PEN Anthology of Imprisoned Writers*, edited by Siobhan Dowd, offers an excellent selection of writings by political prisoners.

38 Julia M. Wright and I make a similar argument about the need for such a pluralistic approach to writings by prisoners and other captives, writing that such a critical stance 'is intended to aid in avoiding the problematic determination of our subject matter into an overly delimited "genre" (17–18).

39 Foucault, *History*, 96.

40 Said, *Humanism and Democratic Criticism*, 77; my emphasis.

Chapter One

1 On Thoreau's political influence on these and other figures, see, for example, Francis B. Dedmond, Stanley Edgar Hyman, Michael Meyer, and Brent Powell. The debate concerning the title of Thoreau's essay rages on. In the now standard Princeton edition of *Reform Papers*, Wendell Glick reverts to

'Resistance to Civil Government,' the title used in the essay's original 1849 publication, rather than the still more commonly known title 'Civil Disobedience,' which was used in the posthumous publication *A Yankee in Canada, with Anti-Slavery and Reform Papers* (1866). Fritz Oehlschlaeger, however, has recently made another case not only for the adoption of the posthumous title, but also for the reintroduction of certain material from the 1866 edition which Glick omits. For ease of referencing, my page citations will be to the standard Princeton edition; however, in keeping not only with Oehlschlaeger's conclusions, but with the general tradition of political and prison authors themselves, I will be using 'Civil Disobedience' as the title.

2 Bob Pepperman Taylor, *America's*, 2.

3 Orlando F. Lewis, 327.

4 Ibid., 323.

5 Ibid., 324.

6 Walter Harding, 202–3.

7 Orlando F. Lewis, 328.

8 For discussions of North American and European perceptions at this time of prisons and penitentiaries, and the related issues of crime and criminality, see Orlando F. Lewis, esp. 323–45; Oliver, esp. 105–29; Rothman; Seán McConville; McGowen; and Wiener, 1–45.

9 Sloop, 22.

10 De Beaumont and de Tocqueville, 55.

11 Foucault, *Discipline*, 238. Benjamin Rush, at the end of the eighteenth century, also uses the idea of the sympathetic subject, the person defined by interiority, in his argument against public punishments, but does so from a different angle than that emphasized in this part of Foucault's argument: Rush argues that public punishments can give rise to sympathy for the criminal, which can cause the unravelling of civil society: 'While we pity, we secretly condemn the law which inflicts the punishment: hence, arises a want of respect for [laws] in general, and a more feeble union of the great ties of government' (83).

12 Ibid.

13 Rush, 89.

14 Orlando F. Lewis, 326–7.

15 Oliver, 112.

16 Rusche and Kirchheimer, 112.

17 Angela Y. Davis has recently argued that 'the penitentiary as an institution was aimed largely at white men,' while women and people of colour were 'excluded from the moral realm within which punishment in the peniten-

tiary was equated with rehabilitation' ('Race,' 37, 38). She then argues that it is when 'black people began to be integrated into southern penal systems in the aftermath of the Civil War – and as the penal system became a system of penal servitude – [that] the punishment associated with slavery became integrated into the penal system' ('Race,' 39). Davis's assertions of the racialized and gendered nature of the assumptions of prison reform are beyond dispute, as are her conclusions regarding the violence perpetrated on prisoners in the post-bellum period. However, as both Lewis and Oliver note, the theory of labour as reform in American penitentiaries was belied by its violent practices long before the Civil War. Despite the justifying rhetoric of prison proponents, the earlier prisons did in fact systemically engage in physical punishments which were explicitly related to prisoners' productivity and labour rather than rehabilitation.

18 Franklin, *Victim*, 134–5.
19 Oliver elaborates this point, writing of Canadian officials' support of the Auburn system that '[b]ecause they believed convict labour in a congregate institution would make the facility self-supporting, the organization of such labour took priority over every other consideration. All other disciplinary possibilities, such as the inculcation of religious values and the provision of educational training, received lip service at most' (112). Further, Orlando F. Lewis states that, in the Auburn-style prisons, such as Sing Sing, '[e]fforts at reformation were sacrificed to the struggle of the State to make money out of the prisons' (327). Foucault, *Discipline*, 239–44; Lewis, 130–46; and Rusche and Kirchheimer, 84–113, detail the general nineteenth-century relationships between prison labour and the larger market.
20 Rothman, 117; my emphasis.
21 See Dario Melossi and Massimo Pavarini's *The Prison and the Factory* for a discussion of the prison as a 'factory of men,' 143ff.
22 Wiener, 11.
23 The rugged individual was figured not only in the writings of Emerson and Thoreau, but also through the popular image of the frontiersman. See Pease, 3–48, on the constitution of representative figures of the individual in the nineteenth-century US.
24 Sloop, 25.
25 Foucault gestures to this understanding when he writes that, in the Philadelphia system, 'life,' here meaning identity, was 'annihilated and begun again' (*Discipline*, 239). Before prisoners can be rehabilitated, their identities (as the origin of their improper behaviour) must be wiped clean, ideally by silence and hard labour and practically by brutal and harsh treatment.
26 Thus Wiener, summarizing arguments made by Michael Ignatieff and

David Garland, can write that 'penal policy has always been determined by unacknowledged deep structures of power. The point of criminal policy ... has always been to reproduce existing social power relations' (7). Garland argues, for instance, that 'penal institutions are functionally, historically and ideologically conditioned by numerous other social relations and agencies, which are, in turn, supported and conditioned by the operation of penal institutions' (*Punishment and Welfare*, viii).

27 Len Gougeon, 200.
28 Gougeon, 201–2, provides a more detailed summary of the issues surrounding the inclusion of Texas, the war with Mexico, and their historical relationship to Thoreau.
29 Harding, 200–1.
30 Ibid., 205.
31 On the reception of *Aesthetic Papers*, and specifically of Thoreau's essay, see Fink, 206–10.
32 Thoreau, 'Civil,' 63. Unless otherwise noted, subsequent references to 'Civil Disobedience' will be to this edition, and will be noted parenthetically.
33 Thoreau, 'A Plea for Captain John Brown,' 129.
34 For a description of the events and decisions leading up to the Fugitive Slave Law and Thoreau's dealings with it, see Kritzberg, 540ff.
35 Thoreau, 'Slavery,' 96–7.
36 Ibid., 91.
37 Golemba, 144.
38 Thoreau, *Walden*, 46.
39 Wiener, 7.
40 Bob Pepperman Taylor, *America's*, 84.
41 Pease, 34.
42 Thoreau, *Yankee*, 126.
43 Thoreau, *Walden*, 91–2.
44 Ibid., 323–4.
45 Ibid., 324.
46 Barry Wood, 109.
47 Duban, 213.
48 Thoreau, 'A Plea for Captain John Brown," 115; also quoted in Duban, 219.
49 Caponigri, 545.
50 Wright, 182. Wright's reference is to Brombert, 68–9.
51 Thoreau, *Walden*, 12.
52 Ibid., 66.
53 Lewis Perry has recently added to the literature on the history of American civil disobedience, arguing that the links between such acts and the 'Protes-

tant past' are only one stream in the history of disobedience (105). Perry's excellent essay is most interested in tracing the relation between civil disobedience and black abolitionists.

54 Grusin, 30. Grusin refers explicitly to the readings of Thoreau done by Michael T. Gilmore and Sacvan Bercovitch. Thomas Augst refers to similar revisionist readings of Emerson's work, citing Bercovitch as well as Mary Cayton and Christopher Newfield. Their work, he writes, 'has tended to read Emerson's use of metaphors drawn from business life as expressing his ideological accommodation to liberal capitalism' (93).

55 Michael T. Gilmore, 44–5.

56 Bob Pepperman Taylor, 'Henry,' 60, 61.

57 Thoreau, *Walden*, 3.

58 Ibid., 4.

59 Ibid., 3.

60 Ibid., 49.

61 Caponigri, 544.

62 Caponigri goes on to overstate, at least for Thoreau, the mediational aspect of the transcendental philosopher: 'This self-reliance is not a form of egotism. The transcendentalist is self-dependent precisely because he is not an egotist. He is self-reliant because he humbly recognizes the universal truth which speaks in him and through him, of which he is the bearer but not the source' (545).

63 Sidonie Smith, *Subjectivity*, 9–10.

64 Hochfield, 435.

65 As Thomas Augst writes, critics who agree with conclusions like Sidonie Smith's also generally argue that 'concepts of self-culture and character were key terms in the formation of a middle-class hegemony, which lent moral justification to patterns of class formation and acquisitive individualism' (89–90). Augst refutes these claims as they are applied to Emerson. He writes that revisionist readings of Emerson that would situate his philosophy as part of the matrix of oppression 'are emblematic of the profound difficulty that modern scholars have in appreciating the degree to which general knowledge about character, of the sort retailed by Emerson in his later lectures, constituted a practical civic pedagogy concerned with the ... challenges of democracy under modern capitalism' (90). Augst's conclusions about the 'practical' nature of this civic pedagogy are largely not applicable to Thoreau, as evidenced by the generally negative contemporary reviews of *Walden*. For reprints of reviews of *Walden* and *A Week on the Concord and Merrimack Rivers*, see Myerson, *Emerson*, 341–415; also see

Henry Abelove's excellent essay on Thoreau and queer politics for a summation of some of the reviews (17–19).

66 Ignatieff, 212.

67 Thoreau, *Walden*, 204.

68 Ibid., 205–6.

69 David R. Roediger writes: 'In the mid nineteenth century, the racial status of Catholic Irish incomers became the object of fierce, extended debate. The "simian" and "savage" Irish only gradually fought, worked and voted their ways into the white race in the US' (*Towards*, 184). On the racialized identification of the Irish in nineteenth-century America see also, for example, Noel Ignatiev's *How the Irish Became White* and Roediger's *Wages of Whiteness*, 133–63.

70 Thoreau, *Walden*, 209.

71 Abelove, 23.

72 Anita Goldman's argument that Thoreau, in this passage, claims 'a status within a race which is distinct from the white people among whom he lives,' and that this status 'allows him to speak on behalf of the oppressed' (245) is belied by the grammatical structure of the passage. The 'Chinamen and Malays' are equated to Thoreau's neighbours, not to Thoreau.

73 Thoreau, *Walden*, 102–3.

74 Ibid., 103.

75 Ibid., 131.

76 Hildebidle, 'Thoreau at the Edge,' 349.

77 For discussions of this passage of *Walden*, see Michael T. Gilmore, 38–9; and Grusin, 38–9, 40–1.

78 D.A. Miller, 220. Foucault makes a similar point when he states that the 'radical criticism' of the nineteenth century may have, on the one hand, aimed to show 'that the legal system itself was merely a way of exerting violence, of appropriating that violence for the benefit of the few, and of exploiting the dissymmetries and injustices of domination'; but, on the other hand, such criticism 'is still carried out on the assumption that, ideally and by nature, power must be exercised in accordance with a fundamental lawfulness' (*History*, 88).

79 Olaf Hansen defends Thoreau's construction of himself as authority, writing, 'The voice of authority that assumes the burden of setting things right cannot be a disembodied one; it needs an agent' (128). However, Hansen's assertion that this mantle of authority is a self-sacrifice in which Thoreau 'adopted ... the role of the victim' (128) in a Christ-like attempt to save others rings false given Thoreau's more than occasionally derogatory

depiction of those others, and given the ontological baggage of his transcendentalism.

80 Hildebidle, *Thoreau*, 109.

81 Indeed, Hildebidle recognizes these multiple interpretive possibilities opened up in Thoreau's text when he notes early in his work that Thoreau 'can be labeled only partially and tentatively' (*Thoreau*, 5). As Richard F. Teichgraeber III writes about Thoreau's conception of the market, one must recognize that 'a number of different paths lead into Thoreau's thinking' (46).

Chapter Two

1 While *Incidents* stands out as – to date – the first authenticated woman's slave narrative written by the slave herself, several dictated accounts were published during the antebellum period, including *The History of Mary Prince, A West Indian Slave Related by Herself* (1831) and *Louisa Picquet, the Octoroon* (1861). In addition to these dictated accounts, there were some postbellum slave narratives that were penned by women, the most notable among them being Elizabeth Keckley's *Behind the Scenes or, Thirty Years a Slave and Four Years in the White House* (1868). William L. Andrews has collected some examples of all of these forms of women's slave narratives in *Six Women's Slave Narratives*. These narratives, furthermore, were not the only form of black women's autobiography in the nineteenth century, but coexisted with and were informed by the genre of spiritual autobiography, as exemplified by the texts of Jarena Lee, Zilpha Elaw, and Julia A.J. Foote (which are collected together by Andrews in *Sisters of the Spirit*). Beth Maclay Doriani writes that Harriet Wilson's novel *Our Nig: or, Sketches from the Life of a Free Black* (1859) should also be read in terms of life writing.

More recently, Henry Louis Gates Jr has published *The Bondwoman's Narrative*, by Hannah Crafts. This text, the handwritten manuscript of which was purchased first by Dorothy Porter in 1948 and then by Gates in 2001, purports to be a narrative written by a fugitive slave woman, and has been dated to between 1853 and 1861, and thus was likely written before Jacobs's. While written as a slave narrative, the work is heavily influenced by nineteenth-century gothic novels. As of the moment I write, the author of the text remains in question, though the scholarship to date largely argues that the author was likely a black woman. For analyses of this fascinating work and for discussions of its authorship, see my essay '"The strange ideas of right and justice": Prison, Slavery, and Other Horrors in *The Bondwoman's Narrative*,' and the essays collected by Gates and Hollis

Robbins in *In Search of Hannah Crafts: Critical Essays on* The Bondwoman's Narrative. For discussions of women's slave narratives and other black women's autobiographies in general, see, for example, Joanne Braxton's *Black Women Writing Autobiography* and Frances Smith Foster's *Written by Herself*. On abolitionists' and slave narrators' discussions of the sexual abuse of slave women, see, for example, Andrews, *To Tell*, 241ff.; Braxton, 20–1; and Ruth Bogin's and Jean Fagan Yellin's introduction to *The Abolitionist Sisterhood*, edited by Yellin and J.C. Van Horne, 5, 9. Mary Prince's narrative, transcribed by Susanna Strickland (who would later, as Susanna Moodie, write the foundational Canadian woman's autobiography, *Roughing It in the Bush* [1852]), offers an account of the sexual abuse of women slaves that resonates strongly with Jacobs's text.

2 Douglas Taylor, 430.
3 Sorisio, 'There Is,' 5.
4 Douglas Taylor points out that Benjamin Rush was an opponent of slavery, but failed to recognize the 'intersection of race, slavery, and punishment in U.S. society,' a failure that 'put him at risk of perpetuating the evils of slavery under the guise of reformation' (430). Maggie Sale writes that one school of slavery apologists 'represented Africans and their descendants as naturally savage and unpredictable but capable of becoming docile, contented, and childlike under the influence of the "civilized" Anglo-Saxon race' (699). Comparing this statement to the doctrine of the Philadelphia penitentiary system, where the final goal was to 'break the convict's unruly spirit and allow the discipline to work on "a contrite heart,"' highlights the similarities in purpose (Oliver, 108). The fact that the Auburn prison system emphasized constant and unpaid convict labour, which could be used as a means of building 'revenue' (Oliver, 110), cements the similarity between the two institutions. For a detailed analysis of the relations between American slavery and the growth of the penitentiary, see Hirsch, 71–111. J. Thorsten Sellin takes a longer and wider perspective, analysing the relationships between slavery and punishment from ancient Greece to Europe and Russia, from the Middle Ages to the twentieth century, but also devotes a large portion of his study to the specific connections between American slavery and prisons.
5 Franklin, *Victim*, 99–100.
6 Davis, 'Racialized,' 99. See also Davis, 'From the Prison,' 75–6.
7 Sale, 699.
8 Davis, 'From the Prison,' 76.
9 For discussions of the convict lease system see, in addition to Davis, Franklin, 102. Also, Hirsch explains that under the convict lease system, even

though prison labourers 'never became the private property of an individual master,' as slaves were, '[i]n several states, authorities ... leased entire penitentiaries to a single entrepreneur who thereby came close to becoming the lord of a private plantation' (74). In a recent essay, Karen Ho and Wende Elizabeth Marshall provide an in-depth analysis of how blackness continues to be implicitly criminalized through contemporary legislation that 'sustain[s] and reinscrib[es] limits to citizenship and status in the United States,' arguing that the 'foundational logic' of such legislation is 'a thinly veiled, hydra-headed, and well-organized resurgence of white nationalism' (209). Recent statistics more than support the conclusion that prisons are in part an attempt to reinscribe the controlling culture's racist practices. A recent anthology of prison writing notes: 'In the general population, African Americans constitute less than 13 percent, yet 51 percent of all prisoners nationwide are black. Thirty-two percent of black men in their twenties are under some form of criminal justice supervision' (Chevigny, 175). Davis similarly traces the historical trend of black imprisonment: 'In 1926, the first year in which there was a national recording, 21 percent of prison admissions were black. By 1970, black people constituted 39 percent of admissions and in 1992, 54 percent' ('Racialized,' 105). See also Mauer and Chesney-Lind's collection – especially their own introduction and the essays by Mauer, Forman, and Western et al. – for a discussion of the effects on African American communities and US society as a whole of the racialized nature of the prison system. Loïc Wacquant has excellently detailed the complex and reinforcing relationships between the 'four peculiar institutions' of slavery, Jim Crow, the inner city or ghetto of modern America (especially in the north), and the recent joining of the ghetto and the mass imprisonment of African Americans. Davis points out that race is a factor in prisons outside of the US, as well, particularly in Europe. She writes, '[A]s postcolonial immigration has radically transformed the racial composition of European populations in general, the prison population in the Netherlands approaches the US in its disproportionate numbers of people of color' ('Racialized,' 102).

10 Reinforcing the relationship between prison and slave narratives, William L. Andrews points out that early slave narratives, specifically those from the eighteenth century, were often constructed as criminal confessions (*To Tell*, 39–44). Franklin's text engages in an extended and well-documented exploration of the generic connection between later slave narratives and prison writings, focusing as well on the transmission of the African American oral culture and traditions through the forced transportation from

Africa, through slavery, and eventually to contemporary society, including the prison.

11 In a letter written shortly before he was murdered by a prison guard in 1970 in San Quentin, George Jackson equates slavery and prison, stating:

> Blackmen born in the U.S. and fortunate enough to live past the age of eighteen are conditioned to accept the inevitability of prison. For most of us, it simply looms as the next phase in a sequence of humiliations. Being born a slave in a captive society and never experiencing any objective basis for expectation had the effect of preparing me for the progressively traumatic misfortunes that lead so many blackmen to the prison gate. I was prepared for prison. It required only minor psychic adjustments. (*Soledad*, 4)

Eldridge Cleaver also makes the connection between slavery and imprisonment explicit: 'In Soledad state prison,' he writes, 'I fell in with a group of young blacks who, like myself, were in vociferous rebellion against what we perceived as a continuation of slavery on a higher plane' (17–18). And, in one of her own early prison writings, Angela Y. Davis draws a similar conclusion when she states that slavery was transformed into the prison, 'a more subtle yet equally pernicious apparatus to dominate Black people' ('Political,' 29). Mumia Abu-Jamal, in his prison writings (for example, *Live from Death Row*, *Death Blossoms*, and *We Want Freedom*), similarly deals with the racialization of the criminal justice system and the current mass imprisonment in the US. Such comparisons were not limited to writings by 20th-century prisoners, though; Hirsch cites a passage from the *Memoirs of the Notorious Stephen Burroughs of New Hampshire*, published in 1798, which states that being a penitentiary inmate was like being subjected to 'abject slavery' (quoted in Hirsch, 74). Douglas Taylor also briefly discusses the relationship between some of the general goals of prison writings of black activists in the 1960s and Jacobs's narrative (430).

Furthermore, due to the expansion throughout the West of the panoptic structure of the prison, African American prison writers form a chain with others who combat the chains placed on them. In addition to the connections between Thoreau, Lytton, and King, for example, as discussed in the fourth and fifth chapters of the current study, and Breytenbach's reference in his *True Confessions* to George Jackson's assassination (238), Jackson's own collection of letters was introduced by the French prison writer Jean Genet, who in turn refers to the writings from prison by the Marquis de Sade and Antonin Artaud (*Soledad*, 333).

12 For discussions of the generic connections and dissonances between men's and women's slave narratives (as connected to Jacobs's text), see Braxton, esp. 18–22, and Winifred Morgan.

13 Hirsch, 76. For Douglas Taylor, Benjamin Rush provides the quintessential, if unaware, example of this relationship.

14 Richard H. Broadhead similarly notes the social ubiquity of discipline when he writes that, in antebellum, middle-class America, even the representation of love can be read as a disciplinary tool in the Foucauldian sense, what he coins 'disciplinary intimacy': 'the cultural assertion embodied in disciplinary intimacy generates on one front an animus against corporal punishment; on another front a normative model of character formation; on another, a particular configuration of training institutions designed to support that character-building plan; and on yet another, a new place for literary reading in cultural life' (18). Broadhead's drawing of a connection between love, literature, and disciplinary institutions (as the figure for which I would place the prison) lends further support to my argument concerning Jacobs's highlighting of the centrality of disciplinary practices in American society.

15 Foucault, *Discipline*, 301.

16 Gilroy, 63.

17 Cutter, 214.

18 Bentham, 34.

19 Douglass, 36.

20 Ibid., 38.

21 Ioan Davies, in a discussion of the 'major internments' of history (including the African slave trade and the Holocaust), describes some of the actions involved in the process of subjugation. These actions include 'the stripping from all individuals of their unique possessions, including hair, herding them like cattle and forcing conformity, the reduction of the self to "pure" natural man, the attempt to deny all history, all culture, the imposition of a universalism of impotent nakedness' (195). For discussions of Douglass's depiction of his fight with Covey, see, for example, Gilroy, 61–4; Kibbey and Stepto, 183–7; and Ziolkowski, 158–60.

22 Hirsch, 91.

23 Harriet Jacobs, 8. Unless otherwise noted, subsequent references will be to this edition, and will be noted parenthetically.

24 Franklin, *Victim*, 15–18.

25 Garfield, 'Vexed,' 277; Sánchez-Eppler, 90.

26 Hirsch discusses the recognition of slavery's effects on the slaveowner, and the similarities to the effects of prison: 'Thomas Jefferson believed that the

master–slave relationship corrupted *owners* by turning them into tyrants. A French visitor to the Walnut Street jail made the same observation: "In putting a man in prison, you subject him to the power of the gaoler ... This state of humiliation ... renders his *masters* imperious, unjust, vexatious, and wicked"' (73).

27 Garfield, 'Vexed,' 277.

28 Accomando, 158.

29 Ibid., 156.

30 Ibid., 127.

31 Ibid.

32 Sorisio, contrasting this passage to dominant depictions of women, suggests that Brent's feeling of strength could indicate that 'it is Linda who *dares to feel like a man*, by exhibiting a fierce need for liberty' (12); Sorisio's gendered figuring of this desire points to the various legal means through which Brent is denied legal freedom.

33 Morgan, 84. Morgan reads Jacobs's emphasis on community in a gendered context, comparing it to Douglass's emphasis on 'the acquisition and development of written language' (84). Braxton similarly argues that Jacobs 'celebrates the cooperation of all the people' and the 'collective effort' involved in the attainment of freedom, and opposes this to the general male narrator's representation of his 'individual' effort (19–20). Despite this difference in the manner of their struggles for freedom, both male and female narrators construct community as a positive force. In addition, as Andrews notes, even Douglass constructs his freedom in terms of community: 'In the "heaven" of freedom, according to the *Narrative*, the black isolato was restored to community.' Andrews argues that for Douglass – as for Jacobs – the 'deprivation epitomized by the absence of mother, father, family, and ... community with others' helps to constitute the 'hell' of slavery (*To Tell*, 218).

34 Accomando, 169.

35 Jane Tompkins describes this use of domestic space as a common political motif in women's sentimental fiction, writing that the 'image of the home ... is conceived as a dynamic center of activity ... whose influence spreads out in ever-widening circles' (145).

36 Nat Turner, a slave in Virginia, led an insurrection in August 1831 during which fifty-five white people were killed; Turner was subsequently caught and executed. In her notes to Jacobs's text, Yellin writes: 'In the aftermath of the insurrection, a wave of white terror swept across the entire South. No one knows how many blacks were murdered; historians' estimates range in the hundreds' (269 n. 1).

37 Carby, 60; Smith, 'Resisting,' 97.

38 Doriani, 211.

39 Andrews, 'Dialogue,' 93.

40 Jacobs's brother, John S. Jacobs, in his own narrative 'A True Tale of Slavery' (now published with his sister's in Yellin's enlarged edition of *Incidents*), discusses similar forms of community destruction by his sister's owner. He writes that the doctor did not allow one of the Jacobs's aunts to see her husband, 'although they had lived together for twenty years, and had never been known to quarrel' (212). For discussions of 'A True Tale,' see Jennifer Fleischner, 61–92; Jacqueline Goldsby; and Yellin, 'Through.'

41 Levander, 32.

42 Mullen, 261. Carby reads this passage as one of several scenes depicting the strained relationships between white and black women in the text (51).

43 Andrews, *To Tell*, 240.

44 Walter, 202.

45 The phrase 'cult of true womanhood' was coined by Barbara Welter, who first used it in her essay 'The Cult of True Womanhood: 1820–1860,' although Welter notes that mid-nineteenth-century writers who dealt with 'the subject of women' used the term 'True Womanhood' 'as frequently as writers on religion mentioned God' (151n1). For other discussions of the cult of true womanhood and related literary depictions of domesticity see, for example, Skinfill, 63–7; and Tompkins, esp. 165–72.

46 Walter, 202.

47 Sorisio, 6.

48 Walter, 202.

49 Douglas Taylor, 440.

50 Walter, 193.

51 John S. Jacobs writes that, while held in jail after his sister's escape, he enacted a mimicry of the 'good slave,' which metaphorically parallels Brent's physical hiding within the gaze of slavery. He writes: 'My mind was fully made up, that I must, in order to effect my escape, hide as much as possible my hatred of slavery, and affect a respect to my master, who ever he might be' (213). Each mimicry specifically denies the controlling gaze of the institutions of captivity – tying prison and slavery again – and each has as its goal the freedom of the captive, but each also risks the permanent denial of that freedom.

52 Walter, 200.

53 Burnham reads the 'loophole' through which Brent looks as a metaphor for linguistic and literary 'loopholes,' and further notes that the phrase 'loopholes of retreat' was used by anti-slavery poet William Cowper, and by Lydia Maria Child (Jacobs's editor) in her own novel, *Hobomok*, 56–7.

54 Burnham, 58.

55 Carla Kaplan, 56.

56 Kawash, 77.

57 For analyses of Jacobs's use of sentimental discourse, see, for example, Bruce Burgett, 137–54; Franny Nudelman; and Skinfill.

58 Adam Smith, 9.

59 For a detailed discussion of the correlations between the works of Bentham and Adam Smith, see Bender, 201–28. He argues that the idea of the self-reflexive, reformable prisoner is directly related to notions of sympathy: 'The interior personification of juridical presence as character – perhaps the element most central to the penitentiary idea – is best understood histori-cally with reference to Adam Smith's explanation of the reciprocal nature of conscience' (218).

60 Adam Smith, 74.

61 Detailing the relationships in Britain between theories of sensibility and sentiment and the literature arising from them, Janet Todd writes: 'Senti-mentalism entered all literary genres – the novel, essay, poetry and drama. But the cult of sensibility was largely defined by fiction from the 1740s to the 1770s' (4); the form of the sentimental novel remained 'firmly en-trenched,' however, 'throughout the nineteenth century' (148). Reading these later sentimental novels, Tompkins argues that they should be read as 'a political enterprise, halfway between sermon and social theory, that both codifies and attempts to mold the values of its time' (126). Nudelman details the relation between sentimental writing and the abolition move-ment (esp. 944–5). Both Russ Castronovo and Henry Louis Gates Jr com-pare slave narratives and pro-slavery plantation novels, though where Gates reads the latter as 'the antithesis or negation of the slave narrative' (*Figures*, 82), Castronovo writes that '[w]hile Jacobs, [William Wells] Brown, and others racialized adventure and sentimental novels, popular Southern writing responded to black cultural critique by sentimentalizing and dera-cializing the slave narrative as the plantation romance of the white woman' (241).

62 In the introduction to their edited volume *Sentimental Men*, Mary Chapman and Glenn Hendler detail how the theory of sensibility – and the fiction related to it – was transformed from a specifically masculine enterprise (albeit one centred around a form of 'affective androgyny' [3]) into a femi-nine one. They write that '[i]n its early years as a literary and philosophical movement, the cult of sentiment was propelled by male writers,' but '[b]y the middle of the nineteenth century ..., American sentimentality seemed to have become ensconced solely in a feminine' sphere (3).

63 Doriani, 203–4.
64 Garfield, 'Speech,' 33.
65 Carby, 58.
66 Doriani, 205; Sorisio, 8.
67 Nudelman, 944.
68 Warhol, 65.
69 Nudelman, 958.
70 Walter, 205.
71 Daniel 12:1–4.
72 Jacobs, like many ex-slave authors, continually quotes biblical sources. This action can be seen in part as a further means of textually reversing the master/slave power structure, by revealing that the ex-slave authors have a more 'authentic' religious faith than the slaveholders. *Incidents* deals explicitly and at length with this in the chapter 'The Church and Slavery' (68–75), which also shows how some religious institutions were used to further subjugate slaves. For other discussions of religion and slavery, see the essays collected in *Religion and the Antebellum Debate over Slavery*, edited by John R. McKivigan and Mitchell Snay.
73 Carby, 50.
74 Walter, 204.
75 Ibid., 207.
76 Douglas Taylor, 438–9.
77 Ibid., 442–3.
78 Goldman, 239.
79 On Brent's relationship to Mrs Bruce as one of servitude, see Carby, 47–8; and Kawash, 73–4. Hirsch notes that *apologists* of slavery also make the connection between paid servitude in the North and slavery, writing: 'Slave, inmate, wage earner. For defenders of slavery, they differed only in name.' He goes on to note, though, that 'convicts and wage earners themselves' engaged in a similar equation of their status to slavery, as a rhetorical means of highlighting their oppression (102).
80 Hirsch, 73–4.
81 Other critics point to similar forms of concealment in the text. 'Like her grandmother's attic,' writes Sánchez-Eppler, 'the figure of Linda Brent places Jacobs in close proximity to those who are seeking her and yet leaves her carefully concealed' (87). See also Carby, 50. Beyond this, Carla Kaplan discusses the silence surrounding the identity of Brent's grandfather, who may have been a white slave-owner, writing, 'This use of silence suggests that thinking about freedom "not in the usual way" may entail imagining what it would be like not to give an account of yourself' (66). Joycelyn K.

Moody suggests that the chapters of *Incidents* which 'are not an integral part of the author's life story' constitute another technique of concealment (53). Garfield, citing Foreman, sees a camouflage of Jacobs's historical identity in the 'representativeness' of Brent's self-construction, which 'not only discloses the lot of the slave community through Brent's example; it also acts as a guise concealing the details of the individual life' ('Speech,' 28; Foreman, 317). Sorisio even reads the title of Jacobs's text as a function of concealment, writing that the emphasis on the 'incidents of' the protagonist's life, instead of the more common 'narrative of' the life of the ex-slave, 'implies not a complete linear story, but rather a series of episodes, with spaces and silences between the various events' (11).

82 Foreman, 316.
83 See Yellin, 'Written'; and Blassingame, 373.
84 Carla Kaplan, 57.
85 Ibid.
86 Sorisio, 16.

Chapter Three

1 Wilde to Robert Ross, 8 October 1897, *Letters of Oscar Wilde*, 654.
2 Losey, 440.
3 Thus, Bruce Bashford can write: 'For Wilde to fill in the theory he outlines in *De Profundis*, he must provide some insight into how the soul, once freed from encumbrances, expresses itself through transmuting experience. But of the soul as he conceives it, nothing illuminating can be said' (402).
4 Gagnier, *Idylls*, 179.
5 Wiener, 49.
6 J.J. Tobias has collected, along with other items, an interesting series of descriptions by Rev. John Clay of the English version of the separate system in the nineteenth century. The excerpts from Clay's writing that Tobias presents range in time from 1838 to 1850. Tobias also offers a report by Rev. John Field, who was Reading Gaol's chaplain from 1840 to 1858; Field describes the use of numbers to identify prisoners and of face-coverings to disguise them, both of which were designed as means of preventing 'recognition by other prisoners' and 'to prevent an acquaintance being formed' (159). In this way, the prisoners were kept separate without incurring the full expense of a more stringent panoptic system.
7 Wiener, 174.
8 Ibid., 185.

9 Wilde, 'The Soul of Man Under Socialism,' 1182.

10 Ibid.

11 Wiener gestures towards this anachronistic aspect of Wilde's trials, noting that Wilde's writings, which touch on the new sense of a loss of 'personal mastery' over oneself, 'provided a key subtext for the seemingly irrational anti-Wildean "moral panic" at the time of his trial' (162, 163 n. 15).

12 Wilde to Lord Alfred Douglas [*De Profundis*], January–March 1897, *Letters*, 424. Hereafter this text will be referred to as *De Profundis*. Unless otherwise noted, subsequent references will be to this edition and will be cited parenthetically.

13 Gagnier, *Idylls*, 179.

14 Wilde, 'Soul of Man,' 1188–9.

15 Foucault, *History*, 42–3.

16 Cohen, 131.

17 Wood, 101.

18 Cohen, 145.

19 'Central Criminal Court, April 5,' *Times*, 6 April 1895.

20 'Central Criminal Court, May 1,' *Times*, 2 May 1895. The moralizing and anti-Wilde discourse of the English papers was more or less repeated abroad, as well. In the *New York Times* of 8 April 1895, a four-part headline reads 'Oscar Wilde's Disgrace,' 'A Mother, Wife, and Two Children Must Share his Shame,' 'Poverty at Cadogan House,' and 'A Mother's Desperate Struggle to Keep up Appearances and Educate her Sons.' The first paragraph of the article following reads, 'Aside from the depravity that it has been necessary to make public in the downfall of Oscar Wilde, people who met him here, and accepted his letters of introduction as an accredited English gentleman, are curious to know something of his family, his mother, his wife, his children, and almost everybody else upon whom he has brought absolute ruin.' That Wilde's character is to blame for everything that has occurred is unquestioned – even the newspaper's publishing of 'the depravity' and the American public's prurient interest in 'everybody' associated with Wilde are the result of his active bringing about of 'absolute ruin.' Some papers, unfortunately, have not changed much over time: in a recent review of a volume of Wilde's previously unpublished letters, the *Sunday Times*'s media editor Nicholas Hellen writes that the letters 'give an intimate portrait of the happy family life led by Wilde before he embarked on a destructive series of homosexual adventures.' The blaming of Wilde's 'adventures' instead of, say, the destructive nature of the Victorian court's homophobia seems a misplaced emphasis, at best.

21 Buckton, 171, quoting Dollimore, 11. Sos Eltis notes that Wilde's active

reconstruction of identity can also be read in terms of his use of his Irish-ness as a critique of English society and imperial rule: 'Wilde retained a cer-tain pride in his native roots, often portraying himself as an Irish rebel against English authority ... Wilde followed Matthew Arnold in using the word "Celtic" to describe the imaginative opposite to narrow-minded English puritanism; supporters of the Prison Reform Bill were "Celtic to a man"' (13). David Alderson explicitly ties Wilde's dandiacal and national identities together, writing that 'Wilde consciously exploited an ensemble of identifications which, in the context of English culture, were conspicu-ously anti-bourgeois and amoral – Catholic, dandy and Celt; criminal, sin-ner and idle artist – and his theorisation of them as related enabled him to make explicit ... his dissident relations to dominant culture' (56). On Wilde's Irishness, also see Richard Pine.

22 Brown, 93. Wilde was concerned with labelling before the trials, as well. His most famous play, *The Importance of Being Earnest*, is, on one level, about the dangers of being labelled, even if one does it to oneself. Discussing Jack's naming of himself as Ernest, Algernon says, 'It is perfectly absurd your say-ing that your name isn't Ernest. It's on your cards. Here is one of them ... I'll keep this as proof that your name is Ernest if ever you attempt to deny it' (Act 1, 361).

23 David Foster, 88.

24 Bristow, 45.

25 Altman, 43.

26 Kauffman, xviii.

27 Buckton, 178.

28 David Foster, 98.

29 'Central Criminal Court, April 5,' *Times*, 6 April 1895.

30 Wiener, 160.

31 Jane Wood, 107. See M.C. Andersen for a discussion of Wilde's figuration in *De Profundis* of his life as tragedy. Andersen misplaces the emphasis of the letter, claiming that Wilde not only sees 'himself as tragic victim,' but also portrays Christ as '*the* victim' (7; my emphasis). In fact, Wilde's Christ escapes the social dynamics inherent in victimization.

32 Wilde, *Dorian Gray*, 17.

33 Wilde, 'Soul of Man,' 1189.

34 Sarah Kofman has noted that Dorian himself 'is precisely not this "com-plete" man, the new hedonistic ideal. Though his mother was able to be a bacchante, following in the train of Dionysus, he himself is not really beautiful or strong enough to truly affirm life, to dare to reveal himself and look at himself naked. His fragility forces him to become an imposter and

to hide behind the protecting mask of youth and beauty' (47–8).

35 Danson, 89.
36 Denisoff, 95.
37 Dollimore, 95.
38 Buckton, 180.
39 Jane Wood, 107.
40 Chai, 110.
41 Brown, 110–11.
42 Wilde, 'Decay of Lying,' 1082. Vivian here uses a stereotypical construction of a passive femininity in order to make his point about this form of artistic autonomy, seemingly supporting Rhonda K. Garelick's statement that, within decadent portrayals of art, '[f]emaleness allies itself ... primarily with a mute, hieratic power, which exists ... only to be read and deciphered by a male interpreter' (5–6). In Vivian's view, though, the mute perfection of art exists only for itself, and cannot be interpreted by anything or anybody (of any gender) external to it.
43 Wilde, 'The Critic as Artist,' 1139.
44 Wilde, 'Soul of Man,' 1174.
45 Jane Wood, 109, with quotation from Kohl, 284. David Foster reaches a similar conclusion, arguing that 'Wilde reconstructs Christ as the supreme aesthete, the quintessence of the artistic consummation Wilde has already claimed for himself' (103).
46 Gagnier, *Idylls*, 179.
47 Joseph Butwin explicates this generic description of the prisoner, writing that in the prison detailed in *De Profundis*, '[v]ariety is deliberately removed from life, details dissolve, and the particular prisoner becomes the representative prisoner' (1).
48 Losey's article traces the various references to Dante's *Divine Comedy* in *De Profundis*, stating, 'Reading Dante enabled Wilde to observe how a fellow exile transformed the daily bread of life into art' (447). See also 'The Critic as Artist' for a lengthy examination of the *Divine Comedy* as life transformed into art, 1132–6.
49 Brown, 99.
50 For a discussion of Wilde's indebtedness to Emerson, especially in 'The Soul of Man Under Socialism' and *De Profundis*, see Murray (esp. 203–7).
51 Foucault, *History*, 4.
52 Jane Wood, 104.
53 Wilde, *The Importance of Being Earnest*, Act 2, 383.
54 Buckler, 'Oscar,' 112.
55 Dollimore, 8.

56 Buckton, 185.
57 Wilde, *Dorian Gray*, 95–6.
58 Andersen, 5.
59 Wilde, 'Decay of Lying,' 1082.
60 Buckler remarks on a similar denial of authority through the use of dia-
    logue in 'The Decay of Lying': for Wilde, '[t]he most disheartening course
    vulgarity takes in aesthetic matters is the literalizing of the artist's observa-
    tions in a way that almost makes him despair of saying anything at all.
    Wilde hoped through fantasy to avoid such a result by making his point
    incomprehensible to the reader without imagination or, by signalling that
    he meant more than he was actually saying, to encourage qualified readers
    to play the spirited imaginative game along with him' ('Wilde's,' 314). Kof-
    man notes that Wilde's method of leaving 'the readers in doubt as to the
    genre he adopted' in *Dorian Gray* creates a similar denial of authorial (and
    authoritative) determination (31).

Chapter Four

1 Bennett, 170ff.
2 Bennett goes on to note that, despite such efforts as King's, the 'hopes for
   racial equality most profoundly addressed in the United States during the
   1960s were never translated into a spatial reality. Instead, since World
   War II, "central-city residence, race, joblessness, and poverty have become
   inextricably intertwined" in American ghettos' (170). Given the inequality
   of imprisonment, one could add the prison system to that 'inextricably
   intertwined' list. Bennett is quoting Thomas J. Sugrue, 3.
3 Sloop, 60.
4 Ibid., 77.
5 Davis, 'Racialized,' 100.
6 Bass's study offers a tremendously detailed, contextual history of the various clergymen behind the letter. Bass quite correctly states that it is problematic to read 'the eight white ministers [as] a monolithic group of
   obstructionists' (207), further pointing out that the clergymen were 'individuals with diverse ideas on the volatile segregation issue' (224). Despite
   the historical diversity of these men's thoughts, however, their co-authored
   letter does still stand as a singular text that engages in the specific historical
   and ideological forces that I analyse here. Rather than a simple condemnation of the clergymen themselves, I offer a close examination of their letter
   in order to demonstrate the reasons why it became such a flashpoint in the
   struggle. The full text of the clergymen's letter is reprinted in Bass, 235–6,

and Snow, 321. In the present essay, the parenthetical citations to this letter refer to paragraph number. Bass also reprints the clergymen's original letter that urges people to obey the desegregation law, and 'to pursue their convictions' only in court (234). For other readings of the clergymen's letter, see, for example, Clark, 34, and Hoover, 50–1.

7 Ho and Marshall, 212.

8 King, 'Letter from Birmingham City Jail,' 302. Unless otherwise noted, quotations are from this edition and will be cited parenthetically.

9 Althusser, 128.

10 Fairclough, 38.

11 Fairclough's notion of the construction of various subject positions from particular forms of discourse arises from such theorists as Bakhtin, who writes: 'At any given moment of its evolution, language is stratified ... into languages that are socio-ideological: languages of social groups, "professional" and "generic" languages, languages of generations and so forth' (271–2). For descriptions of Birmingham and the demonstrations, see, in addition to Bass, Baldwin, *Balm*, 198–203; Colaiaco, 77–95; Garrow, 231–86; and Hoover.

12 E. Culpepper Clark, 40.

13 Quoted in Bass, 233.

14 Andrews, *To Tell*, 180.

15 During the years that I wrote this book, both Thomas Blanton and Bobby Frank Cherry were convicted – almost forty years after the fact – for the deadly bombing of the 16th Street Baptist Church, when they were members of the KKK. Robert Chambliss was also convicted – in 1977. For one example of the contemporary depiction by the mainstream press of Birmingham's race relations, see 'Six Dead.'

16 Clark, 39.

17 Fairclough states that the examination of pronouns can uncover the masked subject positions in a given text. Among other functions, pronouns can obviously be used to include people within specific power relations (127–8), and they can also be used to exclude people, thus providing a linguistic parallel to segregation.

18 Altman, 43.

19 Williams, 166.

20 Bass, 46–7.

21 Hawkins and Thomas, 66.

22 Davis writes that 'both Emancipation and the authorization of penal servitude combined to create an immense black presence within southern prisons and to transform the character of punishment into a means of

managing former slaves as opposed to addressing problems of serious crime' ('Racialized,' 99). On the exclusionary nature of the supposedly 'universal' concept of the Enlightenment individual, see Sidonie Smith.

23 Keith D. Miller, *Voice*, 160.

24 Fulkerson, 123.

25 Keith D. Miller, *Voice*, 163.

26 Hoover, 55.

27 Hoover also structurally represents some aspects of King's letter, specifically the rhetorical construction of positive and negative values (60–1).

28 The Nation of Islam, a religious and militant black organization founded by Elijah Muhammad in 1931, has a history of connection with prison writing. Malcolm X (*Autobiography*, 158–90, and Interview, 38), Eldridge Cleaver (57–66), and Sanyika Shakur (203–34); among others, discuss in their autobiographies their prison conversions and relationships to the Nation of Islam and related groups.

29 Kauffman, xviii.

30 Approaching this redefinition from another angle, Baldwin writes: 'Overcoming racism as a world problem, King thought, involved removing both internal prejudices as well as external systems and symbols of white domination and privilege' (*Wounded*, 262).

31 While she focuses on epistolary fiction rather than historical letters, Altman's distinction between the 'internal' and 'external' reader – a division that is also reframed as the 'involved' and 'removed' addressees – similarly points to the epistle's ability to have multiple audiences even when there is only one actual addressee. See Altman, esp. 111–12, 200–12.

32 Keith D. Miller, *Voice*, 164.

33 Fulkerson, 123.

34 Lentz, 116–17.

35 For discussions of this tradition see, for example, John Ernest and Dolan Hubbard.

36 David L. Lewis, 188.

37 Andrews, *To Tell*, 46.

38 Ernest, 5. Ernest is writing specifically at this point about the nineteenth-century preacher and abolitionist J.W.C. Pennington.

39 Snow, 319.

40 Wesley T. Mott makes this point clear, writing, 'Against the outrages King so powerfully exposes, the recalcitrance of the eight clergymen reveals them as the true felons for their toleration of evil' (413). Paul's prison epistles are: Colossians; Ephesians; Philemon; and Philippians.

41 Erwin Smith, 17.

42 King, interview by Haley, 91.
43 See Zepp, 84–5, 118–19.
44 King, *Stride Toward Freedom*, 91.
45 This technique is clarified by Keith D. Miller, who writes that King 'merge[d] his voice and identity with a tradition of a white majority ... Surely this strategy endeared King to his white audiences' ('Composing,' 79). For an in-depth analysis of King's use of sources from the Western canon, see Ira G. Zepp, Jr, who notes that 'King marshals arguments of Catholic, Jewish, and Protestant traditions,' thus addressing all of the clergymen (120).
46 Jackson, *Soledad Brother*, 168.
47 Cleaver, 81.
48 Baldwin, *Balm*, 3.
49 See, for example, Miller, 'Composing' and *Voice*, and Hortense Spillers.
50 Page, 5.
51 Hubbard, 9.
52 Page, 32.
53 This textual practice could also be read through what several theorists of African American literature have called – picking up on a Bakhtinian phrase as revoiced by Henry Louis Gates Jr – a 'double voiced' discourse. Gates defines African American double voicedness in terms of the linguistic practice of signifyin(g). Dale E. Peterson offers a useful summary of Gates' argument:

> Finding useful an elaborate dialogic pun, Gates has devised a mature theory of African American discourse patterns that depends on rapid, context-specific apprehension of 'signifyin(g)' significations ... His core argument is that African American expression has traditionally cultivated a high degree of 'metaphoric literacy' because public articulation within earshot of a master discourse requires 'monkeyshines' and the 'aping' of rhetorical figures. Signifyin(g) is, then, 'essentially, a technique of repeating inside quotation marks in order to reverse or undermine pretended meaning, constituting an implicit parody of a subject's complicity'; it is repetition heard as revision in one deft discursive act. (93)

A large portion of the 'Letter' is geared around reworking the clergymen's language, turning, for example, their religious plea for peace and passivity into King's religious defence of his and others' civil disobedience. King's 'Letter' is very much a double-voiced document, but it does not engage – at least consistently – in the parodic and humorous aspects of signifyin(g), and so I do not deal with this issue at length. A study that does engage

King's 'Letter' in this manner would be useful. Peterson's essay also provides an excellent summary of the use of Bakhtin's theories by contemporary analysts of African American literature and culture. See Gates's foundational study, *The Signifying Monkey,* for an in-depth analysis of double-voicedness and signifyin(g). For his use of Bakhtin, see *Figures,* 247–50; and *Signifying,* 50–1, 110–13.

54 DuBois, 364–5.

55 King, 'When Peace Becomes Obnoxious,' 208.

56 King, 'Statement,' 426.

57 Clark, 43.

58 Clark, 44; added words in original. A passage from King's address 'Non-Aggression Procedures to Interracial Harmony' echoes his desire to discuss the struggle as one which exceeds racial divisions:

> We must come to see ... that the tension at bottom is not between races. As I like to say in Montgomery, the tension in Montgomery is not between seventy thousand white people and fifty thousand Negroes. The tension is at bottom a tension between justice and injustice. It is a tension between the forces of light and the forces of darkness. And if there is a victory, it will not be a victory merely for fifty thousand Negroes. If there is a victory for integration in America, it will not be a victory merely for sixteen million Negroes, but it will be a victory for justice, a victory for good will, a victory for democracy. (326)

King also uses a version of this passage in his essay 'The Current Crisis in Race Relations,' 87.

59 Gates, 'Writing "Race,"' 5.

60 For a list of King's pronoun usage in the 'Letter,' see Klein, 31–2.

61 Bogumil and Molino, 809.

62 O'Connor, 75.

63 Altman, 43. Jacobs's text contains a passage which similarly shifts pronouns to create a sympathetic identification between narrator and reader (55–6).

64 Moses, 54.

65 O'Connor, 75, 104.

66 Ralph McGill was the editor of the Atlanta *Constitution* newspaper, and an author whose works include *The South and the Southerner* (1963). Lillian Smith was a Southern author of such texts as her autobiographical work *Killers of the Dream* (1949). Harry Golden was a well-known Jewish American author and humorist who wrote, among others, *Mr. Kennedy and the Negroes* (1964) and *Only in America* (1958). James McBride Dabbs was a journalist and

the author of *Who Speaks for the South?* (1964). All of the authors were well known for their outspoken belief in civil rights and calls for racial equality.

67 Clark makes a related point, writing that the 'Letter' 'can be viewed as a rhetorical document that served both to end one phase of the Second Reconstruction and to herald a new and ... unsettled beginning' (36).

68 Zepp, 204. Zepp notes that King's formulation of a struggle leading to a future state of peace reflects a Hegelian notion of history, but I would argue that it is important to recognize that King does not subordinate human agency to the movement of history. Miller views this reformulation of Hegel as, more directly, 'echo[ing] the typology of the folk pulpit' ('Composing,' 78).

69 Fairclough, 39.

70 Page, 19.

Chapter Five

1 A more specific historical aside also links these two prison authors: Herbert Henry Asquith, who was Home Secretary during Wilde's trials and who was one of the signatories of Wilde's arrest warrant, was Prime Minister during Lytton's imprisonments and indeed through most of the period of suffragette militancy.

2 Wiener, 379, 380.

3 1912 Fabian tract, quoted in Wiener, 379.

4 For other examples of women's prison writing, beyond the suffrage movement, see Judith A. Scheffler's anthology, *Wall Tappings*. For discussions of women's punishment and confinement in general see, for example, Christopher Castiglia, Karlene Faith, and Elissa D. Gelfland. On the history of women in prison, see Harlow, *Barred*, Estelle B. Freedman, and Nicole Hahn Rafter.

5 Lytton, *Prisons and Prisoners*, 86–7. All subsequent quotations are from this edition, unless otherwise noted, and are cited parenthetically.

6 Green, 67.

7 The term 'passing,' of course, derives especially from African American culture and literature, and describes the act of a 'black' person crossing racial boundaries and being recognized and treated as 'white.' The concept of passing is therefore often used to demonstrate the porous nature of supposedly essential or natural racial categories. The term is now more generally used, beyond discussions of race, to describe the act of a member of any supposedly rigidly defined social group 'passing' as a member of another. For discussions of passing see, for example, the essays collected by Elaine K. Ginsberg.

8 June Purvis summarizes some of these readings, as well many of the prison narratives, in her article 'The Prison Experiences of the Suffragettes in Edwardian Britain.'

9 The WSPU was formed in 1903 by Emmeline Pankhurst, whose daughter, Christabel, would effectively go on to lead the group for the next ten years. Not being satisfied with the Liberal government's continued inaction on the issue of women's suffrage, the WSPU began a militant campaign in 1905. In what is generally cited as the first act of militancy, Annie Kenney (a working-class suffragette, and one of the early members of the WSPU) and Christabel Pankhurst disrupted a Liberal meeting at the Manchester Free Trade Hall in October 1905. Their action culminated with Pankhurst spitting at a policeman, which was legally constructed as an assault. As Barbara Green notes, because both women were taken into custody, 'the newspapers carried the story on the front page, and militancy was born' (3). The militants were subsequently labelled 'suffragettes' by the press in order to differentiate them from such groups as the National Union of Women's Suffrage Societies, who avoided 'illegal' action and were generally labelled 'suffragists.' The militants appropriated the derogatory term, with the WSPU even naming one journal *The Suffragette*. For a discussion of the complexities of the distinction between suffragist and suffragette, see Green, 185 n. 1; Colmore offers a contemporary depiction of the differences between 'suffragette' and 'suffragist,' 21, 24, 43–56, 60–1. The 1 May 1914 issue of *The Suffragette* also discusses the difference, in a brief editorial titled 'Suffragist or Suffragette?':

> We have all heard of the girl who asked what was the difference between a Suffragist and a Suffragette, as she pronounced it, and the answer made to her that the 'Suffragist jist wants the vote, while the Suffragette means to get it.' The matter has attracted some attention in the ordinary Press, and the 'Yorkshire Post' says, after dealing with the origin of the word 'Suffragette':
> [']The militants of the Women's Social and Political Union, with their usual aptitude for effects, saw that the word with its suggestion of youth and daintiness was an asset rather than the reverse, and they promptly adopted it and paraded it.['] (56)

The history of women's suffrage in Britain and elsewhere has been detailed by several critics, including Caine, Kent, *Sex* and *Gender*, Liddington, Rosen, and Tickner, as well as Green, esp. 1–27, Lyon, 94–7, and Holton, *Suffrage*. For early representations of the movement's history, see Jane Lewis, Marcus, Norquay, Pethick-Lawrence, and Strachey. McQuiston offers a useful timeline of the campaigns for women's suffrage. *The Suffrag-*

ette was retitled *Britannia* as the WSPU put its support behind Britain's war effort.

10 See, for example, Green, Howlett, Norquay, and Tickner.

11 Joannou, 104. Anti-suffrage material appeared in papers and pamphlets, and even in novels, such as W. Burton Baldry's *From Hampstead to Holloway: Depicting the Suffragette in Her Happiest Moods.*

12 Green, 84.

13 Norquay, 3.

14 See Norquay, 13–16, 39–40.

15 For the contexts surrounding discussions of gender, power, and text in the Victorian and Edwardian eras, see the collection edited by Shires (especially engaging in this context are the essays by Crosby, Ferris, Newton, and Shaw); Felski, *Gender*; and Ingram and Patai's introduction to their volume.

16 Kenney describes this same meeting in her own autobiography, *Memories of a Militant*. She writes that before Lytton's conversion to militancy, the upper-class woman was 'understanding and sympathetic even in her opposition' (87).

17 Hekman, 195.

18 Sidonie Smith, 'Resisting,' 76.

19 Ibid., 82.

20 Green, 31. Baldry's anti-suffrage novel depicts just such an 'unruly feminine crowd': 'Trafalgar Square was crowded with women ... And London was annoyed for it wanted to get home to its tea – and the huge crowd had stopped the traffic ... There was not a smile among the whole of that assembly. All their faces looked as though they were draped in black' (Baldry, 119–21). The crowd then begins a deputation, leading to a conflict with the police, which makes the statue of 'Poor Lord Nelson nearly [fall] off his monument!' (123).

21 Comparing these popular depictions of suffragettes to the representation of rape, Caroline J. Howlett, quoting Lynn Higgins and Brenda Silver, writes that such an 'elision of the scene of violence' 'is associated with a displacement of the violence, which is attributed to the raped woman rather than to the rapist' (11–12). Furthering this displacement, '[i]mages of women being punished or silenced were ... a staple of contemporary cartoon humour'; 'ridicule' of the suffragettes and comic denials of their abuse at the hands of the police were used as 'potent weapon[s] in the maintenance of hegemony' (Tickner, 163).

22 Indeed, in a letter dated 10 January 1908, kept in the British Library, Lytton tells a Mr Broadbent that Thoreau is one of her 'favourite authors.'

23 The pamphlet Lytton refers to is her '"No Votes for Women."'

24 Corbett, 165.

25 Marie Mulvey-Roberts describes the social position of Lytton's family in some detail (see esp. 162–3).

26 Wiener, 309.

27 Mulvey-Roberts, 160.

28 Green, 54.

29 Ibid., 62.

30 'Views and Comments,' 184.

31 Waters writes that, in this role of protector, Lytton falls into a general group of middle- and presumably leisure-class women who 'were encouraged to become involved in the provision of "improving" recreations for the working class as a whole. Here was one area of activity where the ideal virtues attributed to women ... could be put to a good social use' (Waters, 167). For a discussion of some other, much more positive public responses to Lytton's story, see Sue Thomas, esp. 61–5.

32 Green, 99.

33 Susan Kingsley Kent cites one medical doctor's opinion that the suffragettes' militancy was the result of a '"mental disorder" caused by "physiological emergencies" within their reproductive systems' (Gender, 269). Lytton's attack on the medical gaze strongly echoes that of Charlotte Perkins Gilman, especially as portrayed in 'The Yellow Wallpaper.' Lytton refers to reading Gilman's The Man-made World during her last imprisonment (333). Gilman's narrator in 'The Yellow Wallpaper' equates the pseudo-medical 'rest cure' with imprisonment in order to expose the oppression of traditional gender roles. Similarly, Lytton exposes the hypocrisy of the medical profession's classification of women in order to highlight the specific oppression of the prison and the larger social subjugation of women. At one point, Lytton sarcastically reminds the governor and the prison doctor that 'prison was not a "rest cure"' (145).

34 Foucault, 'Politics,' 166.

35 Joannou notes that the phrase 'no surrender' was 'made famous by the militant suffragette Mary Leigh' (110) who, as Myall discusses, was 'a working-class suffragette' (174). See Purvis for a general overview of working-class involvement in suffragette activity.

36 See Wiener, 310–13.

37 Howlett, 6.

38 Departments of States and Official Bodies, Home Office, 'Suffragist Women Prisoners.'

39 Howlett, 5, 7.

40 While my use of the word 'performance' in this context recalls Judith Butler's theoretical reading of the linguistic category of the performative in
terms of gender (see Butler, 'Imitation'), I am using the term in its more
mundane dress. Butler's theoretical frame, in which gender is itself an
unconscious performative social structure, could provide a valuable reading of Lytton's text, in terms not only of gender but also of class. In my
more general use of the word, Lytton's act of becoming Jane is performative
in that she is Jane Warton as far as society is concerned – the various signs
she uses to represent the working class are in themselves the act that makes
her Jane Warton in the eyes of others. Unlike Butler's performative, Lytton's sign/act is very much a conscious one.

41 Howlett, 31.

42 Mulvey-Roberts, 167.

43 As Mulvey-Roberts writes, 'By embracing anonymity through her Jane
Warton disguise, Lytton was better equipped not only to identify with
women across the class divide but also to draw attention to the ordeals
endured by forgotten women' (162).

44 Felman, 14.

45 Lytton's dual subjectivity further functions against Maud Ellmann's assertion that, despite the hunger strikers' 'refus[al] to be influenced by the
authorities ... their sufferings reveal that this denial of the other necessarily
entails the isolation and annihilation of the self' (93). The value of Ellmann's construction of 'hunger artists' (women who use self-starvation as a
means of gaining power) is further belied by her occasional denial of historical context and textual evidence in order to further an overly general psy-
choanalytic point. This lends to potential misreadings of hunger strikes. For
example, after discussing Lytton's text, she writes:

> Nonetheless, it is hard to silence the suspicion, unwelcome as it is, that
> these women are obeying an unconscious *wish* to be force-fed and to
> experience the shattering of subjectivity that it entails. Indeed, what
> makes these episodes particularly harrowing is that they reawaken a
> trauma familiar to us all. Our first experience of eating is force-feeding:
> as infants, we were fed by others and ravished by the food they thrust
> into our jaws. We eat, therefore, in order to avenge ourselves against this
> rape inflicted at the very dawn of life ... *All eating is force-feeding.* (35–6)

The slippage between the forcible feeding of the suffragettes (an act of violence largely without value as a food source) and the everyday feeding of a
child (not to mention between the feeding of an infant and rape) can be
seen as dangerously denying the violence perpetrated against these
women. The pathologizing of 'all eating' could also be read as a misrecog-

nition of the suffering of people who have eating disorders, whom Ellmann also discusses. Mulvey-Roberts offers a more contextualized reading of Lytton as a masochist, and similarly notes that 'Ellmann is over-stating the case' (179n37).

46 Howlett, 9.
47 Corbett, 161.
48 Howlett, 7.
49 Mason, 22.
50 Caren Kaplan, 121.
51 Sidonie Smith writes that traditional autobiography 'involves a contractual obligation in which the autobiographer engages in a narrative itinerary of self-disclosure, retrospective summation, self-justification' (*Subjectivity*, 162). Felski sees the critique of the traditional autobiographical subject as a condition of what she refers to as feminist confessions. She writes: '[T]he shift toward a conception of communal identity which has emerged with new social movements such as feminism brings with it a modification of the notion of individualism as it is exemplified in the male bourgeois autobiography' (*Beyond*, 93–4).
52 Corbett, 170.
53 Green, 90.
54 Billington-Grieg's and other dissidents' problems with the non-democratic practices of the WSPU led to the formation in 1907 of the Women's Freedom League. See Eustance, 51. Billington-Grieg's questioning of the WSPU looks forward to contemporary critiques of the extant patriarchal nature of Western culture, in which, as Judith Kegan Gardiner writes, 'the woman laborer [is] all too often exploited and ignored' (3).
55 Corbett, 173.
56 Thomas, 60.
57 Corbett, 169.
58 Howlett, 33.
59 On Schreiner's dedication, see Felski, *Gender*, 156.
60 Gagnier, *Subjectivities*, 45–6.
61 Howlett, 36.
62 Sidonie Smith, *Subjectivity*, 155–6.
63 Mulvey-Roberts, 162–3.
64 Ibid., 162.
65 Thomas, 65.
66 Howlett, 34.
67 Mulvey-Roberts, 161. Shortly after making this somewhat Thoreauvian point, Mulvey-Roberts writes that the 'secularised religiosity that pervaded the WSPU ... filled an emotional void for Constance following an unhappy

love affair' (161). Mulvey-Roberts makes this point within the overall context of her laudable efforts to break 'down the hagiographic approach' that she sees in some readings of Lytton's text and life (176). Even within this context, though, and despite the excellence of her analysis, the phrasing of the statement above (no matter its authenticity) could risk being seen as reducing Lytton's motives for her suffrage activities solely to gendered stereotypes.

68 Friedman, 40.

Chapter Six

1 Breytenbach, *The True Confessions of an Albino Terrorist*, 334. Subsequent references will be to this edition, and will be cited parenthetically.
2 Breytenbach is most likely referring to the establishment of the Universal Inquisition by Pope Paul III in 1542.
3 Breytenbach makes a more condemnatory statement about state security in an article originally published in 1985, one year after the publication of the *Confessions*: 'Repression, with its concomitants of violence and corruption, will inevitably be justified in the name of the state's supposed security, which is the highest good and ideal; the state is God's carcass inhabited by the good and the just ... The army and the police, particularly the security police and the intelligence advisers, become the mainstay of the regime' ('South African,' 29).
4 Coetzee, 225.
5 Some critics deal with the relationship that Breytenbach draws between the interrogator and the interrogated. Jolly views it as 'reflect[ing] to some extent the perverse mutual dependence of the dominant and submissive selves found in sadomasochistic relationships' (64). J.U. Jacobs analyses the prevalence of this relationship in South African prison writing as a genre, viewing it through Louis J. West's 'D D D [Debility, Dependancy, Dread] syndrome' ('Confession,' 121ff.). Doherty reads into the relationship a Lacanian relationship of an alienated self and a desired Other. Despite the variances in their readings, all of the critics note that, as J.U. Jacobs writes, 'The various modes of interrogation ... form an interrogative matrix for an eventual process of self-investigation in narrative' ('Confession,' 118). This self-investigation is necessarily combined with, I would add, a narrative of political investigation.
6 Many authors have sketched Breytenbach's biography, their descriptions usually culminating with his imprisonment and eventual release. Most of these brief histories rely on Breytenbach's own autobiographical works, *A Season in Paradise*, *The True Confessions of an Albino Terrorist*, and *Return to*

Paradise. See, for example, Jolly, 61; Egan, 'Breytenbach's,' 89; Moore, 3–4; and, dating before Breytenbach's release from prison, André Brink's introduction to *A Season in Paradise*, 9–17. Breytenbach has recently added *Dog Heart: A Memoir* to his autobiographical writings.

7 Breytenbach, 'I am not,' 4; also quoted in Jolly, 61.
8 Also quoted in Jolly, 100. Jan Breytenbach is an author in his own right, largely of military and adventure books such as, for example, *Buffalo Soldiers: The Story of South Africa's 32-Battalion: 1975-1993, Forged in Battle*, and *The Plunderers*.
9 Sloop, 78.
10 Lovesay, 36.
11 For a description of the various classifications of prisoners by race and security categories, see Cook, 31–2. Cook also includes an appendix documenting the different rations allotted to members of each racial category in prison (74). For a summary of apartheid laws, see McLachlan. As to his distinction between Afrikaners and English-speaking 'red-necks,' Breytenbach's decision to write the *Confessions* in English, thus distancing himself somewhat from his Afrikaner heritage, supports Harlow's general assertion about resistance writing, that '[t]he very choice of the language in which to compose is itself a political statement' (*Resistance*, xviii). Not only does Breytenbach reject the language of oppression; but, furthermore, in adopting English he could be seen as attacking Afrikaner history, which lauds the Afrikaner rebellion against English colonialism. Recently, however, Breytenbach has attempted to resurrect Afrikaans as a creole language that was born from oppression, and is therefore resonant with various political struggles. In an interview on CBC Radio, he stated that Afrikaans 'is not a white man's language ... and it carries within it, as creole languages do, a wonderful adaptability to the environment within which it finds itself.' Still, he is wary of taking 'this point a little too far,' of perhaps overly romanticizing Afrikaans as the apartheid regime did.
12 Breytenbach, *A Season*, 27.
13 Breytenbach, *Dog Heart*, 1.
14 Ibid.
15 Reckwitz, 12.
16 O'Connor, 77. As J.U. Jacobs establishes, scenes such as this one are in fact characteristic of South African prison writing. He cites several authors, including Moses Dlamini, Indres Naidoo, and Frank Chikane, who identify themselves in their works in terms of the numbers or the classifications that the prison gives them ('Confession,' 116). Michael Dingake, who served fifteen years on Robben Island with Nelson Mandela, refers in his text to his 'new identity as prisoner number 277/66' (140). Breytenbach's specific

engagement with this tradition not only demonstrates the pervasiveness of the apartheid police state, but also reinforces his own depiction of the state's power. The prison officials become figures of the almighty power of those in charge of heaven itself.

17 Breytenbach, *Mouroir*, 70.
18 Golz, 52.
19 *Mouroir*, 70.
20 Wilde, 'Soul of Man,' 1182.
21 Butler, 'Imitation,' 23.
22 Breytenbach retells the story of the Minotaur in *Dog Heart* (146), placing it as one of several 'weighty matters' (145) his daughter discusses with him during a visit to post-apartheid South Africa. The emphasis in *Dog Heart*, in contrast to the *Confessions*, is placed in part on the king's death after Theseus kills the Minotaur – perhaps a metaphor for the whites' loss of power and the transformation of the country afterwards, which, I'd argue, Breytenbach allegorically describes here as '"good" in a practical and possibly a moral sense,' but which is still a 'painful' process (145).
23 Breytenbach, *Mouroir*, 55–6.
24 Ibid., 56.
25 Davis, 'Racialized,' 99.
26 Brink, 16.
27 Mandela, 126.
28 First, 135.
29 Pheto, 69. For discussions of both Pheto's and First's texts, see Harlow, *Barred*, 22–3, 145–57.
30 Lewin, 38.
31 Naidoo, 20–6. See also Cook, who includes an appendix of 'prisoners' testimony' in his work (64–73), as well as the section titled 'Treatment of Prisoners' in Amnesty International's *Political Imprisonment in South Africa* (56–91).
32 Dingake, 102.
33 Schalkwyk, 25. In a similar vein, Attridge and Jolly, in the introduction to their recent collection of essays on South Africa, write that 'the history of South African culture is illuminating for its numerous instances of those who have rejected ethnic identification as a means of negotiating their future because of the bigoted formulation it takes within a racist imagination' (9).
34 Fischer, 46.
35 Mandela, 472.
36 Jolly, 70.
37 Ibid., 99.

38 Ibid., 90.
39 Schalkwyk, 26. Doherty misreads the addressee of the *Confessions* as, even-
    tually, being stably constructed as 'the voice of future authority in South
    Africa, of a black political group questioning Breytenbach about his behav-
    ior in prison' (236). In addition to the constant trope of what Jolly calls the
    dislocation of identity, however, Breytenbach writes, in the 'Note' at the
    end of the text (which Doherty mentions, but briefly), 'I was in the first
    instance, in all intimacy, talking to [my wife]; telling her all which I'd had to
    hold back over the years' (338). Thus Davies, who also sees the addressee as
    a member of the 'revolutionary black South African movement,' admits
    that, 'even "Mr. Investigator" had his origins in a Vietnamese woman,' and
    equates this to what he sees as the '*briccolage*' of the text (160, 161). The
    addressee is, *at times*, constructed as a black person in a position of power,
    but that is not the sole construction.
40 Emma Mashinini, in her South African prison memoir, describes a similarly
    problematic relationship between the interrogator and interrogated: 'These
    outings – to the doctor, to the interrogation, to my visitors – served a very
    good purpose, because it was going out to meet people, to see other things
    and most of all to see people. Even interrogation I looked forward to. And if
    they didn't call me for interrogation, I really wanted to remind them,
    because interrogation was better than to be isolated and all by myself for all
    those months' (85). While Mashinini thus complicates the relationship
    between interrogator and prisoner, unlike Breytenbach's text hers empha-
    sizes the terror of isolation as the cause.
41 Tambling, 209.
42 Breytenbach, *Memory*, 86.
43 See 'An Open Letter to Nelson Mandela, 1991,' and 'An Open Letter to Nel-
    son Mandela, 1994' (*Memory*, 74–87). In the CBC Radio interview, when dis-
    cussing the present social state of South Africa, Breytenbach stated that he
    thought that the country is 'probably moving in a direction of what one
    could call a kind of a less democratic form of stability. The stability part,
    which is what the present community and the outside world really wants
    to see, will have to be enforced probably with some kind of authoritative
    means, and that's not good either.'
44 Leigh Gilmore, 55.
45 Jolly, 99.
46 Ibid.
47 Ibid., 98.
48 Lovesay, 34.
49 Derrida, 'Otobiographies,' 19.

50 Caren Kaplan, 121.
51 Harlow, *Resistance*, 125, 129.
52 Sidonie Smith, *Subjectivity*, 155–6.
53 See Derrida's 'Racism's Last Word' for his specific comments on apartheid.
    See also the critiques of that essay by Jolly, xvi n. 2; and McClintock and
    Nixon, as well as Derrida's response to them.
54 Breytenbach, *Mouroir*, 62.
55 Egan, *Mirror*, 12.
56 Breytenbach, *Mouroir*, 62–3.
57 Jolly, 85.
58 Ibid.
59 De Man, 81.
60 Breytenbach, 'Interview.'
61 Bataille, 145.
62 Pheto, 170.
63 Dingake, 182.

Closing Statements / Opening Arguments

 1 Harlow, *Barred*, 31. For further discussions of the relationships between the
    university and the prison, see *Workplace: A Journal for Academic Labor* 3.2.
    This issue (edited by Bruce Simon) was dedicated to the analysis of the
    prison and its ideological and practical connections to a variety of social
    issues. Two articles in particular address the relation between prisons and
    universities. H. Bruce Franklin's essay, 'The American Prison in the Culture
    Wars,' details the economic and larger relationships in the past 40 years
    between the prison and university systems. Robert Gangi, Vincent
    Schiraldi, and Jason Ziedenberg update the 1998 Justice Policy Institute
    report in their article, 'New York State of Mind? Higher Education vs.
    Prison Funding in the Empire State, 1988-1998,' analysing New York's con-
    current slashing of the education budget and increasing of the prison bud-
    get. As Simon notes in his introduction to the issue, all of the essays deal
    with the relationship between the academic and imprisoning institutions:

    '[C]ontributors refused to treat prisons and universities simply as institu-
    tions competing for state support in a conceptual vacuum. Instead, they
    repeatedly pointed out the complicity of academic disciplines and insti-
    tutions in the formation and development of the U.S. prison system and
    situated both prisons and universities within a larger political economy.'
    (para. 6).

2 Butler, *Excitable*, 16.

3 Foucault, *History*, 96.

4 Said, 10–11.

5 Davis, 'Racialized,' 103.

6 Ibid., 103–4.

7 For further discussions of prison abolition, see, for a few examples among many, Thomas Mathiesen's influential work, and the essays collected by Bianchi and René van Swaaningen. Several websites are also dedicated to prison abolition (see, for example, the site for the Coalition for the Abolition of Prisons, Inc., http://www.noprisons.org); also, the International Circle of Penal Abolitionists holds a biennial conference on the subject (see their website at http://www.interlog.com/~ritten/icop/icopaix3.htm).

8 Duff and Garland, 333.

9 Bianchi, 'Abolition,' 340.

10 This type of communication was the goal of the Truth and Reconciliation Commission in South Africa, which allowed both the victims and perpetrators of racial violence to discuss the past, in order to be able, hopefully, to come to communal forms of understanding and grieving. The commission was created, in the words of Dullah Omar, the former South African minister of justice, as an 'exercise to enable South Africans to come to terms with their past on a morally accepted basis and to advance the cause of reconciliation' (quoted from the Truth and Reconciliation Commission home page). The TRC website (http://www.doj.gov.za/trc) contains much information about the program, including papers that debate its effectiveness. Also see the 'Discussion with Alex Boraine and Breyten Breytenbach,' in which Breytenbach and Boraine, a co-chair of the TRC, engage in a conversation about the Commission's role.

11 Mathiesen, 211–12.

12 Of course, an expensive prison system would seem better than the newest trend of 'prisons for profit' run by private companies, whose monetary interest in maintaining at least a steady influx of inmates appears superficially obvious.

13 O'Connor calls for a similar engagement in her analysis of prisoners' self-constructions in spoken narratives, writing that such narratives 'indicate opportunities for dynamic interaction in the construction of new selves' (22). She limits this interaction, to a degree, to a form of prisoner rehabilitation, noting that analysing prisoner's speech 'could lead to locating, even constructing, a more responsible self' (24), and that '[f]ruitful uptake depends ... upon hearing the stories and reacting to them – validating or challenging, but nonetheless interacting with the prisoner, not isolating him

from the potential for changed behaviour' (155). While certainly positive, this statement could seem to ignore the possibility that the prisoner may have useful comments on how *others* can change. O'Connor's valuable conclusions could be expanded, though, to include the recognition that such discussions can also lead to reformations of the non-prisoner, of the society which the authors studied here critique.

14 Abu-Jamal, *Live from Death Row*, 84–5. For discussions of mass imprisonment see, for example, the essays in Garland's *Mass Imprisonment*, and Christian Parenti's *Lockdown America*.

15 Charles Culhane, 'Of Cold Places.' Franklin offers a brief biography of this poet (*Prison*, 290), which I summarize here. Culhane was convicted of felony murder in 1971, for his supposed participation in an escape attempt during which another prisoner killed a deputy sheriff. After two trials, Culhane was sentenced to be executed. His conviction was overturned, and he was subsequently found guilty in a third trial (despite having such people as Allen Ginsberg and William Buckley on his defence committee). He was paroled in 1992. Culhane went on to do a master's degree and to lecture in the American Studies department at the State University of New York at Buffalo.

Works Cited

Abelove, Henry. 'From Thoreau to Queer Politics.' *Yale Journal of Criticism* 6.2 (1993): 17–27.

Abu-Jamal, Mumia. *Death Blossoms: Reflections from a Prisoner of Conscience.* Farmington: Plough Publishing, 1997.

– *Live from Death Row.* New York: Addison-Wesley, 1995.

– *We Want Freedom: A Life in the Black Panther Party.* Cambridge, MA: South End Press, 2004.

Accomando, Christina. *'The Regulations of Robbers': Legal Fictions of Slavery and Resistance.* Columbus: Ohio State University Press, 2001.

Alderson, David. 'Momentary Pleasures: Wilde and English Virtue.' In *Sex, Nation, and Dissent in Irish Writing*, ed. Éibhear Walshe, 43–59. New York: St Martin's Press, 1997.

Althusser, Louis. 'Ideology and Ideological State Apparatuses (Notes towards an Investigation).' In *Lenin and Philosophy and Other Essays*, trans. Ben Brewster, 121–73. London: New Left Books, 1971.

Altman, Janet Gurkin. *Epistolarity: Approaches to a Form.* Columbus: Ohio State University Press, 1982.

Amnesty International. *Political Imprisonment in South Africa.* London: Amnesty International, 1978.

Andersen, M.C. 'Document of Division: Oscar Wilde's *De Profundis.*' *UNISA English Studies* 27.2 (1989): 1–11.

Andrews, William L. 'Dialogue in Antebellum Afro-American Autobiography.' In *Studies in Autobiography*, ed. James Olney, 89–98. Oxford: Oxford University Press, 1988.

– *To Tell a Free Story: The First Century of Afro-American Autobiography, 1760–1865.* Urbana: University of Illinois Press, 1986.

Andrews, William L., ed. *Critical Essays on Frederick Douglass*. Boston: G.K. Hall & Co., 1991.

– *Sisters of the Spirit: Three Black Women's Autobiographies of the Nineteenth Century*. Bloomington: Indiana University Press, 1986.

– *Six Women's Slave Narratives*. Oxford: Oxford University Press, 1988.

Attridge, Derek, and Rosemary Jolly, ed. *Writing South Africa: Literature, Apartheid, and Democracy, 1970–1995*. Cambridge: Cambridge University Press, 1998.

Augst, Thomas. 'Composing the Moral Senses: Emerson and the Politics of Character in Nineteenth-Century America.' *Political Theory* 27.1 (1999): 85–120.

Bakhtin, M.M. 'Discourse in the Novel.' In *The Dialogic Imagination*, trans. Caryl Emerson and Michael Holquist, ed. Michael Holquist, 259–422. Austin: University of Texas Press, 1981.

Baldry, W. Burton. *From Hampstead to Holloway: Depicting the Suffragette in Her Happiest Moods*. Illus. G.E. Shepheard. London: John Ouseley Ltd, 1909.

Baldwin, Lewis V. *There Is a Balm in Gilead: The Cultural Roots of Martin Luther King, Jr.* Minneapolis: Fortress, 1991.

– *To Make the Wounded Whole: The Cultural Legacy of Martin Luther King, Jr.* Minneapolis: Fortress, 1992.

Bashford, Bruce. 'Oscar Wilde as Theorist: The Case of *De Profundis*.' *English Literature in Transition 1880–1920* 28.4 (1985): 395–406.

Bass, S. Jonathan. *Blessed Are the Peacemakers: Martin Luther King Jr., Eight White Religious Leaders, and the 'Letter from Birmingham Jail'*. Baton Rouge: Louisiana State University Press, 2001.

Bataille, Georges. 'The Psychological Structure of Fascism.' Trans. Carl R. Lovitt. In *Visions of Excess: Selected Writings, 1927–1939*, ed. Alan Stoekl, 137–60. Minneapolis: University of Minnesota Press, 1985.

Bender, John. *Imagining the Penitentiary: Fiction and the Architecture of Mind in Eighteenth-Century England*. Chicago: University of Chicago Press, 1987.

Bennett, Michael. 'Manufacturing the Ghetto: Anti-urbanism and the Spatialization of Race.' In *The Nature of Cities: Ecocriticism and Urban Environments*, ed. Michael Bennett and David W. Teague, 169–88. Tucson: University of Arizona Press, 1999.

Bentham, Jeremy. *The Panopticon Writings*. Ed. Miran Božovič. London: Verso, 1995.

Bercovitch, Sacvan. *The American Jeremiad*. Madison: University of Wisconsin Press, 1978.

Bianchi, Herman. 'Abolition: Assensus and Sanctuary.' In Duff and Garland, *Reader on Punishment*, 336–51.

Bianchi, Herman, and René van Swaaningen, eds. *Abolitionism: Toward a Non-Repressive Approach to Crime*. Amsterdam: Free University Press, 1986.

Blassingame, John W. *The Slave Community: Plantation Life in the Antebellum South*. Revised and enlarged edition. Oxford: Oxford University Press, 1979.

Bogin, Ruth, and Jean Fagan Yellin. Introduction. In Yellin and Van Horne, *Abolitionist Sisterhood*, 1–19.

Bogumil, Mary L., and Michael R. Molino. 'Pretext, Context, Subtext: Textual Power in the Writing of Langston Hughes, Richard Wright, and Martin Luther King, Jr.' *College English* 52.7 (1990): 800–11.

Braxton, Joanne. *Black Women Writing Autobiography: A Tradition Within a Tradition*. Philadelphia: Temple University Press, 1989.

Breytenbach, Breyten. *Dog Heart: A Memoir*. New York: Harcourt Brace, 1999.

– '"I am not an Afrikaner any more."' *Index on Censorship* 12.3 (1983): 3–6.

– Interview. *Writers and Company*. CBC Radio, Radio One, Toronto. 6 Feb. 2000.

– *The Memory of Birds in Times of Revolution*, 74–81. London: Faber and Faber, 1996.

– *Mouroir: Mirrornotes of a Novel*. London: Faber and Faber, 1984.

– *Return to Paradise*. London: Faber and Faber, 1993.

– *A Season in Paradise*. Trans. Rike Vaughn. London: Jonathan Cape, 1980.

– 'The South African Wasteland.' 1985. In Mermelstein, *Anti-Apartheid Reader*, 27–38.

– *The True Confessions of an Albino Terrorist*. London: Faber and Faber, 1984.

Breytenbach, Jan. *Buffalo Soldiers: The Story of South Africa's 32-Battalion: 1975-1993*. Johannesburg: Galago, 2002.

– *Forged in Battle*. Cape Town: Saayman and Weber, 1986.

– *The Plunderers*. Johannesburg: Covos-Day, 2001.

Brink, André. 'Interrogating Silence: New Possibilities Faced by South African Literature.' In Attridge and Jolly, *Writing South Africa*, 14–28.

Bristow, Joseph. *Effeminate England: Homoerotic Writing after 1885*. New York: Columbia University Press, 1995.

Broadhead, Richard H. *Cultures of Letters: Scenes of Reading and Writing in Nineteenth-Century America*. Chicago: University of Chicago Press, 1993.

Brombert, Victor. 'The Happy Prison: A Recurring Romantic Metaphor.' In *Romanticism: Vistas, Instances, Continuities*, ed. David Thorburn and Geoffrey Hartman, 62–79. Ithaca: Cornell University Press, 1973.

Brown, Julia Prewitt. *Cosmopolitan Criticism: Oscar Wilde's Philosophy of Art*. Charlottesville: University Press of Virginia, 1997.

Buckler, William E. 'Oscar Wilde's Aesthetic of the Self: Art as Imaginative Self-Realization in *De Profundis*.' *Biography* 12.2 (1989): 95–115.

– 'Wilde's "Trumpet Against the Gate of Dullness": "The Decay of Lying."'
   English Literature in Transition 1880–1920 33.3 (1990): 311–23.
Buckton, Oliver S. '"Desire Without Limit": Dissident Confession in Oscar
   Wilde's *De Profundis.*' In *Victorian Sexual Dissidence*, ed. Richard Dellamora,
   171–87. Chicago: University of Chicago Press, 1999.
Burgett, Bruce. *Sentimental Bodies: Sex, Gender, and Citizenship in the Early Repub-
   lic.* Princeton: Princeton University Press, 1998.
Burnham, Michelle. 'Loopholes of Resistance: Harriet Jacobs's Slave Narrative
   and the Critique of Agency in Foucault.' *Arizona Quarterly* 49.2 (1993): 53–73.
Butler, Judith. *Excitable Speech: A Politics of the Performative.* New York: Rout-
   ledge, 1997.
– 'Imitation and Gender Insubordination.' In *Inside/Out: Lesbian Theories, Gay
   Theories*, ed. Diana Fuss, 13–31. New York: Routledge, 1991.
Butwin, Joseph. 'The Martyr Clown: Oscar Wilde in *De Profundis.*' *Victorian
   Newsletter* 42 (1972): 1–6.
Caine, Barbara. *English Feminism 1780–1980.* Oxford: Oxford University Press,
   1997.
Calloway-Thomas, Carolyn, and John Louis Lucaites, eds. *Martin Luther King,
   Jr., and the Sermonic Power of Public Discourse.* Tuscaloosa: University of Ala-
   bama Press, 1993.
Caponigri, A. Robert. 'Individual, Civil Society, and State in American Tran-
   scendentalism.' In *Critical Essays on American Transcendentalism*, ed. Philip F.
   Gura and Joel Myerson, 541–60. Boston: G.K. Hall, 1982.
Carby, Hazel V. *Reconstructing Womanhood: The Emergence of the Afro-American
   Woman Novelist.* Oxford: Oxford University Press, 1987.
Carnochan, W.B. 'The Literature of Confinement.' In Morris and Rothman,
   Oxford History of the Prison, 427–55.
Castiglia, Christopher. *Bound and Determined: Captivity, Culture-Crossing, and
   White Womanhood from Mary Rowlandson to Patty Hearst.* Chicago: University
   of Chicago Press, 1996.
Castronovo, Russ. 'Incidents in the Life of a White Woman: Economies of Race
   and Gender in the Antebellum Nation.' *American Literary History* 10.2 (1998):
   239–65.
'Central Criminal Court, April 5.' *Times*, 6 April 1895: 10D.
'Central Criminal Court, May 1.' *Times*, 2 May 1895: 3.
Chai, Leon. *Aestheticism: The Religion of Art in Post-Romantic Literature.* New
   York: Columbia University Press, 1990.
Chapman, Mary, and Glenn Hendler. Introduction. In *Sentimental Men: Mascu-
   linity and the Politics of Affect in American Culture*, ed. Mary Chapman and
   Glenn Hendler, 1–16. Berkeley: University of California Press, 1999.

Chevigny, Bell Gale, ed. *Doing Time: 25 Years of Prison Writing*. New York: Arcade, 1999.

Clark, E. Culpepper. 'The American Dilemma in King's "Letter from Birmingham Jail."' In Calloway-Thomas and Lucaites, *Martin Luther King*, 33–49.

Cleaver, Eldridge. *Soul on Ice*. 1968. New York: Dell, 1991.

The Coalition for the Abolition of Prisons, Inc. Web site. Ed. Mutaamba-By Wa Maasha, Balam N. Kenter, and Dirk Schmaljohann. 2001. http://www.noprisons.org (accessed 7 Sept. 2003).

Coetzee, J.M. 'Breyten Breytenbach and the Reader in the Mirror.' In *Giving Offense: Essays on Censorship*, 215–32. Chicago: University of Chicago Press, 1996.

Cohen, Ed. *Talk on the Wilde Side: Toward a Genealogy of a Discourse on Male Sexualities*. New York: Routledge, 1993.

Colaiaco, James A. *Martin Luther King, Jr.: Apostle of Militant Nonviolence*. 1988. New York: St Martin's Press, 1993.

Colmore, Gertrude. *Suffragette Sally*. 1911. Reprinted as *Suffragettes: A Story of Three Women*, London: Pandora, 1984.

Cook, Allen. *South Africa: The Imprisoned Society*. London: International Defence and Aid Fund, 1974.

Corbett, Mary Jean. *Representing Femininity: Middle-Class Subjectivity in Victorian and Edwardian Women's Autobiographies*. Oxford: Oxford University Press, 1992.

Crosby, Christina. 'Reading the Gothic Revival: "History" and *Hints on Household Taste*.' In Shires, *Rewriting the Victorians*, 101–15.

Culhane, Charles. 'Of Cold Places.' In *Prison Writing in 20th-Century America*, ed. H. Bruce Franklin, 292. New York: Penguin, 1998.

Cutter, Martha J. 'Dismantling "The Master's House": Critical Literacy in Harriet Jacobs's *Incidents in the Life of a Slave Girl*.' *Callaloo* 19.1 (1996): 209–25.

Dabbs, James McBride. *Who Speaks for the South?* New York: Funk and Wagnalls, 1964.

Danson, Lawrence. 'Wilde as Critic and Theorist.' In *The Cambridge Companion to Oscar Wilde*, ed. Peter Raby, 80–95. Cambridge: Cambridge University Press, 1997.

Davies, Ioan. *Writers in Prison*. Toronto: Between the Lines, 1990.

Davis, Angela Y. *The Angela Davis Reader*. Ed. Joy James. Oxford: Blackwell, 1998.

– 'From the Prison of Slavery to the Slavery of Prison: Frederick Douglass and the Convict Lease System.' In Davis, *Reader*, 74–95.

– 'Political Prisoners, Prisons and Black Liberation.' In Davis, *If They Come*, 27–43.

- 'Race, Gender, and Prison History: From the Convict Lease System to the Supermax Prison.' In *Prison Masculinities*, ed. Don Sabo, Terry A. Kupers, and Willie London, 35–45. Philadelphia: Temple University Press, 2001.
- 'Racialized Punishment and Prison Abolition.' In Davis, *Reader*, 96–107.
- 'Trials of Political Prisoners Today.' In Davis, *If They Come*, 77–105.
Davis, Angela Y., Ruchell Magee, the Soledad Brothers, and Other Political Prisoners. *If They Come in the Morning: Voices of Resistance*. New York: Signet, 1971.
de Beaumont, Gustave, and Alexis de Tocqueville. *On the Penitentiary System in the United States and its Application in France*. Trans. Francis Lieber. 1833. Reprint, ed. Herman R. Lantz, Carbondale: Southern Illinois University Press, 1964.
Dedmond, Francis B. '"Many Things to Many People": Thoreau in His Time and Ours.' *Forum* 30.3 (1989): 60–9.
Deleuze, Gilles. *Foucault*. Ed. and Trans. Seán Hand. Minneapolis: University of Minnesota Press, 1988.
de Man, Paul. 'Autobiography as De-Facement.' In *The Rhetoric of Romanticism*, 67–81. New York: Columbia University Press, 1984.
Denisoff, Dennis. 'Posing a Threat: Queensberry, Wilde, and the Portrayal of Decadence.' In *Perennial Decay: On the Aesthetics and Politics of Decadence*, ed. Liz Constable, Dennis Denisoff, and Matthew Potolsky, 83–100. Philadelphia: University of Pennsylvania Press, 1999.
Departments of States and Official Bodies, Home Office. 'Suffragist Women Prisoners.' 18 December 1909. *Home Office Papers and Memoranda*, 1889–1910.
Derrida, Jacques. 'But beyond ...: (Open Letter to Anne McClintock and Rob Nixon).' Trans. Peggy Kamuf. In Gates, *'Race,'* 354–69.
- 'Otobiographies: The Teaching of Nietzsche and the Politics of the Proper Name.' Trans. Avital Ronnell. In *The Ear of the Other: Otobiography, Transference, Translation*, ed. Christie McDonald, trans. Peggy Kamuf, 1–38. Lincoln: University of Nebraska Press, 1985.
- 'Racism's Last Word.' Trans. Peggy Kamuf. In Gates, *'Race,'* 329–38.
Dingake, Michael. *My Fight Against Apartheid*. London: Kliptown, 1987.
'Discussion with Alex Boraine and Breyten Breytenbach.' 30 Nov. 1999. Humanitarianism and Human Rights Seminar Homepage. Bard College Human Rights Project. http://www.bard.edu/hrp/resources (accessed 24 April 2005).
Doherty, Brian F. 'Paradise and Loss in the Mirror Vision of Breyten Breytenbach.' *Contemporary Literature* 36.2 (1995): 226–48.
Dollimore, Jonathan. *Sexual Dissidence: Augustine to Wilde, Freud to Foucault*. Oxford: Clarendon, 1991.
Doriani, Beth Maclay. 'Black Womanhood in Nineteenth-Century America:

Subversion and Self-Construction in Two Women's Autobiographies.' *American Quarterly* 43.2 (1991): 199–222.

Douglass, Frederick. *Narrative of the Life of Frederick Douglass*. 1845. New York: Dover, 1995.

Dowd, Siobhan, ed. *This Prison Where I Live: The PEN Anthology of Imprisoned Writers*. London: Cassell, 1996.

Duban, James. 'Conscience and Consciousness: The Liberal Christian Context of Thoreau's Political Ethics.' *New England Quarterly* 60.2 (1987): 208–22.

DuBois, W.E.B. *The Souls of Black Folk. Writings*, 357–547. New York: Library of America, 1986.

Duff, R.A., and David Garland, eds. *A Reader on Punishment*. Oxford: Oxford University Press, 1994.

Dunbabin, Jean. *Captivity and Imprisonment in Medieval Europe 1000–1300*. New York: Palgrave Macmillan, 2002.

Egan, Susanna. 'Breytenbach's *Mouroir*: The Novel as Autobiography.' *Journal of Narrative Technique* 18.2 (1988): 89–104.

– *Mirror Talk: Genres of Crisis in Contemporary Autobiography*. Chapel Hill: University of North Carolina Press, 1999.

Ellmann, Maud. *The Hunger Artists: Starving, Writing, and Imprisonment*. Cambridge: Harvard University Press, 1993.

Eltis, Sos. *Revising Wilde: Society and Subversion in the Plays of Oscar Wilde*. 1996. Oxford: Clarendon, 1999.

Ernest, John. *Resistance and Reformation in Nineteenth-Century African-American Literature: Brown, Wilson, Jacobs, Delany, Douglass, and Harper*. Jackson: University Press of Mississippi, 1995.

Eustance, Claire. 'Meanings of Militancy: The Ideas and Practice of Political Resistance in the Women's Freedom League, 1907–14.' In Joannou and Purvis, *Women's Suffrage Movement*, 51–64.

Fairclough, Norman. *Language and Power*. New York: Longman, 1989.

Faith, Karlene. *Unruly Women: The Politics of Confinement and Resistance*. Vancouver: Press Gang, 1993.

Felman, Shoshana. *What Does a Woman Want? Reading and Sexual Difference*. Baltimore: Johns Hopkins University Press, 1993.

Felski, Rita. *Beyond Feminist Aesthetics: Feminist Literature and Social Change*. Cambridge: Harvard University Press, 1989.

– *The Gender of Modernity*. Cambridge: Harvard University Press, 1995.

Ferris, Ina. 'From Trope to Code: The Novel and the Rhetoric of Gender in Nineteenth-Century Critical Discourse.' In Shires, *Rewriting the Victorians*, 18–30.

Fink, Steven. *Prophet in the Marketplace: Thoreau's Development as a Professional Writer*. Princeton: Princeton University Press, 1992.

First, Ruth. *117 Days: An Account of Confinement and Interrogation under the South African Ninety-Day Detention Law*. 1965. London: Bloomsbury, 1988.

Fischer, Bram. [Statement from the Dock.] In *The Sun Will Rise: Statements from the Dock by Southern African Political Prisoners*, revised and enlarged edition, ed. Mary Benson, 35–50. London: International Defence and Aid Fund for Southern Africa, 1981.

Fleischner, Jennifer. *Mastering Slavery: Memory, Family, and Identity in Women's Slave Narratives*. New York: New York University Press, 1996.

Foreman, P. Gabrielle. 'The Spoken and the Silenced in *Incidents in the Life of a Slave Girl* and *Our Nig*.' *Callaloo* 13.2 (1990): 313–24.

Forman, James, Jr. 'Children, Cops, and Citizenship: Why Conservatives Should Oppose Racial Profiling.' In Mauer and Chesney-Lind, *Invisible Punishment*, 150–62.

Foster, David. 'Oscar Wilde, *De Profundis*, and the Rhetoric of Agency.' *Papers on Language and Literature* 37.1 (2001): 85–110.

Foster, Frances Smith. *Written by Herself: Literary Production by African American Women, 1746–1892*. Bloomington: Indiana University Press, 1993.

Foucault, Michel. *Discipline and Punish: The Birth of the Prison*. Trans. Alan Sheridan. New York: Vintage, 1979.

– *The History of Sexuality*. Vol. 1. Trans. Robert Hurley. New York: Vintage, 1990.

– 'The Politics of Health in the Eighteenth Century.' Trans. Colin Gordon. In Foucault, *Power/Knowledge*, 166–82.

– *Power/Knowledge: Selected Interviews and Other Writings, 1972–1977*. Ed. Colin Gordon. Trans. Colin Gordon, Leo Marshall, John Mepham, and Kate Soper. New York: Pantheon, 1980.

– 'Prison Talk.' Interview by J.J. Brochier. Trans. Colin Gordon. In Foucault, *Power / Knowledge*, 37–54.

– 'Technologies of the Self.' In *Technologies of the Self: A Seminar with Michel Foucault*, ed. Luther H. Martin, Huck Gutman, and Patrick H. Hutton, 16–49. Amherst: University of Massachusetts Press, 1988.

– 'What Is an Author?' In *The Foucault Reader*, ed. Paul Rabinow, 101–20. New York: Pantheon, 1984.

Franklin, H. Bruce. 'The American Prison in the Culture Wars.' In Simon, *The Prison Issue*.

– *The Victim as Criminal and Artist: Literature from the American Prison*. Oxford: Oxford University Press, 1978.

Franklin, H. Bruce, ed. *Prison Writing in 20th-Century America*. New York: Penguin, 1998.

Freedman, Estelle B. *Their Sisters' Keepers: Women's Prison Reform in America, 1830–1930*. Ann Arbor: University of Michigan Press, 1981.

Friedman, Susan Stanford. 'Women's Autobiographical Selves: Theory and Practice.' In *The Private Self: Theory and Practice of Women's Autobiographical Writings*, ed. Shari Benstock, 34–62. Chapel Hill: University of North Carolina Press, 1988.

Fulkerson, Richard P. 'The Public Letter as a Rhetorical Form: Structure, Logic, and Style in King's "Letter from Birmingham Jail."' *Quarterly Journal of Speech* 65.2 (1979): 121–36.

Gagnier, Regenia. *Idylls of the Marketplace: Oscar Wilde and the Victorian Public*. Stanford: Stanford University Press, 1986.

– *Subjectivities: A History of Self-Representation in Britain, 1832–1920*. Oxford: Oxford University Press, 1991.

Gangi, Robert, Vincent Schiraldi, and Jason Ziedenberg. 'New York State of Mind? Higher Education vs. Prison Funding in the Empire State, 1988-1998.' In Simon, *The Prison Issue*.

Gardiner, Judith Kegan. Introduction. *Provoking Agents: Gender and Agency in Theory and Practice*, ed. Judith Kegan Gardiner, 1–20. Urbana: University of Illinois Press, 1995.

Garelick, Rhonda K. *Rising Star: Dandyism, Gender, and Performance in the Fin de Siècle*. Princeton: Princeton University Press, 1998.

Garfield, Deborah M. 'Speech, Listening, and Female Sexuality in *Incidents in the Life of a Slave Girl*.' *Arizona Quarterly* 50.2 (1994): 19–49.

– 'Vexed Alliances: Race and Female Collaborations in the Life of Harriet Jacobs.' Conclusion. In Garfield and Zafar, *Harriet Jacobs*, 275–91.

Garfield, Deborah M., and Rafia Zafar, eds. *Harriet Jacobs and Incidents in the Life of a Slave Girl: New Critical Essays*. Cambridge: Cambridge University Press, 1996.

Garland, David. *Punishment and Modern Society: A Study in Social Theory*. Chicago: University of Chicago Press, 1990.

– *Punishment and Welfare: A History of Penal Strategies*. Aldershot: Gower, 1985.

Garland, David, ed. *Mass Imprisonment: Social Causes and Consequences*. London: Sage, 2001.

Garrow, David J. *Bearing the Cross: Martin Luther King, Jr., and the Southern Christian Leadership Conference*. New York: William Morrow, 1986.

Gates, Henry Louis, Jr. *Figures in Black: Words, Signs, and the 'Racial' Self*. Oxford: Oxford University Press, 1987.

– *The Signifying Monkey: A Theory of African-American Literary Criticism.* Oxford: Oxford University Press, 1988.

– 'Writing "Race" and the Difference It Makes.' In Gates, *'Race,'* 1–20.

Gates, Henry Louis, Jr, ed. *'Race,' Writing, and Difference.* Chicago: University of Chicago Press, 1985.

Gates, Henry Louis, Jr, and Hollis Robbins, eds. *In Search of Hannah Crafts: Critical Essays on* The Bondwoman's Narrative. New York: Basic, 2004.

Gelfand, Elissa D. *Imagination in Confinement: Women's Writings from French Prisons.* Ithaca: Cornell University Press, 1983.

Genet, Jean. Introduction to the 1st edition. Trans. Richard Howard. In Jackson, *Soledad Brother*, 331–9.

Gilman, Charlotte Perkins. 'The Yellow Wallpaper.' 1892. In *Daughters of Decadence: Women Writers of the* Fin de Siècle, ed. Elaine Showalter, 98–117. New Brunswick: Rutgers University Press, 1993.

Gilmore, Leigh. 'Policing Truth: Confession, Gender, and Autobiographical Authority.' In *Autobiography and Postmodernism*, ed. Kathleen Ashley, Leigh Gilmore, and Gerald Peters, 54–78. Amherst: University of Massachusetts Press, 1994.

Gilmore, Michael T. *American Romanticism and the Marketplace.* Chicago: University of Chicago Press, 1985.

Gilmore, Paul. 'The Indian in the Museum: Henry David Thoreau, Okah Tubbee, and Authentic Manhood.' *Arizona Quarterly* 54.2 (1998): 25–63.

Gilroy, Paul. *The Black Atlantic: Modernity and Double Consciousness.* Cambridge: Harvard University Press, 1993.

Ginsberg, Elaine K. *Passing and the Fictions of Identity.* Durham: Duke University Press, 1996.

Golden, Harry. *Mr. Kennedy and the Negroes.* Greenwich: Fawcett, 1964.

– *Only in America.* Cleveland: World, 1958.

Goldman, Anita. 'Harriet Jacobs, Henry Thoreau, and the Character of Disobedience.' In Garfield and Zafar, *Harriet Jacobs*, 233–50.

Goldsby, Jacqueline. '"I Disguised My Hand": Writing Versions of the Truth in Harriet Jacobs's *Incidents in the Life of a Slave Girl* and John Jacobs's "A True Tale of Slavery."' In Garfield and Zafar, *Harriet Jacobs*, 11–43.

Golemba, Henry. *Thoreau's Wild Rhetoric.* New York: New York University Press, 1990.

Golz, Hans-Georg. *'Staring at Variations': The Concept of 'Self' in Breyten Breytenbach's* Mouroir: Mirrornotes of a Novel. Aachen British and American Studies 5. Frankfurt am Main: Peter Lang, 1995.

Gougeon, Len. 'Thoreau and Reform.' In Myerson, *Cambridge Companion*, 194–214.

Green, Barbara. *Spectacular Confessions: Autobiography, Performative Activism, and the Sites of Suffrage 1905–1938*. New York: St Martin's, 1997.

Grusin, Richard. 'Thoreau, Extravagance, and the Economy of Nature.' *American Literary History* 5.1 (1993): 30–50.

Haley, Alex. *Alex Haley: The Playboy Interviews*, ed. Murray Fisher, 80–128. New York: Ballantine, 1993.

Hansen, Olaf. *Aesthetic Individualism and Practical Intellect: American Allegory in Emerson, Thoreau, Adams, and James*. Princeton: Princeton University Press, 1990.

Harding, Christopher, and Richard W. Ireland. *Punishment: Rhetoric, Rule, and Practice*. New York: Routledge, 1989.

Harding, Walter. *The Days of Henry Thoreau: A Biography*. New York: Dover, 1982.

Harlow, Barbara. *Barred: Women, Writing, and Political Detention*. Hanover: Wesleyan University Press, 1992.

– *Resistance Literature*. New York: Methuen, 1987.

Haslam, Jason. 'Criminal Autobiography.' *Encyclopedia of Life Writing*, vol. 1, ed. Margaretta Jolly, 237–8. London: Fitzroy Dearborn, 2001.

– 'Discovering Identity in James Tyman's *Inside Out: An Autobiography of a Native Canadian*.' *English Studies in Canada* 26.4 (2000): 473–92.

– '"The strange ideas of right and justice": Prison, Slavery, and Other Horrors in *The Bondwoman's Narrative*.' *Gothic Studies* 7.1 (2005): 29–40.

Haslam, Jason, and Julia M. Wright, eds and intro. *Captivating Subjects: Writing Confinement, Citizenship, and Nationhood in the Nineteenth Century*. Toronto: University of Toronto Press, 2005.

Hawkins, Homer, and Richard Thomas. 'White Policing of Black Populations: A History of Race and Social Control in America.' In *Out of Order? Policing Black People*, ed. Ellis Cashmore and Eugene McLaughlin, 65–86. New York: Routledge, 1991.

Hekman, Susan. 'Subjects and Agents: The Question for Feminism.' In *Provoking Agents: Gender and Agency in Theory and Practice*, ed. Judith Kegan Gardiner, 194–207. Urbana: University of Illinois Press, 1995.

Hellen, Nicholas. 'Lost letters reveal Wilde was earnest about love of a woman.' *Sunday Times*, 29 October 2000. http://www.sunday-times.co.uk/news/pages/sti/2000/10/29/stinwenws03010.html (accessed 29 October 2000).

Hildebidle, John. *Thoreau: A Naturalist's Liberty*. Cambridge: Harvard University Press, 1983.

– 'Thoreau at the Edge.' *Prose Studies* 15.3 (1992): 344–65.

Hirsch, Adam Jay. *The Rise of the Penitentiary: Prisons and Punishment in Early America*. New Haven: Yale University Press, 1992.

Hirst, P.Q. 'The Concept of Punishment.' In Duff and Garland, *Reader on Punishment*, 264–80.

Ho, Karen, and Wende Elizabeth Marshall. 'Criminality and Citizenship: Implicating the White Nation.' In *Race Consciousness: African-American Studies for the New Century*, ed. Judith Jackson Fossett and Jeffrey A. Tucker, 208–26. New York: New York University Press, 1997.

Hochfield, George. 'Anti-Thoreau.' *Sewanee Review* 96.3 (1988): 433–43.

Holton, Sandra Stanley. *Suffrage Days: Stories from the Women's Suffrage Movement*. New York: Routledge, 1996.

Holy Bible. King James version.

Hoover, Judith D. 'Reconstruction of the Rhetorical Situation in "Letter from Birmingham Jail."' In Calloway-Thomas and Lucaites, *Martin Luther King*, 50–65.

Howlett, Caroline J. 'Writing on the Body? Representation and Resistance in British Suffragette Accounts of Forcible Feeding.' In *Bodies of Writing, Bodies in Performance*, ed. Thomas Foster, Carol Siegel, and Ellen E. Berry, 3–41. New York: New York University Press, 1996.

Hubbard, Dolan. *The Sermon and the African American Literary Imagination*. Columbia: University of Missouri Press, 1994.

Hyman, Stanley Edgar. 'Henry Thoreau in Our Time.' In *The Recognition of Henry David Thoreau: Selected Criticism Since 1848*, ed. Wendell Glick, 334–51. Ann Arbor: University of Michigan Press, 1969.

ICOPA, International Circle of Penal Abolitionists. 2002. International Circle of Penal Abolitionists. http://www.interlog.com/~ritten/icop/icopaix3.htm (accessed 24 April 2005).

Ignatieff, Michael. *A Just Measure of Pain: The Penitentiary in the Industrial Revolution, 1750–1850*. New York: Pantheon, 1978.

Ignatiev, Noel. *How the Irish Became White*. New York: Routledge, 1995.

Ingram, Angela, and Daphne Patai, eds. *Rediscovering Forgotten Radicals: British Women Writers, 1889–1939*. Chapel Hill: University of North Carolina Press, 1993.

Jackson, George. *Blood in My Eye*. New York: Random House, 1972.

– *Soledad Brother: The Prison Letters of George Jackson*. 1970. Reprint, Chicago: Lawrence Hill Books, 1994.

Jacobs, Harriet. *Incidents in the Life of a Slave Girl Written by Herself*. 1861. Ed. Jean Fagan Yellin. Enlarged edition with 'A True Tale of Slavery' by John S. Jacobs. Cambridge: Harvard University Press, 2000.

Jacobs, J.U. 'Breyten Breytenbach and the South African Prison Book.' *Theoria* 68 (1986): 95–105.

– 'Confession, Interrogation and Self-interrogation in the New South African Prison Writing.' *Kunapipi* 13.1–2 (1991): 115–27.

Jenkins, Richard. 'From Criminology to Anthropology? Identity, Morality and Normality in the Social Construction of Deviance.' In *Thinking about Criminology*, ed. Simon Holdaway and Paul Rock, 133–60. Toronto: University of Toronto Press, 1998.

Joannou, Maroula. 'Suffragette Fiction and the Fictions of Suffrage.' In Joannou and Purvis, *Women's Suffrage Movement*, 101–16.

Joannou, Maroula, and June Purvis. *The Women's Suffrage Movement: New Feminist Perspectives*. Manchester: Manchester University Press, 1998.

Jolly, Rosemary Jane. *Colonization, Violence, and Narration in White South African Writing: André Brink, Breyten Breytenbach, and J. M. Coetzee*. Athens: Ohio University Press, 1996.

Kaplan, Caren. 'Resisting Autobiography: Out-Law Genres and Transnational Feminist Subjects.' In *De/Colonizing the Subject: The Politics of Gender in Women's Autobiography*, ed. Sidonie Smith and Julia Watson, 115–38. Minneapolis: University of Minnesota Press, 1992.

Kaplan, Carla. *The Erotics of Talk: Women's Writing and Feminist Paradigms*. Oxford: Oxford University Press, 1996.

Kauffman, Linda S. *Special Delivery: Epistolary Modes in Modern Fiction*. Chicago: University of Chicago Press, 1992.

Kawash, Samira. *Dislocating the Color Line: Identity, Hybridity, and Singularity in African-American Literature*. Stanford: Stanford University Press, 1997.

Keckley, Elizabeth. *Behind the Scenes or, Thirty Years a Slave and Four Years in the White House*. 1868. Reprint, New York: Arno and *New York Times*, 1968.

Kenney, Annie. *Memories of a Militant*. 1924. Reprinted as *A Militant*, ed. Marie Mulvey Roberts and Tamae Mizuta. London: Routledge/Thoemmes, 1994.

Kent, Susan Kingsley. *Gender and Power in Britain, 1640–1990*. New York: Routledge, 1999.

– *Sex and Suffrage in Britain, 1860–1914*. Princeton: Princeton University Press, 1987.

Kibbey, Ann, and Michele Stepto. 'The Antilanguage of Slavery: Frederick Douglass's 1845 *Narrative*.' In Andrews, *Critical*, 166–91.

King, Martin Luther, Jr. 'The Current Crisis in Race Relations.' In King, *Testament*, 85–90.

– 'Letter from Birmingham City Jail.' In King, *Testament*, 289–302.

– Interview by Alex Haley. In Haley, *Alex Haley*, 80–128.

– 'Non-Aggression Procedures to Interracial Harmony: Address Delivered at the American Baptist Assembly and American Home Mission Agencies Conference.' In King, *Papers*, vol. 3, 321–8.

– *The Papers of Martin Luther King, Jr.* Vol. 3. Ed. Clayborne Carson et al. Berkeley: University of California Press, 1997.

– *Stride Toward Freedom: The Montgomery Story.* New York: Harper & Row, 1958.
– *A Testament of Hope: The Essential Writings of Martin Luther King Jr.* Ed. James Melvin Washington. San Francisco: Harper & Row, 1986.
– 'When Peace Becomes Obnoxious: Sermon Delivered on 18 March 1956 at Dexter Avenue Baptist Church.' In *Papers,* vol. 3, 207–8.
King, Martin Luther, Jr, A. Philip Randolph, Lester B. Granger, and Roy Wilkins. 'A Statement to the President of the United States.' In *The Papers of Martin Luther King, Jr.* Vol. 4. Ed. Clayborne Carson et al., 426–9. Berkeley: University of California Press, 2000.
Klein, Mia. 'The *Other* Beauty of Martin Luther King, Jr.'s "Letter from Birmingham Jail."' *College Composition and Communication* 32.1: 30–7.
Kofman, Sarah. 'The Imposture of Beauty: The Uncanniness of Oscar Wilde's *Picture of Dorian Gray.*' Trans. Duncan Large. In *Enigmas: Essays on Sarah Kofman,* ed. Penelope Deutscher and Kelly Oliver, 25–48. Ithaca: Cornell University Press, 1999.
Kohl, Norbert. *Oscar Wilde: The Works of a Conformist Rebel.* Trans. David Henry Wilson. Cambridge: Cambridge University Press, 1989.
Kritzberg, Barry. 'Thoreau, Slavery, and Resistance to Civil Government.' *Massachusetts Review* 30.4 (1989): 535–65.
Lauterbach, Frank. '"From the slums *to* the slums": The Delimitation of Social Identity in Late Victorian Prison Narratives.' In Haslam and Wright, *Captivating Subjects,* 113–43.
Lentz, Richard. *Symbols, the News Magazines, and Martin Luther King.* Baton Rouge: Louisiana State University Press, 1990.
Leps, Marie-Christine. *Apprehending the Criminal: The Production of Deviance in Nineteenth-Century Discourse.* Durham: Duke University Press, 1992.
Levander, Caroline. '"Following the Condition of the Mother": Subversions of Domesticity in Harriet Jacobs's *Incidents in the Life of a Slave Girl.*' In *Southern Mothers: Fact and Fictions in Southern Women's Writing,* ed. Nagueyalti Warren and Sally Wolff, 28–38. Baton Rouge: Louisiana State University Press, 1999.
Lewin, Hugh. *Bandiet: Seven Years in a South African Prison.* London: Heinemann, 1974.
Lewis, David L. *King: A Critical Biography.* New York: Praeger, 1970.
Lewis, Jane, ed. *Before the Vote Was Won: Arguments For and Against Women's Suffrage.* New York: Routledge and Kegan Paul, 1987.
Lewis, Orlando F. *The Development of American Prisons and Prison Customs, 1776–1845.* 1922. Montclair: Patterson Smith, 1967.
Liddington, Jill. *The Long Road to Greenham: Feminism and Anti-Militarism in Britain Since 1820.* London: Virago, 1989.

Losey, Jay. 'The Aesthetics of Exile: Wilde Transforming Dante in *Intentions* and *De Profundis.' English Literature in Transition, 1880–1920* 36.4 (1993): 429–50.

Lovesay, Oliver. 'Chained Letters: African Prison Diaries and "National Allegory."' *Research in African Literatures* 26.4 (1995): 31–45.

Lyon, Janet. *Manifestoes: Provocations of the Modern.* Ithaca: Cornell University Press, 1999.

Lytton, Constance. Letter to Mr. Broadbent. 10 January 1908. British Library.

– '"No Votes for Women": A Reply to Some Recent Anti-Suffrage Publications.' London: A.C. Fifield, 1909.

– *Prisons and Prisoners: Some Personal Experiences.* London: Heinemann, 1914.

Malcolm X, as told to Alex Haley. 1965. *The Autobiography of Malcolm X.* New York: Ballantine, 1973.

– Interview with Alex Haley. In Haley, *Alex Haley,* 20–45.

Mandela, Nelson. *Long Walk to Freedom: The Autobiography of Nelson Mandela.* Boston: Little, Brown, 1995.

Marcus, Jane, ed. *Suffrage and the Pankhursts.* New York: Routledge and Kegan Paul, 1987.

Mashinini, Emma. *Strikes Have Followed Me All My Life: A South African Autobiography.* 1989. New York: Routledge, 1991.

Mason, Mary G. 'The Other Voice: Autobiographies of Women Writers.' In *Life / Lines: Theorizing Women's Autobiography,* ed. Bella Brodzki and Celeste Schenk, 19–44. Ithaca: Cornell University Press, 1988.

Mathiesen, Thomas. *The Politics of Abolition.* New York: Halsted, 1974.

Mauer, Marc. 'Mass Imprisonment and the Disappearing Voters.' In Mauer and Chesney-Lind, *Invisible Punishment*, 50–8.

Mauer, Marc, and Meda Chesney-Lind, ed. and intro. *Invisible Punishment: The Collateral Consequences of Mass Imprisonment.* New York: New Press, 2002.

McClintock, Anne, and Rob Nixon. 'No Names Apart: The Separation of Word and History in Derrida's "Le Dernier Mot du Racisme."' In Gates, *'Race,'* 339–53.

McConville, Seán. 'The Victorian Prison: England, 1865–1965.' In Morris and Rothman, *Oxford History of the Prison*, 131–67.

McGill, Ralph. *The South and the Southerner.* Boston: Little Brown, 1963.

McGowen, Randall. 'The Well-Ordered Prison: England, 1780–1865.' In Morris and Rothman, *Oxford History of the Prison*, 79–109.

McKivigan, John R., and Mitchell Snay, eds. *Religion and the Antebellum Debate over Slavery.* Athens: University of Georgia Press, 1998.

McLachlan, Fiona. 'The Apartheid Laws in Brief.' 1985. In Mermelstein, *Anti-Apartheid Reader,* 76–8.

McQuiston, Liz. *Suffragettes to She-Devils: Women's Liberation and Beyond*. Foreword by Germaine Greer. London: Phaidon, 1997.

Melossi, Dario, and Massimo Pavarini. *The Prison and the Factory: Origins of the Penitentiary System*. Trans. Glynis Cousin. London: Macmillan, 1981.

Mermelstein, David, ed. *The Anti-Apartheid Reader: The Struggle against Racist White Rule in South Africa*. New York: Grove, 1987.

Meyer, Michael. *Several More Lives to Live: Thoreau's Political Reputation in America*. Contributions in American Studies 29. Westport: Greenwood, 1977.

Miller, D.A. *The Novel and the Police*. Berkeley: University of California Press, 1988.

Miller, Keith D. 'Composing Martin Luther King, Jr.' *PMLA* 105.1 (1990): 70–82.

– *Voice of Deliverance: The Language of Martin Luther King, Jr. and Its Sources*. New York: Free Press, 1992.

Moodie, Susanna. *Roughing It in the Bush, or Life in Canada*. 1852. Reprint, Toronto: McClelland and Stewart, 1989.

Moody, Joycelyn K. 'Twice Other, Once Shy: Nineteenth-Century Black Women Autobiographers and the American Literary Tradition of Self-Effacement.' *a/b: auto/biography Studies* 7.1 (1992): 46–61.

Moore, Gerald. 'The Martian Descends: The Poetry of Breyten Breytenbach.' *Ariel* 16.2 (1985): 3–12.

Morgan, Winifred. 'Gender-Related Difference in the Slave Narratives of Harriet Jacobs and Frederick Douglass.' *American Studies* 35.2 (1994): 73–94.

Morris, Norval, and David J. Rothman, eds. *The Oxford History of the Prison: The Practice of Punishment in Western Society*. Oxford: Oxford University Press, 1995.

Moses, Greg. *Revolution of Conscience: Martin Luther King, Jr., and the Philosophy of Nonviolence*. New York: Guilford, 1997.

Mott, Wesley T. 'The Rhetoric of Martin Luther King, Jr.: "Letter from Birmingham Jail."' *Phylon* 36.4 (1975): 411–21.

Mullen, Harryette. 'Runaway Tongue: Resistant Orality in *Uncle Tom's Cabin*, *Our Nig*, *Incidents in the Life of a Slave Girl*, and *Beloved*.' In *The Culture of Sentiment: Race, Gender, and Sentimentality in Nineteenth-Century America*, ed. Shirley Samuels, 244–64. Oxford: Oxford University Press, 1992.

Mulvey-Roberts, Marie. 'Militancy, Masochism, or Martyrdom? The Public and Private Prisons of Constance Lytton.' In *Votes for Women*, ed. June Purvis and Sandra Stanley Holton, 159–80. London: Routledge, 2000.

Murphy, P.J., and Jennifer Murphy, eds. *Sentences and Paroles: A Prison Reader*. Vancouver: New Star Books, 1998.

Murray, Isobel. 'Oscar Wilde and Individualism: Contexts for "The Soul of Man."' *Durham University Journal* 83.2 (1991): 195–207.

Myall, Michelle. '"No Surrender!": The Militancy of Mary Leigh, a Working-Class Suffragette.' In Joannou and Purvis, *Women's Suffrage Movement*, 173–87.

Myerson, Joel, ed. *The Cambridge Companion to Henry David Thoreau.* Cambridge: Cambridge University Press, 1995.

– *Emerson and Thoreau: The Contemporary Reviews.* American Critical Archives 1. Cambridge: Cambridge University Press, 1992.

Naidoo, Indres, as told to Albie Sachs. *Robben Island: Ten Years as a Political Prisoner in South Africa's Most Notorious Penitentiary.* New York: Vintage, 1983.

Newton, Judith. 'Engendering History for the Middle Class: Sex and Political Economy in the *Edinburgh Review.*' In Shires, *Rewriting the Victorians,* 1–17.

Norquay, Glenda, ed. *Voices and Votes: A Literary Anthology of the Women's Suffrage Campaign.* Manchester: Manchester University Press, 1995.

Nudelman, Franny. 'Harriet Jacobs and the Sentimental Politics of Female Suffering.' *ELH* 59.4 (1992): 939–64.

O'Connor, Patricia E. *Speaking of Crime: Narratives of Prisoners.* Lincoln: University of Nebraska Press, 2000.

Oehlschlaeger, Fritz. 'Another Look at the Text and Title of Thoreau's "Civil Disobedience."' *ESQ* 36.3 (1990): 239–54.

Oliver, Peter. *'Terror to Evil Doers': Prisons and Punishments in Nineteenth-Century Ontario.* Toronto: University of Toronto Press, 1998.

'Oscar Wilde's Disgrace.' *New York Times,* 8 April 1895: 9.

Ovid. *The Metamorphoses.* Trans. Horace Gregory. New York: Viking, 1958.

Page, Philip. *Reclaiming Community in Contemporary African American Fiction.* Jackson: University Press of Mississippi, 1999.

Parenti, Christian. *Lockdown America: Police and Prisons in the Age of Crisis.* London: Verso, 1999.

Pease, Donald E. *Visionary Compacts: American Renaissance Writings in Cultural Context.* Madison: University of Wisconsin Press, 1987.

Perry, Lewis. 'Black Abolitionists and the Origin of Civil Disobedience.' In *Moral Problems in American Life: New Perspectives on Cultural History,* ed. Karen Halttunen and Lewis Perry, 103–21. Ithaca: Cornell University Press, 1998.

Peterson, Dale E. 'Response and Call: The African American Dialogue with Bakhtin and What It Signifies.' In *Bakhtin in Contexts: Across the Disciplines,* ed. Amy Mandelker, 89–98. Evanston: Northwestern University Press, 1995.

Pethick-Lawrence, Emmeline. *My Part in a Changing World.* London: Gollancz, 1938.

Pheto, Molefe. *And Night Fell: Memoirs of a Political Prisoner in South Africa.*
London: Allison, 1983.

Pine, Richard. *The Thief of Reason: Oscar Wilde and Modern Ireland.* New York:
St Martin's, 1995.

Powell, Brent. 'Henry David Thoreau, Martin Luther King Jr., and the American Tradition of Protest.' *Magazine of History* 9.2 (1995): 26–9.

Prince, Mary. *The History of Mary Prince: A West Indian Slave Related by Herself.*
1831. Ed. Moira Ferguson. Revised edition, Ann Arbor: University of Michigan Press, 1997.

Purvis, June. 'The Prison Experiences of the Suffragettes in Edwardian Britain.'
Women's History Review 4.1 (1995): 103–33.

Rafter, Nicole Hahn. *Partial Justice: Women, Prisons, and Social Control.* 2nd ed.
New Brunswick: Transaction, 1990.

Ransom, John S. *Foucault's Discipline: The Politics of Subjectivity.* Durham: Duke
University Press, 1997.

Reckwitz, Erhard. '"I Am Not Myself Anymore:" Problems of Identity in Writing by White South Africans.' *English in Africa* 20.1 (1993): 1–23.

Rodríguez, Dylan. 'Against the Discipline of "Prison Writing": Toward a Theoretical Conception of Contemporary Radical Prison Praxis.' *Genre: Forms of Discourse and Culture.* Special issue: Prisoners Writing. Ed. Megan Sweeney.
35.3–4 (2002): 407–28.

Roediger, David R. *Towards the Abolition of Whiteness: Essays on Race, Politics,
and Working Class History.* London: Verso, 1994.

– *The Wages of Whiteness: Race and the Making of the American Working Class.*
London: Verso, 1991.

Rosen, Andrew. *Rise Up, Women! The Militant Campaign of the Women's
Social and Political Union 1903–1914.* London: Routledge and Kegan Paul,
1974.

Rothman, David J. 'Perfecting the Prison: United States, 1789–1865.' In Morris
and Rothman, *Oxford History of the Prison*, 111–29.

Rusche, Georg, and Otto Kirchheimer. *Punishment and Social Structure.* 1939.
New York: Russell and Russell, 1968.

Rush, Benjamin. 'An Enquiry into the Effects of Public Punishments upon
Criminals, and Upon Society. Read in the Society for Promoting Political
Enquiries, Convened at the House of Benjamin Franklin, Esq. in Philadelphia, March 9th, 1787.' In *Essays Literary, Moral, and Philosophical*, 1806. Ed.
Michael Meranze. Schenectady: Union College Press, 1988.

Said, Edward. *Humanism and Democratic Criticism.* New York: Columbia University Press, 2004.

Sale, Maggie. 'Critiques from Within: Antebellum Projects of Resistance.'
American Literature 64.4 (1992): 695–718.

Sánchez-Eppler, Karen. *Touching Liberty: Abolition, Feminism, and the Politics of the Body*. Berkeley: University of California Press, 1993.

Schalkwyk, David. 'Confession and Solidarity in the Prison Writing of Breyten Breytenbach and Jeremy Cronin.' *Research in African Literatures* 25.1 (1994): 23–45.

Scheffler, Judith A., ed. *Wall Tappings: Women's Prison Writings, 200 A.D. to the Present*. 2nd ed. New York: Feminist Press, 2003.

Sellin, J. Thorsten. *Slavery and the Penal System*. New York: Elsevier, 1976.

Shakur, Sanyika, aka Monster Cody Scott. *Monster: The Autobiography of an L. A. Gang Member*. New York: Penguin, 1993.

Shaw, Marion. '"To tell the truth of sex": Confession and Abjection in Late Victorian Writing.' In Shires, *Rewriting the Victorians*, 87–100.

Shires, Linda M., ed. *Rewriting the Victorians: Theory, History, and the Politics of Gender*. New York: Routledge, 1992.

Simon, Bruce, ed. and intro. *The Prison Issue*. Feature issue of *Workplace: A Journal for Academic Labor* 3.2 (Dec. 2000). http://www.cust.educ.ubc.ca/workplace/issue6/ (accessed 14 March 2001).

'Six Dead after Church Bombing.' *Washington Post*, 16 Sept. 1963. http://www.washingtonpost.com/wp-srv/national/longterm/churches/archives1.htm (accessed 24 April 2005).

Skinfill, Mauri. 'Nation and Miscegenation: *Incidents in the Life of a Slave Girl*.' *Arizona Quarterly* 51.2 (1995): 63–79.

Sloop, John M. *The Cultural Prison: Discourse, Prisoners, and Punishment*. Tuscaloosa: University of Alabama Press, 1996.

Smith, Adam. *The Theory of Moral Sentiments*. Ed. D.D. Raphael and A.L. Macfie. Indianapolis: Liberty Fund, 1982.

Smith, Erwin. *The Ethics of Martin Luther King, Jr.* Lewiston: Mellen, 1981.

Smith, Lillian. *Killers of the Dream*. New York: Norton, 1949.

Smith, Paul. *Discerning the Subject*. Minneapolis: University of Minnesota Press, 1988.

Smith, Sidonie. 'Resisting the Gaze of Embodiment: Women's Autobiography in the Nineteenth Century.' In *American Women's Autobiography: Fea(s)ts of Memory*, ed. Margo Culley, 75–110. Madison: University of Wisconsin Press, 1992.

– *Subjectivity, Identity, and the Body: Women's Autobiographical Practices in the Twentieth Century*. Bloomington: Indiana University Press, 1993.

Snow, Malinda. 'Martin Luther King's "Letter from Birmingham Jail" as Pauline Epistle.' *Quarterly Journal of Speech* 71.3 (1985): 318–34.

Sorisio, Carolyn. '"There Is Might in Each": Conceptions of Self in Harriet Jacobs's *Incidents in the Life of a Slave Girl, Written by Herself*.' *Legacy* 13.1 (1996): 1–18.

Spillers, Hortense J. 'Martin Luther King and the Style of the Black Sermon.' *The Black Scholar* 3.1 (1971): 14–27.

Stern, Vivien. 'The International Impact of U.S. Policies.' In Mauer and Chesney-Lind, *Invisible Punishment*, 279–92.

Strachey, Ray. *'The Cause': A Short History of the Women's Movement in Great Britain*. London: G. Bell and Sons, 1928.

'Suffragist or Suffragette?' *The Suffragette*, 1 May 1914: 55–6.

Sugrue, Thomas J. *The Origins of the Urban Crisis: Race and Inequality in Postwar Detroit*. Princeton: Princeton University Press, 1996.

Tambling, Jeremy. *Confession: Sexuality, Sin, the Subject*. Manchester: Manchester University Press, 1990.

Taylor, Bob Pepperman. *America's Bachelor Uncle: Thoreau and the American Polity*. Lawrence: University Press of Kansas, 1996.

– 'Henry Thoreau, Nature, and American Democracy.' *Journal of Social Philosophy* 25.1 (1994): 46–64.

Taylor, Douglas. 'From Slavery to Prison: Benjamin Rush, Harriet Jacobs, and the Ideology of Reformative Incarnation.' *Genre: Forms of Discourse and Culture*. Special issue: Prisoners Writing. Ed. Megan Sweeney. 35.3–4 (2002): 429–47.

Teichgraeber, Richard F. *Sublime Thoughts / Penny Wisdom: Situating Emerson and Thoreau in the American Market*. Baltimore: Johns Hopkins University Press, 1995.

Thomas, Sue. 'Scenes in the Writing of "Constance Lytton and Jane Warton, Spinster": Contextualising a Cross-class Dresser.' *Women's History Review* 12.1 (2003): 51–71.

Thoreau, Henry David. 'Civil Disobedience' ['Resistance to Civil Government']. In Thoreau, *Reform Papers*, 63–90.

– 'A Plea for Captain John Brown.' In Thoreau, *Reform Papers*, 111–38.

– *Reform Papers*. Ed. Wendell Glick. Writings of Henry D. Thoreau. Princeton: Princeton University Press, 1973.

– 'Slavery in Massachusetts.' In Thoreau, *Reform Papers*, 91–109.

– *Walden*. Ed. J. Lyndon Shanley. Writings of Henry D. Thoreau. Princeton: Princeton University Press, 1971.

– *A Yankee in Canada, with Anti-Slavery and Reform Papers*. 1892. New York: Greenwood, 1969.

Tickner, Lisa. *The Spectacle of Women: Imagery and the Suffrage Campaign 1907–14*. Chicago: University of Chicago Press, 1988.

Tobias, J.J. *Nineteenth-century Crime: Prevention and Punishment*. Devon: David and Charles, 1972.

Todd, Janet. *Sensibility: An Introduction*. London: Methuen, 1986.

Tompkins, Jane. *Sensational Designs: The Cultural Work of American Fiction 1790–1860*. Oxford: Oxford University Press, 1985.

Tonry, Michael. 'Proportionality, Parsimony, and Interchangeability of Punishments.' In Duff and Garland, *Reader on Punishment*, 136–60.

Travis, Jeremy. 'Invisible Punishment: An Instrument of Social Exclusion.' In Mauer and Chesney-Lind, *Invisible Punishment*, 15–36.

Truth and Reconciliation Commission. Home page. 28 Nov. 2000. http://www.doj.gov.za/trc/ (accessed 24 April 2005).

'Views and Comments.' *The Egoist: An Individualist Review*, 10.1 (15 May 1914): 182–5.

Wacquant, Loïc. 'Deadly Symbiosis: When Ghetto and Prison Meet and Mesh.' In Garland, *Mass Imprisonment*, 82–120.

Walter, Krista. 'Surviving in the Garret: Harriet Jacobs and the Critique of Sentiment.' *American Transcendental Quarterly*, new series, 8.3 (1994): 189–210.

Warhol, Robyn R. '"Reader, Can You Imagine? No, You Cannot": The Narratee as Other in Harriet Jacobs's Text.' *Narrative* 3.1 (1995): 57–72.

Waters, Chris. *British Socialists and the Politics of Popular Culture, 1884–1914*. Manchester: Manchester University Press, 1990.

Welter, Barbara. 'The Cult of True Womanhood: 1820–1860.' *American Quarterly* 18.2 (1966): 151–74.

Western, Bruce, Becky Pettit, and Josh Guetzkow. 'Black Economic Progress in the Era of Mass Imprisonment.' In Mauer and Chesney-Lind, *Invisible Punishment*, 165–80.

Wiener, Martin J. *Reconstructing the Criminal: Culture, Law, and Policy in England, 1830–1914*. Cambridge: Cambridge University Press, 1990.

Wilde, Oscar. *The Ballad of Reading Gaol*. In Wilde, *Complete Works*, 883–99.

– *Complete Works of Oscar Wilde*. Glasgow: Harper, 1994.

– 'The Critic as Artist.' In Wilde, *Complete Works*, 1108–55.

– 'The Decay of Lying.' In Wilde, *Complete Works*, 1071–92.

– *The Importance of Being Earnest*. In Wilde, *Complete Works*, 357–419.

– *The Letters of Oscar Wilde*. Ed. Rupert Hart-Davis. London: Hart-Davis Ltd, 1962.

– *The Picture of Dorian Gray*. Ed. Isobel Murray. Oxford: Oxford University Press, 1981.

– 'To Robert Ross.' 8 October 1897. In Wilde, *Letters*, 654–5.

– 'The Soul of Man Under Socialism.' In Wilde, *Complete Works*, 1174–97.

– Wilde to Lord Alfred Douglas [*De Profundis*], January–March 1897. In Wilde, *Letters*, 423–511.

Williams, Carolyn. 'The Female Antislavery Movement: Fighting against

Racial Prejudice and Promoting Women's Rights in Antebellum America.' In Yellin and Van Horne, *Abolitionist Sisterhood*, 159–77.

Wood, Barry. 'Thoreau's Narrative Art in "Civil Disobedience."' *Philological Quarterly* 60.1 (1981): 105–15.

Wood, Jane. 'Prisons of Subjectivity: Oscar Wilde's *De Profundis*, an Autobiography of Escape.' *Victorian Literature and Culture* 24 (1998): 99–114.

Wright, Julia M. '"National Feeling" and the Colonial Prison: Teeling's *Personal Narrative*.' In Haslam and Wright, *Captivating Subjects*, 175–98.

Yellin, Jean Fagan. 'Through Her Brother's Eyes: *Incidents* and "A True Tale."' In Garfield and Zafar, *Harriet Jacobs*, 44–56.

– 'Written by Herself: Harriet Jacobs's Slave Narrative.' *American Literature* 53.3 (1981): 479–86.

Yellin, Jean Fagan, and John C. Van Horne, eds. *The Abolitionist Sisterhood: Women's Political Culture in Antebellum America*. Ithaca: Cornell University Press, 1994.

Zepp, Ira G., Jr. *The Social Vision of Martin Luther King, Jr.* 1971. New York: Carlson, 1989.

Ziolkowski, Thad. 'Antitheses: The Dialectic of Violence and Literacy in Frederick Douglass's *Narrative* of 1845.' In Andrews, *Critical Essays*, 148–65.

Index